Complete Canadian Curriculum

Grade **8**

Revised and Updated!

Math
English
History
Geography
Science

Credits

Photos (Cover "boy" Dan Kosmayer/123RF.com, "polar bear" Buchachon Petthanya/123RF.com, "students" Andres Rodriguez/123RF.com, "Parliament Hill" rambleon/123RF.com, "duckling" belchonock/123RF.com)

Copyright © 2015 Popular Book Company (Canada) Limited

Printed in China

ISBN: 978-1-77149-036-8

Contents

Mathematics

1 Exponents — 6

2 Square Roots — 10

3 Pythagorean Theorem — 14

4 Integers — 18

5 Order of Operations — 22

6 Expanded Form and Scientific Notation — 26

7 Ratio and Proportion — 30

8 Rate — 34

9 Application of Percent — 38

10 Fractions — 42

11 Decimals, Fractions, and Percents — 46

12 Nets — 50

13 Circumference and Area — 54

14 Surface Area and Volume — 58

15 Volume and Surface Area of Solids (1) — 62

16 Volume and Surface Area of Solids (2) — 66

17 Angle Properties of Intersecting Lines — 70

18 Angle Properties in Parallel Lines — 74

19 Angle Properties in a Triangle — 78

20 Constructing Bisectors — 82

21 Transformations (1) — 86

22 Transformations (2) — 90

23 Number Patterns — 94

24 Algebraic Expressions — 98

25 Equations — 102

26 Data Management (1) — 106

27 Data Management (2) — 110

28 Probability — 114

English

1 Polar Bears – Did You Know? — 120

2 Cambodia's Angkor Wat: Endangered by Tourism — 124

3 Canadian Nobel Prize Laureates — 128

4 Naming a Public Holiday — 132

5 The History of Christmas Giving — 136

6 The Remarkable Journey of Al Gore — 140

7 The Wisdom of a Baseball Player: Yogi Berra's Quotes — 144

8 Too Much of a Good Thing: the "Law of Unintended Consequences" — 148

9 How to Talk Like a Fashion Trendsetter — 152

10 Watch Out for Those Language Bloopers! — 156

11 Don't Be a Dope: Drugs in Sports — 160

12 One of the World's Most Published Editorials — 164

13 Steven Fletcher, an Exceptional Public Servant — 168

14 The Seven Sacred Teachings — 172

15 Twenty Thousand "Oskar Schindlers": the Holocaust Rescuers — 176

16 An Ancient Story about the Sun and the Moon — 180

17 Do Aliens Exist? — 184

18 Saving Lake Winnipeg — 188

19 Depression in Teenagers: a Very Treatable Condition — 192

20 The Start of the Sagas — 196

21 Green Iceland: a Letter from Uncle Josh — 200

22 Magnificent Trees — 204

23 High Flight – a Poem by John Gillespie Magee, Jr. — 208

24 Hannah Taylor and the Ladybug Foundation — 212

25 The Truth about Water — 216

26 Yoga: a Most Healthful Form of Exercise — 220

27 Tips for Effective Public Speaking — 224

28 A Volunteer and a Tourist? — 228

ISBN: 978-1-77149-036-8

History

Creating Canada, 1850 – 1890

1 Creating Canada 234
2 Expansion of Canada 236
3 Events and Development of Early Canada 238
4 Distinguished Canadians 240
5 Social, Economic, and Political Changes 242
6 Conflict and Cooperation (1) 244

Canada, 1890 – 1914: A Changing Society

7 The Underprivileged in Canada 246
8 Changes in Canada 248
9 Diverse Faces of Canada 250
10 Groups in Action 252
11 Individuals Making a Difference 254
12 Conflict and Cooperation (2) 256

Geography

Global Settlement: Patterns and Sustainability

1 Physical Environment and Human Settlements 260
2 Global Human Settlement Patterns 262
3 Global Settlement Trends 264
4 Impact of Human Settlements 266
5 Sustainable Human Settlements 268
6 Land-use Issues 270

Global Inequalities: Economic Development and Quality of Life

7 Quality of Life 272
8 Quality of Life – Interrelationships among Factors 274
9 Quality of Life – Correlations between Indicators 276
10 Fair Trade and Quality of Life 278
11 Organizations for Improving Quality of Life 280
12 Economic Systems and Sectors 282

Science

1 Cell Theory 286
2 Animal and Plant Cells 288
3 Structures and Organelles in Cells 290
4 Diffusion and Osmosis 292
5 The Organization of Cells 294
6 About Systems 296
7 Systems: Input and Output 298
8 The Work Systems Do 300
9 Work, Mechanical Advantage, and Efficiency 302
10 Evolving Systems 304
11 Where on Earth Is Water? 306
12 What Is a Watershed? 308
13 The Water Table 310
14 Glaciers and Polar Ice Caps 312
15 Water Conservation 314
16 Fluids and Density 316
17 Viscosity 318
18 Buoyancy 320
19 Compressed Fluids - Hydraulics and Pneumatics 322
20 Using Fluids 324

Answers

Mathematics 328
English 344
History 354
Geography 358
Science 362

ISBN: 978-1-77149-036-8

MATHEMATICS

* The Canadian penny is no longer in circulation. It is used in the units to show money amounts to the cent.

ISBN: 978-1-77149-036-8

Exponents

- write integers as powers
- evaluate expressions using the order of operations
- find the volumes and side lengths of cubes
- write numbers as a product of prime factors
- find common factors using prime factors

$2^5 = 2 \times 2 \times 2 \times 2 \times 2$
$= \underline{32}$

We double ourselves every minute. There'll be 32 of us after 5 minutes.

Write each as a product of powers.

1. $3 \times 3 \times 3 \times 4 \times 4 = \underline{3^3 \times 4^2}$

2. $6 \times 6 \times 6 \times 6 \times 8 \times 8 = \underline{6^4 \times 8^2}$

3. $2.5 \times 2.5 \times 8 \times 8 = \underline{2.5^2 \times 8^2}$

4. $1.7 \times 1.7 \times 1.7 \times 1.7 \times 5 \times 5 = \underline{1.7^4 \times 5^2}$

5. $9 \times 5 \times 5 \times 9 \times 9 = \underline{9^3 \times 5^2}$

6. $4.6 \times 7 \times 7 \times 4.6 \times 7 = \underline{4.6^2 \times 7^3}$

7. $10 \times 7.8 \times 7.8 \times 10 \times 2 \times 2 \times 10 \times 7.8 \times 7.8 = \underline{10^3 \times 2^2 \times 7.8^4}$

8. $6.3 \times 5 \times 5 \times 5 \times 6.3 \times 6.3 \times 13 \times 14^2 = \underline{6.3^3 \times 5^3 \times 13 \times 14^2}$

9. $3 \times 3 \times 3^2 \times 4 \times 4 \times 5.5 \times 4^3 \times 5.5 = \underline{3^4 \times 4^5 \times 5.5^2}$

Write the integers as powers.

10. $81 = 3 \times \underline{27}$

$= 3 \times \underline{3} \times \underline{9}$

$= 3 \times \underline{1} \times \underline{1} \times \underline{1}$

$= \underline{1}$

Hint

Write 16 as a power of 2.

$16 = 2 \times 8$
$= 2 \times 2 \times 4$
$= 2 \times 2 \times 2 \times 2$
$= 2^4$

11. 125 as a power of 5 _____

12. 1296 as a power of 6 _____

13. 243 as a power of 3 _____

14. 10 000 as a power of 10 _____

15. 1024 as a power of 4 _____

16. 128 as a power of 2 _____

Follow the order of operations to evaluate, commonly called: **BEDMAS**

B - Brackets
E - Exponents
D - Divide
M- Multiply
A - Add
S - Subtract

e.g. $20 \div (8 - 6)^2 + 10$
= $20 \div (\mathbf{2})^2 + 10$ ⟵ Do the brackets first.
= $20 \div \mathbf{4} + 10$ ⟵ Evaluate the exponent.
= $\mathbf{5} + 10$ ⟵ Divide.
= $\mathbf{15}$ ⟵ Add.

Evaluate.

17. $2^4 = 2 \times 2 \times 2 \times$ _____ = _____

18. $7^3 =$ _____ = _____

19. $1.5^3 =$ _____ = _____

20. $(\frac{1}{3})^4 =$ _____ = _____

Follow the order of operations to evaluate.

21. $2^3 \times 3$

= _____ $\times 3$ ⟵ Evaluate 2^3 first.

= _____

22. $6^3 - (2 + 1)^2$

= _____ − _____

= _____

23. $10 + 1.2^2 \times 5$

=

24. $(5 - 2)^4 \div 9^0 + 8$

=

25. $(3 + 1)^2 \div 2^2 - 1$ = _____

26. $45 \div (2 + 1)^2 - 3$ = _____

27. $(10 - 3)^4 \div (3 + 4)$ = _____

28. $(7^2 - 4^2) \times 2 + 10$ = _____

29. $36 - (5^2 - 4^2) \times 4$ = _____

30. $5^2 \times (31 - 3^3) + 99^0$ = _____

31. $(6^2 - 5^2)^2 \div 11$ = _____

32. $(4^3 - 5^2 \times 2)^2 \times 5$ = _____

Find the volume of each cube.

33.

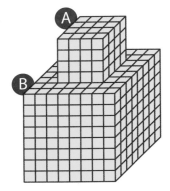

Volume of A

= 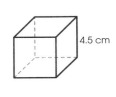^{3} = _____ (unit cube)

Volume of B

= 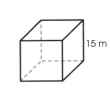^{3} = _____ (unit cube)

34.

4.5 cm

V =

35.

15 m

V =

36.

0.6 m

V =

Evaluate the cube of each number. Find the side length of each cube with the help of the evaluated answers. Then fill in the blank.

37.　　$1^3 = $ _____　　　$2^3 = $ _____　　　$3^3 = $ _____　　　$4^3 = $ _____　　　$5^3 = $ _____

　　　$0.5^3 = $ _____　　$1.2^3 = $ _____　　$2.5^3 = $ _____　　$3.4^3 = $ _____　　$4.2^3 = $ _____

38. **8 cm³**　Think: $8 = $ _____^{3}

　　side length = _____ cm

39. **15.625 cm³**　Think: $15.625 = $ _____^{3}

　　side length = _____ cm

40. **64 cm³**　Think: $64 = $ _____^{3}

　　side length = _____ cm

41. 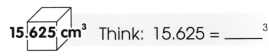 **1.728 cm³**　Think: $1.728 = $ _____^{3}

　　side length = _____ cm

42.　The side length of a cube is the value of the _____ of the power.
<u>base/exponent</u>

Finding common factors of 2 or more numbers using prime factors:

1st Find the prime factors of each number.

2nd Multiply any 2 or more common factors to form another common factor.

e.g. Find the common factors of 24 and 36.
Write each number as a product of prime factors.

$24 = 2 \times 2 \times 2 \times 3$ ← 2, 2, and 3 are
$36 = 2 \times 2 \times 3 \times 3$ common factors.

So, the common factors of 24 and 36 are
2, 3, 4 (2 x 2), **6** (2 x 3), **and 12** (2 x 2 x 3).

Write each number as a product of prime factors.

43. 25 = _____

44. 40 = _____

45. 42 = _____

46. 18 = _____

47. 72 = _____

48. 56 = _____

49. 96 = _____

50. 100 = _____

51. 300 = _____

Hint

You can use a factor tree to find all the prime factors of a composite number.

e.g.　　63
　　　　 / \
　　　 7   9
　　　　　 / \
　　　　　3   3

63 = 3 x 3 x 7
　 = 3^2 x 7

Write each number as a product of prime factors. Then find the common factors of each pair of numbers.

52. **30** = 2 x _____

　　45 = _____

　　common factors of 30 and 45: _____

53. **120** = _____

　　420 = _____

　　common factors of 120 and 420: _____

Don't you know that 120 and 420 have 11 common factors excluding 1?

ISBN: 978-1-77149-036-8　　　　Complete Canadian Curriculum • **Grade 8**　　**9**

Square Roots

- evaluate square roots
- estimate square roots
- find the areas and dimensions of squares and triangles involving square roots
- solve problems involving square roots

This wall is in the shape of a square and its area is 7 m². How long is this wall border?

Guess (square – side length)	Square of Guess (area)
2.6	6.76 (< 7)
2.7	7.29 (> 7)
2.65	7.02 (> 7) ✔
2.64	6.97 (< 7)
7.02 is closer to 7.	

The border should be about 2.65 m long.

Use a calculator to evaluate.

1. $\sqrt{81}$ = _____

2. $\sqrt{121}$ = _____   3. $\sqrt{361}$ = _____   4. $\sqrt{625}$ = _____

5. $\sqrt{900}$ = _____   6. $\sqrt{1.69}$ = _____   7. $\sqrt{0.25}$ = _____

Write the answers and circle the correct answer for each sentence.

8. $\left(\sqrt{16}\right)^2$ = ( )² = _____   9. $\left(\sqrt{100}\right)^2$ =

10. $\left(\sqrt{2.25}\right)^2$ =   11. $\left(\sqrt{a}\right)^2$ =

12.
The square of the square root of a number is the number   itself / squared .

13. $\sqrt{3^2}$ = $\sqrt{}$ = _____   14. $\sqrt{11^2}$ =

15. $\sqrt{100^2}$ =   16. $\sqrt{b^2}$ =

17.
The square root of a number squared is the number times 2 / itself .

ISBN: 978-1-77149-036-8

Approximating square roots using a guess-and-check method:

1st Find the two perfect squares that are closest to the number.

2nd Find the square roots of the two perfect squares.

3rd Choose a number that lies between the square roots and find the answer by guessing and checking.

e.g. Evaluate $\sqrt{21}$,

1st the two square roots closest to 21 are 16 and 25

2nd $\sqrt{16} = 4$ and $\sqrt{25} = 5$

3rd root: between 4 and 5

Guess   **Check**

4.5 $4.5^2 = 20.25$
4.6 $4.6^2 = 21.16$ ← closest to 21
4.7 $4.7^2 = 22.09$

So, the value of $\sqrt{21}$ is about 4.6.

Complete the number line. Find the value that each square root lies between. Then find the square root and round it to 1 decimal place.

18.

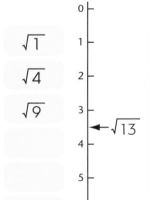

$\sqrt{1}$
$\sqrt{4}$
$\sqrt{9}$

$\sqrt{49}$
$\sqrt{64}$

$\sqrt{100}$

$\sqrt{169}$

← $\sqrt{13}$

19. $\sqrt{13}$: between $\sqrt{9}$ and $\sqrt{16}$ **Guess**   **Check**

$\sqrt{9}$ = _____ and $\sqrt{16}$ = _____

$\sqrt{13} \approx$ _____

20. $\sqrt{28}$: between ____ and ____   **Guess**   **Check**

21. $\sqrt{150}$: between ____ and ____   **Guess**   **Check**

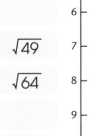

22. $\sqrt{85}$: between ____ and ____   **Guess**   **Check**

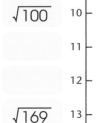

Put "<", "=", or ">" in the circles to make the statements true.

23. $\sqrt{25}$ ◯ $\sqrt{40}$

24. $\sqrt{44}$ ◯ 7

25. $\sqrt{510}$ ◯ $\sqrt{300}$

26. $\sqrt{250}$ ◯ 18

27. $\sqrt{100}$ ◯ $\sqrt{10^2}$

28. $(\sqrt{40})^2$ ◯ 14

Hint

If $a > b$, then $\sqrt{a} > \sqrt{b}$.

e.g. $16 > 9$, so $\sqrt{16} > \sqrt{9}$.

Put the numbers in order from least to greatest.

29. $\sqrt{100}$ 11 4^2

30. | 7^2 | 14 | $\sqrt{13^2}$ | $\sqrt{225}$ |

31. $\sqrt{33^2}$ 5^2 $(\sqrt{26})^2$

32. $\sqrt{169}$ 12 $\sqrt{11^2}$ $(\sqrt{10})^2$

Look at the figure. Find the area and dimensions of each shape.

33. The figure is formed by a rectangle, 2 small squares, and 1 big square.

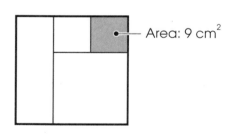

Area: 9 cm^2

	Area
small square	
big square	
rectangle	
whole figure	

34. The figure is formed by 1 square, 2 small triangles, and 1 big triangle.

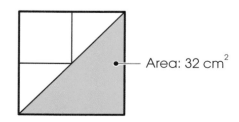

Area: 32 cm^2

	Area
big triangle	
small triangle	
square	
whole figure	

ISBN: 978-1-77149-036-8

Help the children find the side lengths of the squares. Then solve the problems.

35.

I have a spool of ribbon with a length of 1.5 m. Do I have enough ribbon to give each piece of cardboard a border? If so, how much ribbon will I have left?

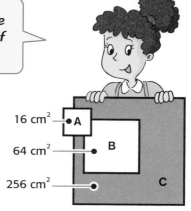

16 cm² — • A

64 cm² — • B

256 cm² — • • C

_____

36. Farmer Jack wants to fence his two fields.
   a.   About how much fencing is needed in total?

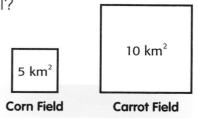

5 km²   10 km²

Corn Field   **Carrot Field**

_____

   b.   The total amount of fencing for both the corn and carrot field is the same as that needed for a wheat field. If the wheat field is also in the shape of a square, what is its side length?

_____

   c.

My field is in the shape of a square, too. The side length of my field is 2 times that of Farmer Jack's wheat field. Is the area of my field two times that of Farmer Jack's wheat field?

Tom

_____

ISBN: 978-1-77149-036-8

Pythagorean Theorem

- identify the legs and hypotenuse of a right triangle
- find the lengths of the sides of a right triangle using Pythagorean Theorem
- determine whether or not a triangle is a right triangle using Pythagorean Theorem
- solve problems using Pythagorean Theorem

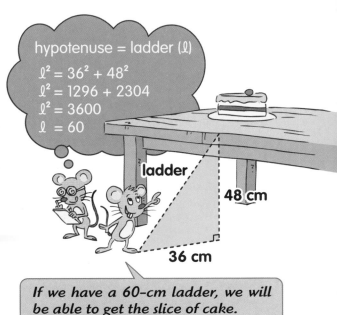

hypotenuse = ladder (ℓ)

$\ell^2 = 36^2 + 48^2$
$\ell^2 = 1296 + 2304$
$\ell^2 = 3600$
$\ell = 60$

ladder

48 cm

36 cm

If we have a 60-cm ladder, we will be able to get the slice of cake.

Fill in the blanks with the given words in the diagram. Then trace the hypotenuse of each triangle red and the legs blue.

1.

A Right Triangle

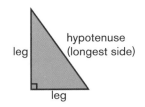

leg

hypotenuse (longest side)

leg

In a right triangle, the _____ form the right angle. The side opposite to the right angle is called the _____ , which is always the _____ side in a right triangle.

2.

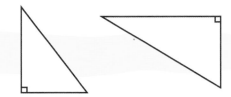

Draw a line to cut the rectangle into two identical right triangles. Then measure and record the lengths of the legs and hypotenuse of one of the triangles.

3.

legs: _____

hypotenuse: _____

4.

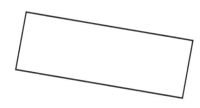

legs: _____

hypotenuse: _____

ISBN: 978-1-77149-036-8

Pythagorean Theorem:

In any right triangle, the square of the hypotenuse equals to the sum of the square of each of its legs.

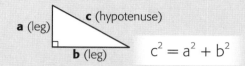

$c^2 = a^2 + b^2$

e.g. Find the length of the hypotenuse.

$h^2 = 3^2 + 4^2$
$h^2 = 9 + 16$
$h^2 = 25$
$h = 5$

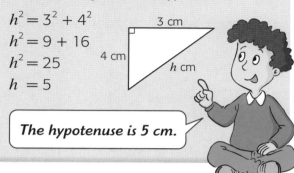

The hypotenuse is 5 cm.

Choose the correct equations.

5.

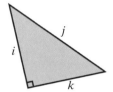

Ⓐ $i^2 = j^2 + k^2$

Ⓑ $j^2 = i^2 + k^2$

6.

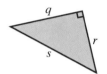

Ⓐ $s = \sqrt{r^2 + q^2}$

Ⓑ $s = \sqrt{r^2} + \sqrt{q^2}$

7.

Ⓐ $u^2 = t^2 - v^2$

Ⓑ $u^2 = v^2 - t^2$

Find the lengths of the missing sides. Show your work.

8.

$h^2 =$ _____ + _____

9.

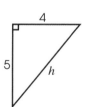

10.

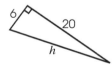

11.

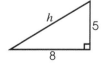

12.

It is an isosceles triangle.

Complete Canadian Curriculum • Grade 8   **15**

Find the lengths of the missing sides. Round the decimals to 2 decimal places.

13.
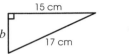

$b =$ _____

14.

$a =$ _____

15.

$k =$ _____

16.
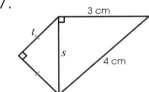

$p =$ _____

$q =$ _____

17.

$s =$ _____

$t =$ _____

The lengths of the three sides of each triangle are given. Decide whether or not each is a right triangle. Explain.

18.

19.
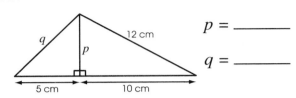

20. 7 cm, 11 cm, 5 cm

21. 6 cm, 10 cm, 8 cm

Hint

You may use Pythagorean Theorem
$a^2 + b^2 = c^2$ to tell whether or not a
triangle is a right triangle.

e.g.

1.

	$a^2 + b^2$	c^2
	$5^2 + 3^2$	6^2
	$25 + 9$	36
	34	36 ✗

It is not a right triangle.

2. lengths of a triangle:

4 cm, **5 cm**, 3 cm

└ hypotenuse (the longest)

$a^2 + b^2$	c^2
$4^2 + 3^2$	5^2
$16 + 9$	25
25	25 ✔

"4 cm, 5 cm, 3 cm" forms a
right triangle.

ISBN: 978-1-77149-036-8

Find the area of each coloured part.   Round the decimals to 2 decimal places.

22.

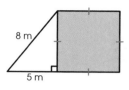

23.

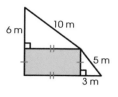

24.

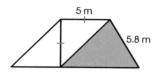

Solve the problems.

25. A ramp is attached to a truck for loading. What is the length of the ramp?

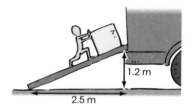

_____

26. If Janet walks across the court diagonally instead of walking along the border to reach the flag, how many fewer metres will she walk?

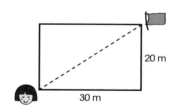

_____

27.

A slice of cake is 20 m due east and 10 m due south. Another slice is 15 m due west and 15 m due north. Which slice of cake am I closer to?

(You may draw a diagram to help you.)

_____

Integers

- add and subtract integers with the help of number lines
- multiply and divide positive and negative integers
- identify pattern rules and complete patterns
- solve problems involving negative integers

We are at B2, which is 2 floors below the ground level. How many floors do we go up to get to my apartment on the 5th floor?

$5 - (-2)$
$= 5 + 2$
$= 7$

We need to go 7 floors up.

Do the addition and subtraction with the help of the number line.

1. $(-3) + 5 =$ _____

2. $-5 - (-8) =$ _____

3. $-2 - (-3) + 5 =$ _____

4. $1 - 6 + 7 =$ _____

Find the answers.

5. $-9 + 5 - (-2) = -9 + 5 +$ _____ $=$ _____

6. $13 - 19 + (-4) = 13 - 19 -$ _____ $=$ _____

7. $21 - (-6) + (-3) =$ _____ $=$ _____

8. $-9 + (-7) - (-4) =$ _____ $=$ _____

9. $4 - 15 + (-7) =$ _____ $=$ _____

10. $(-19) - 7 + 8 =$ _____ $=$ _____

Hint

- Adding a negative integer means subtracting its opposite.

  e.g. $7 + (-2) = 7 - 2$
  $ = \underline{5}$

- Subtracting a negative integer means adding its opposite.

  e.g. $7 - (-2) = 7 + 2$
  $ = \underline{9}$

ISBN: 978-1-77149-036-8

When 2 integers with the same sign are multiplied, the product is always positive.

Multiplying Integers:

- **(+) x (+) → (+)**
  e.g. $(+2)(+3) = +6$

- **(–) x (+) → (–)**
  e.g. $(-2)(+3) = -6$

- **(+) x (–) → (–)**
  e.g. $(+2)(-3) = -6$

- **(–) x (–) → (+)**
  e.g. $(-2)(-3) = +6$

Fill in the blanks with "positive" or "negative".

11. a positive integer   x a positive integer   = a _____ integer

12. a positive integer   x a negative integer = a _____ integer

13. a negative integer x a positive integer   = a _____ integer

14. a negative integer x a negative integer = a _____ integer

15. a negative integer x a negative integer x a positive integer

    = a _____ integer

16. a positive integer x a negative integer x a positive integer

    = a _____ integer

Do the multiplication.

17. $(-3) \times 5 =$ _____

18. $(-7) \times (-8) =$ _____

19. $6 \times (-12) =$ _____

20. $6 \times (-4) =$ _____

21. $(-9) \times (-5) =$ _____

22. $(-10) \times 7 =$ _____

23. $(-8) \times 2 \times (-3) =$ _____

24. $(-4) \times (-2) \times (-8) =$ _____

25. $9 \times (-3) \times (-1) =$ _____

26. $3 \times 4 \times (-9) =$ _____

Fill in the missing integers.

27. $9 \times$ _____ $= -45$

28. _____ $\times (-3) = 15$

29. _____ $\times (-6) = -36$

30. $8 \times$ _____ $= -16$

31. $(-5) \times (-2) \times$ _____ $= -40$

32. _____ $\times 7 \times (-3) = 42$

Fill in the blanks with "positive" or "negative". Then write the sign of each quotient.

33. **Dividing Integers**

    • The quotient of 2 integers with the same sign is _____ .

      e.g. $(+12) \div (+2) = \blacksquare 6$ and $(-12) \div (-2) = \blacksquare 6$

    • The quotient of 2 integers with different signs is _____ .

      e.g. $(+12) \div (-2) = \blacksquare 6$ and $(-12) \div (+2) = \blacksquare 6$

Do the division.

34. $(+12) \div (-3) =$ _____

35. $(-10) \div 2 =$ _____

36. $(-78) \div (-6) =$ _____

37. $81 \div (-3) =$ _____

38. $(-98) \div 7 =$ _____

39. $(-76) \div (-2) =$ _____

40. $24 \div (-2) \div (-6) =$ _____

41. $10 \div (-2) \div (-1) =$ _____

42. $(-32) \div 4 \div (-2) =$ _____

43. $48 \div (-6) \div 2 =$ _____

Circle the part that you do first. Then find the answer.

44. $(-12) + (-4) \times 8$

    $= (-12) +$ _____

    $=$ _____

45. $13 \times (-5) \div 2$

    $=$ _____

    $=$ _____

46. $(-20) \div (-4) + (-18)$

    $=$ _____

    $=$ _____

47. $(-11) \times (-4 + 2)$

    $=$ _____

    $=$ _____

48. $(3^2 - 21) \div (-2)$

    $=$ _____

    $=$ _____

49. $(-30) \div 6 + (-5)$

    $=$ _____

    $=$ _____

ISBN: 978-1-77149-036-8

Find the pattern rule for each pattern. Then write the next three terms.

50. 1, -2, 4, -8, 16, _____ , _____ , _____

pattern rule: _____

51. 2, -5, 9, -19, 37, _____ , _____ , _____

pattern rule: _____

52. 128, -64, 32, -16, 8, _____ , _____ , _____

pattern rule: _____

53. -1276, 425, -142, 47, _____ , _____ , _____

pattern rule: _____

54. -3, -12, -48, -192, _____ , _____ , _____

pattern rule: _____

Solve the problems.

55. Each of the 7 members has a score of -6 in the first round.

a.   What is their total score?   _____

b.   They got a score of 35 in the second round. What is
the total score of the two rounds?   _____

56. Jason recorded the temperatures of the last five days.

   -21°C   -18°C   -17°C   -11°C   -23°C

a.   What is the mean temperature?   _____

b.
   Today's temperature is 3°C lower than the old mean.
   What is the new mean temperature?

_____

Order of Operations

- apply order of operations to integers
- evaluate expressions involving decimals
- evaluate expressions involving negative numbers
- identify the correct expressions to solve problems

No. of Dark Chocolates
$(7^2 - 9) + 4^2 \times 6$
$= (49 - 9) + 16 \times 6$
$= 40 + 96$
$= 136$

$7^2 - 9$

$4^2 \times 6$

Tim, let me give you all of my dark chocolates.

Thank you, Jane. So I'll have 136 dark chocolates.

Evaluate each expression.

1. $(12 - 4)^2 + 4^2 \div 2$

= _____^{2} + $4^2 \div 2$ ⟵ brackets

= _____ + _____ ÷ 2 ⟵ exponents

= _____ + _____ ⟵ divide

= _____ ⟵ add

2. $5^2 \times 8 - (10 - 5)^2$

=

> **Hint**
>
> When solving an expression that has multiple operations, there is an order to follow, often referred to as "BEDMAS".
>
> > **Brackets**
> > **Exponents**
> > **Divide**
> > **Multiply**
> > **Add**
> > **Subtract**

3. $4^3 \div 16 + 2^4 \times 3$ = _____

4. $10 \div (7 - 2) + 3^2$ = _____

5. $51 \div (5^2 - 2^3) + 4$ = _____

6. $(11 - 2) \times 4 - 6^2$ = _____

7. $(4^2 + 2^2) - 2 \times 3$ = _____

8. $5^2 \times 6 + (7 - 5)^2$ = _____

9. $(17 - 2)^2 \div (4 + 1)^2$ = _____

10. $(28 + 12) \times 3 + 2^3$ = _____

ISBN: 978-1-77149-036-8

Evaluate without using calculators. Show your work.

11. $(1.2 + 0.8)^2 - 9.9^0$

12. $22 - (1.7 + 2.3)^2$

13. $1.8^3 - (0.2^2 \times 5)$

14. $1.5^2 \times (0.1^3 + 9.999)^2$

15. $(10 - 8.5)^2 \times 2^2$

16. $1.1^3 + 3 \times 1.1$

17. $9^3 \div (5^2 - 4^2) + 11^2 =$ _____

18. $2^3 \times (8.25 - 3.75)^2 =$ _____

19. $(5 + 6.4 + 0.27)^0 \div 2 + 1.5 =$ _____

Evaluate each power. Then put "+" or "–" in the circles.

20.   **$(-4)^2$**   **-4^2**

= -4 x _____   = -(4 x   )

= + _____   = - _____

21.   **$(-2)^3$**   **-2^3**

= -2 x _____   = -(   )

= _____   = _____

22. $(-3)^4 =$ _____   23. $(-5)^2 =$ _____   24. $(-4)^5 =$ _____

-3^4 = _____ -5^2 = _____ -4^5 = _____

25.   a negative number with an even number exponent ➤ ◯ integer

26.   a negative number with an odd number exponent ➤ ◯ integer

Check the next step for each expression.

27. $(-8)^2 - (-3)^3 \times 2$

    (A) $-64 + 27 \times 2$

    (B) $64 - 27 \times 2$

    (C) $64 - (-27) \times 2$

28. $(-5^3) \div (-2)^2 + 8$

    (A) $(-125) \div 4 + 8$

    (B) $125 \div 4 + 8$

    (C) $(-125) \div (-4) + 8$

29. $(-14) - (-4)^3 \div 5^2$

    (A) $(-14) - 64 \div 25$

    (B) $(-14) - (-64) \div 25$

    (C) $(-14) + (-64) \div 25$

30. $(-3)^2 \times (-5)^2 - (-7)^3$

    (A) $9 \times (-25) - 343$

    (B) $9 \times 25 - (-343)$

    (C) $9 \times 25 - 343$

Evaluate the expressions.

31. $-5^3 - 7^2 \times (-6)^3$

    $=$

32. $(-2 - 3^2) \times (-3)^2$

    $=$

33. $(6^2 - (-2)^3) \div 2^2$

    $=$

34. $(-8^2 + 10^2) \div (5^2 - 4^2)$

    $=$

35. $2 \div (1 - 0.5)^2 = $ _____

36. $(0.96 + 0.2^2)^8 + (-3)^0 = $ _____

37. $(-4.5 - 1.5)^3 + (5 - 2^2)^{99} = $ _____

38. $(-7^2 + 5 \times 10)^9 \times (2^8 - 8^2) = $ _____

1 to the power of any number is always 1.

$$(1)^n = 1$$

ISBN: 978-1-77149-036-8

Check the correct expression for each question. Then find the answer.

39. Annie folds a piece of paper that measures 50 cm by 50 cm into two halves 6 times. What is the area of each small rectangle?

    (A) $50^2 \div 2^6$

    (B) $50^2 \div (2 \times 6)$

    (C) $50^2 \div 6^2$

    1st fold

    2nd fold

    Each small rectangle has an area of _____ .

40. A technician puts one each of two types of bacteria into a test tube. One type doubles itself every 10 minutes and another type triples itself every 15 minutes. After one hour, a drop of a chemical is added and the number of bacteria is reduced by 40%. What is the total number of bacteria left in the jar?

    (A) $(2 \times 6 + 3 \times 4) \times (1 - 0.4)$

    (B) $0.4 \times (2^6 + 3^4)$

    (C) $(2^6 + 3^4) \times (1 - 0.4)$

    The number of bacteria left in the jar is _____ .

41.

    I cut out 2 blocks from this modelling clay, each having a volume of 17.5 cm³. Then I cut out another 3 cubes from the remaining clay, each having a side length of 4 cm. How much has the volume of the original clay been reduced?

    (A) $17.5 \times 2 - 3 \times 4^3$

    (B) $17.5 \times 2 + 3 \times 4^3$

    (C) $17.5 \times (2 + 3) \times 4^3$

    The volume of the clay has been reduced by_____ .

Expanded Form and Scientific Notation

- write numbers in expanded form
- identify numbers that are written in scientific notation
- write numbers in scientific notation
- order numbers that are written in scientific notation
- solve problems involving scientific notation

What? Only $5.31 was raised!

No, Sam. They raised $531 000 000.

NEWS FUNDRAISING $5.31 $\times 10^8$

$5.31 \times 10^8 = \underline{531\ 000\ 000}$ ← scientific notation

$5.31\ 0\ 0\ 0\ 0\ 0\ 0$

Move the decimal point 8 places to the right.

Write each number in expanded form three different ways.

1. $724 = 700 +$ _____ $+$ _____

    $= 7 \times 100 +$ _____ $+$ _____

    $= 7 \times 10^2 +$ _____ $\times 10^1 +$ _____ $\times 10^0$

2. $253 =$

3. $896 =$

4. $1625 =$

5. $47\ 000 =$

Hint

Quick Reference:

$1 = 10^0$

$10 = 10^1$

$100 = 10^2$

$1000 = 10^3$

$10\ 000 = 10^4$

_____

$100\ 000\ 000 = \underline{10^8}$

Think: $1\ 0\ 0\ 0\ 0\ 0\ 0\ 0\ 0$

8 places to the left

Numbers in Scientific Notation*:

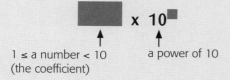 x $10^{\blacksquare}$

$1 \leq$ a number < 10
(the coefficient)

a power of 10

* Scientific notation is used to express very large numbers.

e.g. Write 625 000 in scientific notation.

Think: $625\,000$ Move the decimal point 5 places to the left to get the number 6.25 (which is greater than 1 and less than 10)

$625\,000 = \underline{6.25 \times 10^{5}}$ ← the number 5 indicates how many places the decimal point moved

Circle the number written in scientific notation in each group.

6. 1.75×10^{8}
   17.5×10^{7}
   1.75×2^{10}

7. 106×10^{3}
   1.06×10^{5}
   10.6×10^{4}

8. 0.04×10^{6}
   4×10^{4}
   4×100^{2}

9. 0.097×10^{8}
   9.7×10^{6}
   9.7×100^{3}

10. 1.52×100^{2}
    15.2×10^{3}
    1.52×10^{4}

11. 7.06×10^{4}
    0.706×10^{5}
    7.06×4^{10}

Fill in the blanks.

12. $34\,000$ = $3.4 \times$ _____

   = $3.4 \times 10^{\blacksquare}$

13. 9210   = _____

   = _____

14. 70 800 = _____

   = _____

15. 31 450 = _____

   = _____

Hint

Draw an arrow to help you count the number of places that the decimal point has moved.

e.g. $2\,6\,0\,0\,0.$
         4 3 2 1

The decimal point has moved 4 places to the left.

Fill in the blanks.

16. $250\,000\,000 = $ _____ $\times 10^8$

17. $3.27 \times 10^9 = $ _____

18. $31\,450\,000 = $ _____

19. $1.008 \times 10^6 = $ _____

20. $8\,012\,000 = $ _____

21. $6.324 \times 10^7 = $ _____

22. $19.27 \times 10^8 = $ _____ $\times 10^9$

23. $372 \times 10^{11} = 3.72 \times$ _____

24. $0.8507 \times 10^{10} = 8.507 \times$ _____

25. $200.86 \times 10^5 = 2.0086 \times$ _____

Write the numbers in standard form. Then complete the table.

26. $2 \times 10^2 + 4 \times 10^1$

$= 2 \times 100 + 4 \times$ _____

$= $ _____

27. $5 \times 10^3 + 2 \times 10^2 + 8 \times 10^1$

$= $ _____

$= $ _____

28. $8 \times 10^4 + 2 \times 10^2 + 3 \times 10^1 + 2 \times 10^0 = $ _____

29. $3 \times 10^5 + 2 \times 10^3 + 2 \times 10^1 + 1 \times 10^0 = $ _____

30. $2 \times 10^5 + 1 \times 10^4 + 2 \times 10^3 + 7 \times 10^1 = $ _____

31. The number of marbles produced in a factory on Tuesday was 10 times the number produced on Monday. The number of marbles produced on Monday was 10 times the number produced on Wednesday.

	Monday	Tuesday	Wednesday
Number of Marbles Produced	3.7×10^5		

32. The total number of marbles produced in the past three days is

_____ .

 ISBN: 978-1-77149-036-8

Comparing Numbers in Scientific Notation:

1st Compare the powers of 10. The greater the power, the greater the number.

2nd If the exponents are the same, compare the coefficients.

e.g. 2.3×10^6 and 9.8×10^3

2.3×10^6
9.8×10^3 — $6 > 3$, so 2.3×10^6 is greater.

$2.3 \times 10^6 > 9.8 \times 10^3$

e.g. 6.9×10^6 and 7.3×10^6

6.9×10^6
7.3×10^6 — Compare the coefficients. $7.3 > 6.9$, so 7.3×10^6 is greater.

$6.9 \times 10^6 < 7.3 \times 10^6$

Put each set of numbers in order from least to greatest.

33. 5.46×10^3
$6.54 \times 10^2 \quad 4.56 \times 10^4$

_____

34. 1.09×10^8
$9.01 \times 10^7 \quad 1.09 \times 10^7$

_____

35. 2.43×10^a
$2.34 \times 10^{a+2} \quad 3.42 \times 10^a$

_____

36. 4.65×10^b
$6.54 \times 10^b \quad 4.56 \times 10^b$

_____

Put the planets in order according to their masses. Then answer the question.

37. Planets (from heaviest to lightest)

_____

38. The mass of Saturn is about 100 times the mass of Earth. How heavy is Saturn?

_____

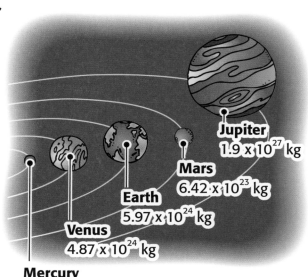

Jupiter
1.9×10^{27} kg

Mars
6.42×10^{23} kg

Earth
5.97×10^{24} kg

Venus
4.87×10^{24} kg

Mercury
3.3×10^{23} kg

ISBN: 978-1-77149-036-8

Ratio and Proportion

- write ratios in different ways
- use proportions to find missing terms
- find measurements of shapes using proportion
- find distances on maps with scales
- solve problems using proportion

Sam, the ratio of the number of hearts on my hat to yours is 2:3. There are 24 hearts on my hat.

$$\frac{2}{3} = \frac{24}{n}$$

$n = 36$

Do you mean that you are going to put 36 hearts on my hat?

Write the ratios in simplest form and in two different ways.

1.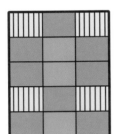

▌▌▌▌ to ▮ = 1:2 = _____

▮ to ▌▌▌▌ = _____ = _____

▮ to all = _____ = _____

Hint

Ratios can be written in 3 different ways.

e.g. ●●▲▲▲

- as a fraction
  ● to ▲ = $\frac{2}{3}$

- using the word "to"
  ● to ▲ = 2 to 3

- using a colon
  ● to ▲ = 2:3

2.

◆ to ◆ = _____ = _____

◆ to ◆ = _____ = _____

◆ to all = _____ = _____

Design a pattern with the given ratios.

3.  to all = 2:15

 to ▨ = 5:2

 to ▫ = 7:10

all to ▦ = 5:1

ISBN: 978-1-77149-036-8

Proportion:
an equation that has two equal ratios

There are 2 ways to find the missing term in a proportion.

e.g. $k:6 = 15:18$

Way 1
using equivalent fractions

$$\frac{k}{6} = \frac{15}{18}$$

×3

$k = \underline{5}$

Way 2
multiplying both sides by a number to isolate k

$$\frac{k}{6} \times 6 = \frac{15}{18} \times 6$$

$k = \underline{5}$

Find the missing terms. Show your work.

4. $2:p = 12:6$

5. $8:3 = s:9$

6. $3:7 = q:14$

7. $n:10 = 8:20$

8.  3 is to 4 as b is to 24

Look at the ratio of different coloured balls in the bag. Then solve it with proportion.

9. There are 10 red balls. Find the number of

    a.   blue balls

    b.   green balls

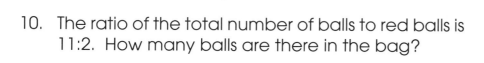

red:blue = 2:3
blue:green = 3:5

10. The ratio of the total number of balls to red balls is 11:2. How many balls are there in the bag?

Look at each pair of similar figures. Find the length of the missing side. Show your work.

11.

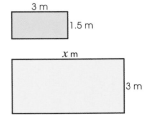

3 m

1.5 m

x m

3 m

12.

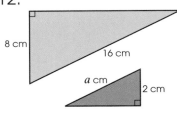

8 cm

16 cm

a cm

2 cm

13.

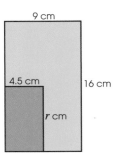

9 cm

4.5 cm

16 cm

r cm

14.

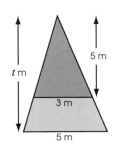

5 m

t m

3 m

5 m

Find the distance between the cities with the given scale. Show your work.

15. The scale tells us that 1 cm on the map represents _____ cm of actual distance.

16. Find the distance between

a. the school and library

_____

b. Mary's house and the theatre

_____

c. the library and theatre

_____

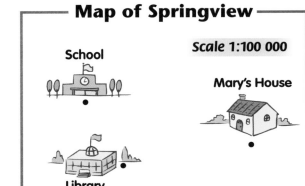

— Map of Springview —

School

Scale 1:100 000

Mary's House

Library

Theatre

ISBN: 978-1-77149-036-8

Find the scale of the map with the given information. Then find the distances.

17. a.   The scale of the map is _____ .

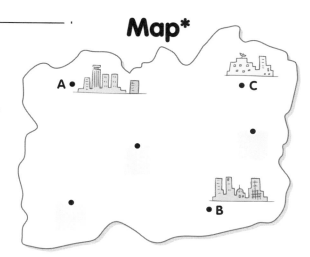

Map*

A ●

● C

● B

b.   The actual distance between

   • City A and City C is _____ .

   • City B and City C is _____ .

c.   The actual distance between City C and City D is 132 km. Mark "D" on the map.

* The actual distance between City A and City B is 120 km.

Solve the problems using proportion. Show your work.

18.   The number of star stickers to heart stickers in a box is in the ratio of 4:5. There are 320 star stickers. How many more heart stickers than star stickers are there?

_____

19.

> The ratio of star stickers to heart stickers on this hat is 3:6 and the ratio of heart stickers to flower stickers is 2:7. There are 14 flower stickers on the hat. How many star stickers are there?

_____

Rate

- find simple rates
- compare rates
- find exchange rates
- solve problems involving rates

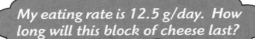

My eating rate is 12.5 g/day. How long will this block of cheese last?

No. of Days = 200 ÷ 12.5
= 16

CHEESE 200 g

It will last 16 days.

Find the unit rate for each situation.

1. typing 34 words in half a minute

_____ words/min

2. earning $385 a week

$_____ /day

3. a dozen eggs for $2.04

_____ ¢/egg

4. running 5 tracks in 7 minutes

_____ min/track

5. printing 20 copies in 45 seconds

_____ s/copy

6. serving 4 customers in 1 hour

_____ min/customer

Find the unit rates. Then check the best buy.

7.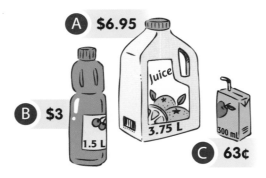

A $6.95

Juice

B $3

1.5 L

3.75 L

C 63¢

300 mL

Unit Price

(A) $_____ /L

(B) $_____

(C) $_____

8.

A $6.88

Flour

Flour 600 g

4.3 kg

Flour 2.25 kg

B $1.44

C $4.50

Unit Price

(A) $_____ /kg

(B) $_____

(C) $_____

ISBN: 978-1-77149-036-8

Find the food items that the children bought. Show your work.

9. Katie bought 3 L of juice that cost $3.90.

 $1.28/L

 0.13¢/mL

 $1.42/L

Cost of 3 L =

Katie bought _____ juice.

10. Joe bought 200 g of deli meat that cost $3.60.

 2¢/g

 $21/kg

 1.8¢/g

Joe bought _____ .

Complete the table and find the exchange rates. Then answer the question.

11.

Exchange Rate

USD ($)	CAD ($)	HKD ($)
1		7.75
3	3.69	
5		
7		
9		
10		
20		
30		

12. Write the exchange rates.

a. USD $1 = CAN $_____

b. CAD $1 = HKD $_____

c. HKD $1 = USD $_____

13.

I have USD $4, HKD $70, and CAD $21. How much do I have in total in CAD?

_____

ISBN: 978-1-77149-036-8

Look at the recipe and read what Karen says. Help her solve the problems.

14.

> I want to make 15 servings of banana bread. How much of each ingredient do I need?

Karen needs:

- butter: _____
- sugar: _____
- banana: _____
- salt: _____
- baking powder: _____

Banana Bread
(10 servings)

- 3 teaspoons of baking powder
- 3 bananas
- 120 g of butter
- $\frac{1}{2}$ teaspoon of salt
- 2 cups of flour
- $\frac{1}{2}$ cup of sugar

15. A tub of 500 g of butter costs $5.48. How much does the butter needed for Karen's loaf cost? _____

16. How much salt does Karen need if she makes 20 servings? _____

17. How many servings can Karen make with 2 cups of sugar? _____

18. How many bananas are needed for

   a. 6 cups of flour?

   b. 240 g of butter?

   _____   _____

Solve the problems.

19. Look at the price of pebbles.

$4.50/kg

   a. How many kilograms of pebbles can be bought with $10?

     _____

   b. How much do $3\frac{1}{5}$ kg of pebbles cost?

     _____

20. A customer gets one free pack of correction pens for every purchase of 5 packs. How much does each correction pen cost if a customer

$5.75/pack

   a. buys 1 pack?

     _____

   b. buys 5 packs and gets 1 pack for free?

     _____

21. Michelle makes 19 cookies in 30 minutes and Jane makes 30 in 45 minutes.

   a. What is the total number of cookies made by both girls in 1.5 hours?

     _____

   b.

What is the ratio of the number of cookies that Michelle makes to what I make in 3 hours?

Jane

     _____

Application of Percent

- find percent change
- find sale price of items in different ways
- find sale tax on items
- calculate simple interest using the formula

Decrease: 250 – 200 = 50

Decrease as a fraction of the original: $\frac{50}{250} = \frac{1}{5}$

Percent decrease: $\frac{1}{5} \times 100\% = 20\%$

How come the weight of the cookies decreased by 20%?

Fill in the blanks and find the percent change.

1. The average test score increased from 78 to 87.

   - Increase: _____

   - Increase as a fraction of the original: _____

   - Percent increase: _____ x 100% = _____

The test score increased by about _____ %.

2. To drop from 51 kg to 46 kg

   - Decrease: _____

   - Decrease as a fraction of the original:

     _____

   - Percent decrease:

     _____ = _____

3. To grow from 160 cm to 178 cm

   - Increase: _____

   - Increase as a fraction of the original:

     _____

   - Percent increase:

     _____ = _____

ISBN: 978-1-77149-036-8

Finding the Sale Price Using Two Different Ways:

e.g.   The regular price of a circus show ticket is $95. If the ticket is sold at a 25% discount, what is its sale price?

Way 1 Find the discount. Then subtract.

Discount: $95 x 25% = $23.75

Sale Price: $\underline{\$95}$ − $\underline{\$23.75}$ = $71.25
            regular   discount
            price

The sale price of the ticket is $71.25.

Way 2 Find the percent. Then multiply.

Discount in Percent: 1 − 25% = 75%

Sale Price: $\underline{\$95}$ x $\underline{75\%}$ = $71.25
            regular   discount
            price   in percent

Find the sale price of each item. Then answer the question.

	Way 1	Way 2

Ideal Clothing

*Get **30% Off** Regular Price*

4.

• $110.50

5.

• $59.24

6.

• $82.88

7.   Ms. Collins buys a 3-piece suit set. How much does it cost? (You may use either method to find the answer.)

Get an extra 10% off on a 3-piece set.

The suit set costs _____ .

Finding Sales Tax:

e.g. A printer costs $112. How much does it cost including the PST and GST?

PST (8%) = $112 x 8% = $8.96
GST (5%) = $112 x 5% = $5.60
Total Cost: $112 + $8.96 + $5.60 = $126.56

The total cost of the printer is $126.56.

In Ontario

PST (Provincial Sales Tax) = 8%
GST (Goods and Services Tax) = 5%

Find the taxes and total cost of each item.

8.

 $59.50    $98.70    $110.54

PST	_____ x 8% = _____		
GST	_____ x 5% = _____		
Total Cost			

All the appliances and toys are 15% and 35% off the regular price respectively. Complete the information chart and answer the question.

9.

Stove Top: $1340	Oven: $1780	Bike: $218.50
Sale Price: _____	Sale Price: _____	Sale Price: _____
PST: _____	PST: _____	PST: _____
GST: _____	GST: _____	GST: _____
Total: _____	Total: _____	Total: _____

10. The regular price of an oven in another store is $1690 and is selling at a discount of 10%. Is this oven a better buy than the one above? Explain.

_____

   ISBN: 978-1-77149-036-8

Simple interest – interest that is calculated only on the principal

Simple interest formula:

$$I = P \times r \times t$$

Interest ($)
Principal ($)
Interest Rate (%)
Time (years)

e.g. Galie deposited $500 into a bank account at the simple interest rate of 6%. How much interest does Galie earn in 3 years?

P = $500   I = P x r x t
r = 6%   = $500 x 6% x 3
t = 3   = $90

Galie earns $90 interest in 3 years.

Find the values of the missing terms.

11. **P = $2500   r = 9%   t = 5**

    I = _____ x _____ x _____

    = _____

12. **P = $39 000   r = 5%   t = 3**

    I = _____

    = _____

13. P= $180

    r = 5.5%

    t = 2

    I = _____

14. P= $3600

    r = 7.25%

    t = _____

    I = $1957.50

15. P= $8300

    r = _____

    t = $1\frac{1}{4}$ ← 1 year 3 months

    I = $207.50

Solve the problems.

16. I deposited $5800 into a simple interest savings account $2\frac{1}{2}$ years ago and earned $522. What was the interest rate?

    _____

17.
> *I borrowed $19 385 at a simple interest rate of 5.5% for the car. If I wait 9 months to repay the loan in full, how much interest will I be paying back?*

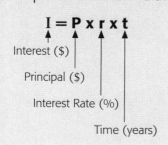

    _____

Fractions

- add and subtract fractions that have different denominators
- multiply fractions and mixed numbers
- divide fractions and mixed numbers
- solve problems involving operations on fractions

James, I'm going to make a bowl of fruit punch for you with these two bottles of juice.

Total amount of juice:

$$2\frac{1}{3} + 1\frac{1}{6} = 2\frac{2}{6} + 1\frac{1}{6}$$
$$= 3\frac{3}{6}$$
$$= 3\frac{1}{2} > 3$$

Thank you, Sue. There will be $3\frac{1}{2}$ L of fruit punch. I think you'll need a bigger bowl.

Add or subtract the fractions. Write the answers in simplest form.

1. $\dfrac{3}{8} - \dfrac{2}{7}$ = _____ − _____ = _____

2. $\dfrac{7}{12} + \dfrac{1}{6}$ = _____ = _____

3. $2\dfrac{3}{7} + \dfrac{16}{21}$ = _____ = _____

4. $1\dfrac{1}{3} - \dfrac{1}{12}$ = _____ = _____

5. $3\dfrac{4}{15} + 1\dfrac{7}{30}$ = _____ = _____

6. $1\dfrac{3}{4} + 1\dfrac{1}{2}$ = _____ = _____

Hint

To add mixed numbers, add the fractions first; then add the whole numbers.

e.g. $1\dfrac{1}{2} + 2\dfrac{2}{5} = 1\dfrac{5}{10} + 2\dfrac{4}{10}$
$$= 3\dfrac{9}{10}$$

add whole numbers
(1 + 2 = 3)

add fractions
($\dfrac{5}{10} + \dfrac{4}{10} = \dfrac{9}{10}$)

Find the sum and difference of each pair.

		Sum	Difference
7. $2\dfrac{1}{2}$	$5\dfrac{4}{6}$	_____	_____
8. 10	$3\dfrac{7}{9}$	_____	_____
9. $3\dfrac{7}{10}$	$1\dfrac{2}{15}$	_____	_____
10. $1\dfrac{3}{8}$	$1\dfrac{1}{4}$	_____	_____

ISBN: 978-1-77149-036-8

Multiplying Fractions:

1st Change all mixed numbers to improper fractions.

2nd Divide the numerators and the denominators by their common factors.

3rd Multiply the numerators and the denominators.

e.g. $\dfrac{9}{14} \times 1\dfrac{1}{6}$

$= \dfrac{9}{14} \times \dfrac{7}{6}$ ← Change the mixed number to improper fraction.

$= \dfrac{\overset{3}{\cancel{9}}}{\underset{2}{\cancel{14}}} \times \dfrac{\cancel{7}^{1}}{\cancel{6}_{2}}$ ← Divide the numerator and the denominators by their common factors, 3 and 7. Then multiply.

$= \dfrac{3}{4}$

Multiply the fractions.

11. $\dfrac{3}{7} \times \dfrac{2}{9}$

12. $\dfrac{5}{22} \times 2\dfrac{3}{4}$

13. $1\dfrac{7}{12} \times \dfrac{2}{5}$

14. $\dfrac{7}{10} \times 3\dfrac{4}{7} = \underline{\qquad}$

15. $2\dfrac{5}{8} \times 1\dfrac{3}{14} = \underline{\qquad}$

16. $1\dfrac{9}{13} \times 1\dfrac{5}{11} = \underline{\qquad}$

17. $6\dfrac{4}{5} \times 2\dfrac{10}{17} = \underline{\qquad}$

Answer the questions.

18. Joe walked $\dfrac{1}{3}$ of the journey to the library from his house to meet his cousin, Lucy. How far did he travel?

Library

$1\dfrac{3}{4}$ **km**

Joe's House

_____

19. A bag of flour weighs $3\dfrac{3}{4}$ kg. Aunt Katie used $\dfrac{1}{3}$ of the bag of flour to make a cake. How much flour was used to make the cake?

_____

Dividing Fractions:

1st Change all mixed numbers to improper fractions.

2nd Find the reciprocal of the divisor.

3rd Multiply the dividend by the reciprocal of the divisor.

e.g. $\dfrac{3}{4} \div 1\dfrac{1}{8}$

$= \dfrac{3}{4} \times \dfrac{8}{9}$ ← $1\dfrac{1}{8} = \dfrac{9}{8}$, reciprocal of $\dfrac{9}{8}$ is $\dfrac{8}{9}$

$= \dfrac{\overset{1}{\cancel{3}}}{\underset{1}{\cancel{4}}} \times \dfrac{\overset{2}{\cancel{8}}}{\underset{3}{\cancel{9}}}$

$= \dfrac{2}{3}$

To find the reciprocal of a fraction, swap the denominator and the numerator. If it is a mixed number, change it to an improper fraction first.

Find the reciprocal of each fraction.

20. $\dfrac{14}{19}$ _____

21. $\dfrac{6}{5}$ _____

22. $1\dfrac{2}{7}$ _____

23. $4\dfrac{6}{11}$ _____

24. $\dfrac{1}{3}$ _____

25. 5 _____

Do the division.

26. $14 \div \dfrac{7}{8} =$ _____

27. $\dfrac{9}{13} \div 1\dfrac{1}{8} =$ _____

28. $\dfrac{3}{11} \div 9 =$ _____

29. $\dfrac{6}{13} \div \dfrac{12}{26} =$ _____

30. $27 \div 4\dfrac{10}{11} =$ _____

31. $1\dfrac{3}{14} \div 6\dfrac{4}{5} =$ _____

Solve the problems.

32. *I'll pack this box of apples into bags each holding $1\dfrac{1}{4}$ kg of apples. How many bags do I need?*

_____

33. There are about 5 apples in a bag. How heavy is an apple on average?

_____

ISBN: 978-1-77149-036-8

Evaluate each expression and write the answers in simplest form.

34. $(\dfrac{2}{7} + \dfrac{5}{14}) \times \dfrac{8}{15}$

35. $3\dfrac{1}{3} \div 2\dfrac{2}{3} - \dfrac{6}{7}$

36. $1\dfrac{3}{8} - \dfrac{1}{2} \times \dfrac{4}{5}$

37. $\dfrac{7}{16} \div \dfrac{1}{4} \times \dfrac{10}{21} = \underline{\hspace{1cm}}$

38. $4\dfrac{7}{8} \times \dfrac{4}{13} - \dfrac{9}{10} \div 3 = \underline{\hspace{1cm}}$

39. $1\dfrac{5}{13} \times (3\dfrac{7}{9} - \dfrac{7}{2}) = \underline{\hspace{1cm}}$

40. $\dfrac{6}{7} + \dfrac{1}{3} \times \dfrac{9}{10} - \dfrac{13}{35} = \underline{\hspace{1cm}}$

Solve the problems.

41. Kary has bought 3 pizzas. She saves $\dfrac{1}{2}$ of a pizza for her family and serves each guest $\dfrac{1}{6}$ of a pizza. How many guests are there?

_____

42. How much juice does Kary have?

_____

43. How many cups can all of the jars fill?

_____

Each jar holds $3\dfrac{2}{3}$ L of juice.

$\dfrac{3}{8}$ L

4 full jars and 1 half-filled jar of juice

Decimals, Fractions, and Percents

- identify the repeated digits in repeating decimals
- identify terminating and repeating decimals
- put numbers in order
- divide numbers by decimal numbers
- solve word problems

Sue, I'm tired of having to keep writing "3".

$0.\overline{3}$

decimal of $\frac{1}{3}$

0.3333333333

You can just put a bar over the repeated digit "3" to show that $\frac{1}{3}$ is a repeating decimal.

Circle the digits that repeat in each repeating decimal. Then rewrite the decimal with a bar over the repeated digits.

1. 0.99999... = $0.\overline{9}$

2. 1.1313131... = _____

3. 1.02402402... = _____

4. 5.08181818... = _____

5. 3.12342342... = _____

6. 2.781321321... = _____

7. 1.1718418418... = _____

8. 4.053053053... = _____

Convert the fractions to decimals. Then write "T" for terminating decimals and "R" for repeating decimals in the circles.

9. $\frac{3}{5}$ = _____ ◯

10. $\frac{2}{9}$ = _____ ◯

11. $\frac{5}{74}$ = _____ ◯

12. $2\frac{7}{8}$ = _____ ◯

13. $\frac{7}{12}$ = _____ ◯

14. $1\frac{12}{25}$ = _____ ◯

15. $3\frac{8}{11}$ = _____ ◯

16. $4\frac{5}{6}$ = _____ ◯

> **Hint**
>
> **Terminating decimal**: a decimal having a finite number of digits
>
> e.g. 0.85, 2.459
>
> **Repeating decimal**: a decimal having an infinite number of digits
>
> e.g. 0.8888... = $0.\overline{8}$
>
> 3.181818... = $3.\overline{18}$

ISBN: 978-1-77149-036-8

Write the fraction, decimal, and percent for the coloured part of each figure.

17.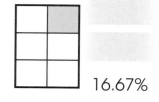

16.67%

18.

0.$\overline{5}$

19.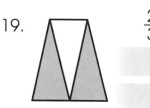

$\frac{2}{3}$

20.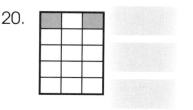

21.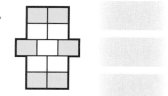

22.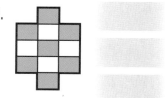

Put ">", "<", or "=" to make each statement true.

23. $\frac{2}{9}$ ◯ 0.$\overline{2}$

24. 0.4 ◯ 0.4$\overline{1}$

25. $\frac{1}{8}$ ◯ 0.12$\overline{5}$

26. 0.1$\overline{9}$ ◯ 1.$\overline{19}$

27. 0.$\overline{3}$ ◯ $\frac{4}{11}$

28. 2$\frac{1}{3}$ ◯ 2.0$\overline{3}$

29. $\frac{2}{11}$ ◯ 0.00$\overline{8}$

30. 0.5$\overline{3}$ ◯ $\frac{8}{15}$

31. 0.$\overline{07}$ ◯ $\frac{7}{90}$

Order each set of numbers from least to greatest. Then do what the girl says.

32. 206%   2.0$\overline{6}$ 2.0$\overline{06}$ 2.00$\overline{6}$ _____

33. 1.16   1$\frac{1}{6}$ 1.0$\overline{6}$ 1$\frac{6}{9}$ _____

34. $\frac{7}{11}$ 0.6$\overline{3}$ 63.3% $\frac{33}{90}$ _____

35.

Change 1.207 into different repeating decimals by putting a bar over the digit(s). Then put them in order.

_____

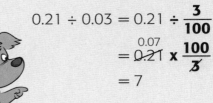

Dividing Decimals by 0.1, 0.01, 0.001:

$$\begin{aligned} &\div\ \mathbf{0.1} && \mathbf{x\ 10} \\ \text{a decimal}\ &\div\ \mathbf{0.01}\ = \text{the decimal}\ \mathbf{x\ 100} \\ &\div\ \mathbf{0.001} && \mathbf{x\ 1000} \end{aligned}$$

e.g. $8.9 \div 0.1 = 8.9\ \mathbf{x\ 10}$
$= 89$

$0.21 \div 0.03 = 0.21 \div \dfrac{3}{100}$

$= 0.\overset{0.07}{\cancel{21}}\ x\ \dfrac{100}{\cancel{3}}$

$= 7$

Do the division.

36. $0.281 \div 0.1 =$ _____

37. $8.07 \div 0.001 =$ _____

38. $0.506 \div 0.01 =$ _____

39. $1.13 \div 0.001 =$ _____

40. $14 \div 0.1 =$ _____

41. $2.8 \div 0.7 =$ _____

42. $0.8 \div 0.02 =$ _____

43. $1.6 \div 0.4 =$ _____

44. $0.09 \div 0.3 =$ _____

45. $0.81 \div 0.009 =$ _____

Find the missing numbers.

46. $0.078 \div$ _____ $= 7.8$

47. _____ $\div 0.001 = 2023$

48. _____ $\div 0.1 = 10.8$

49. $0.73 \div$ _____ $= 14.6$

50. $3.6 \div$ _____ $= 9$

51. _____ $\div 0.09 = 80$

52. $\dfrac{2.5}{\boxed{}} = 5$

53. $\dfrac{4}{\boxed{}} = 8$

54. $\dfrac{\boxed{}}{0.03} = 40$

55. $\dfrac{\boxed{}}{0.005} = 30$

Hint

A fraction can be rewritten as a division.

e.g. $\dfrac{0.8}{\boxed{}} = 4$ — equivalent

$0.8 \div \boxed{} = 4$

ISBN: 978-1-77149-036-8

Complete the charts.

56.

÷ 10	
0.25	
	4.5
3.4	

57.

÷ 0.01	
1.4	
	27.9
0.26	

58.

÷ 0.1	
0.7	
	18.6
	0.29

59.

÷ 0.2	
0.18	
	4
1.56	

60.

÷ 0.05	
0.15	
	10
1.2	

61.

÷ 0.003	
0.9	
	60
1.8	

Help Mr. Welly solve the problems.

62. Mr. Welly had 1.78 kg of ground beef and he used 35% of it to make a shepherd's pie. How many kilograms of ground beef are left?

63.

> 0.65 L of water and $\frac{7}{12}$ of a box of beef stock are needed to make a tasty soup base.

a. How many litres of soup base will Mr. Welly get?

b. Mr. Welly used 45% of the remaining stock to make the shepherd's pie. How much beef stock is there now?

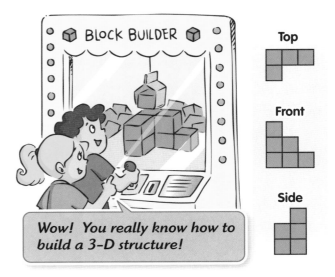

Nets

- identify the top, front, and side views of different solids
- match the views with the solids
- sketch solids with given views
- draw nets of prisms
- understand Euler's formula

Wow! You really know how to build a 3-D structure!

Label the views of the solids. Write "top", "side", or "front" on the lines.

1.

_____

_____

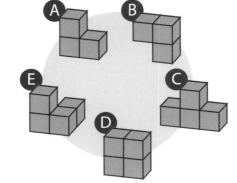

_____

2.

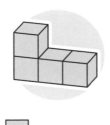

_____

_____

_____

3.

_____

_____

_____

Match the solids with the given views. Write the letters.

4.

solid	top	front	side
◯			
◯			
◯			

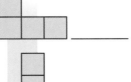

ISBN: 978-1-77149-036-8

Cross out the wrong view of each solid. Then draw the correct one in the circle.

5.
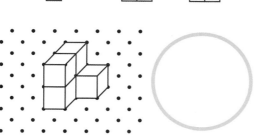

6.

7.
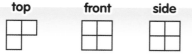

8.
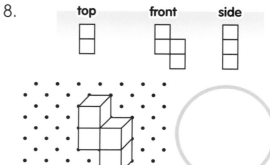

Sketch the objects on the isometric dot paper.

9.
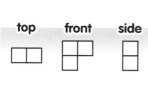

10.
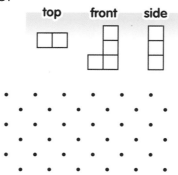

11.

Draw the missing faces to complete the net of each prism. Label the measurements of the sides in bold. Then draw another net that can be folded to give the same prism.

12.

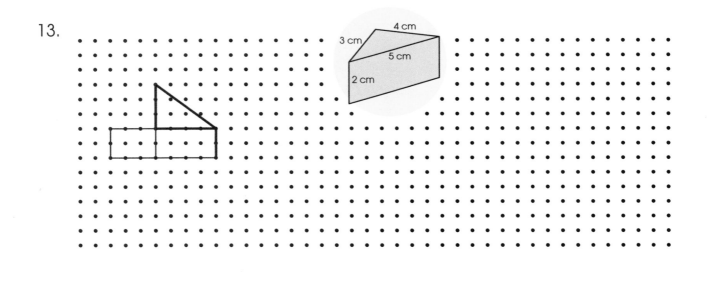

8 cm
5 cm
4 cm
2 cm

Description: _____

_____

13.

4 cm
3 cm
5 cm
2 cm

Description: _____

_____

ISBN: 978-1-77149-036-8

Match the views with the correct object. Then sketch a possible net and name the object.

14.

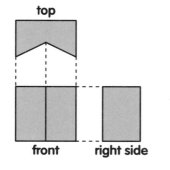

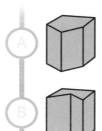

Ⓐ

Ⓑ

15.

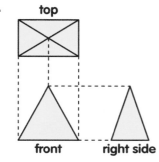

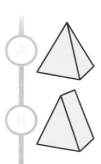

Ⓐ

Ⓑ

Complete the chart and Euler's formula to show the relationships among the vertices, faces, and edges of a solid. Then answer the question.

16. a.

Solid	Rectangular Prism	Triangular Pyramid	Pentagonal Pyramid
No. of Vertices (V)			
No. of Faces (F)			
No. of Edges (E)			
V + F − E			

b. Euler's fomula: V + F − E = _____

17.

There are 7 vertices and 7 faces in a solid. How many edges does it have? Name the solid.

_____

Circumference and Area

- identify the radius and diameter of a circle
- find the circumference and area of a circle
- solve problems involving circumference and area
- draw circles with given information

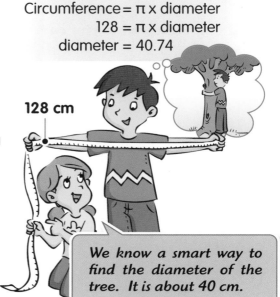

Circumference = π x diameter
128 = π x diameter
diameter = 40.74

128 cm

We know a smart way to find the diameter of the tree. It is about 40 cm.

Fill in the blanks with the help of the words given in the diagram.

1. _____ (r):
   the length of any line segment from the centre of a circle to its edge

2. _____ (d):
   the length of any line segment that passes through the centre where its endpoints are on the edge

3. _____ (C):
   the perimeter of a circle

4. *pi* (π):
   a number, 3.141592... , which is the ratio of a
   circle's circumference to its _____

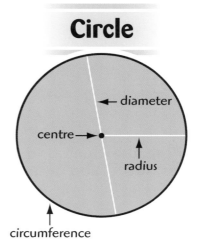

Circle

diameter

centre

radius

circumference

Draw a radius with a red pen and a diameter with a blue pen on each circle. Measure and record the lengths. Then answer the questions.

5. **A** r = _____   d = _____
   B r = _____   d = _____

6. What is the relationship between radius and diameter?

   _____

   _____

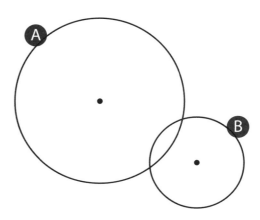

ISBN: 978-1-77149-036-8

Finding the Circumference of a Circle:

C = πd

or

C = 2πr

e.g. What is the circumference of the circle with a diameter of 4 cm?

C = πd
= π x 4
≈ 12.57 (cm)

π = 3.14

You may find the answer using the "π" button on your calculator or by substituting π with 3.14.

Find the circumference of each circle.

7. **d = 3 cm**

C = _____ x _____

= _____

8. **r = 10 m**

C = _____

= _____

9. **r = 0.5 cm**

C = _____

= _____

10. **d = 0.68 m**

C = _____

= _____

11. 7 cm   C = _____

= _____

12. 1 m   C = _____

= _____

Solve the problems.

13. The circumference of a circle is 46 cm. What is its radius? _____

14. 50.27 cm of string was needed to wrap around a circular object twice. What is the radius of the object? _____

15. Molly makes 3 identical circles with a string of 152 cm long. What is the diameter of each circle? _____

16. The circumference of a big circle is 62.83 cm and it is twice as long as that of a small circle. What is the radius of the small circle? _____

Finding the Area of a Circle:

$A = \pi r^2$
or
$A = \pi(\dfrac{d}{2})^2$

e.g.   Find the areas.

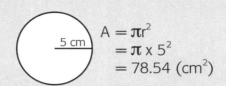

5 cm

$A = \pi r^2$
$= \pi \times 5^2$
$= 78.54\ (cm^2)$

12 cm

$A = \pi(\dfrac{d}{2})^2$
$= \pi(\dfrac{12}{2})^2$
$= \pi \times 6^2$
$= 113.1\ (cm^2)$

Find the area of each circle.

17. r = 1 cm

A =

18. r = 3.9 cm

A =

19. r = 20 cm

A =

Sally has made 3 circles out of modelling clay. Find the areas of the circles. Then answer the questions.

20.

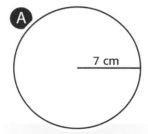

A

7 cm

B

4.5 cm

C

8 cm

21.

I make one big circle that has the same area as the sum of the 3 circles. What is the radius of the big circle?

_____

22.

I'm making 3 identical circles. Their total area is the same as the big circle's. What is the radius of each circle?

_____

ISBN: 978-1-77149-036-8

Drawing Circles:

e.g.   Draw a circle with a radius of 5 cm.

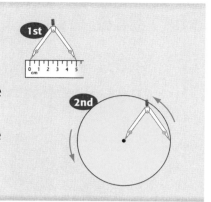

1st   Use a ruler to set the point of the compass and the point of the pencil to be 5 cm apart.

2nd   Place the point of the compass at the centre of the circle and turn the compass 360°.

Draw circles with the given dots as their centres. Then answer the questions.

23. **A**: centre at A with r = 2.5 cm

B: centre at B with r = 2 cm

C: centre at C with d = 3 cm

24. Points A, B, and C are the vertices of △ABC. Explain how to find the side lengths of △ABC without using a ruler.

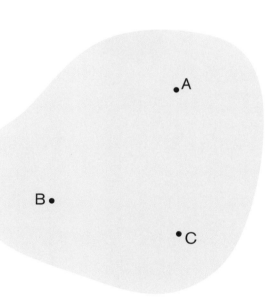

Solve the problems.

25. Tom wants to cut out the largest circle possible from the cardboard to make a spinner. What is the area of the spinner?

_____

26. Timmy the Dog wants to put a ribbon around the spinner. How much ribbon will he need?

_____

Surface Area and Volume

- find the volume of a cylinder
- find the surface area of a cylinder
- solve problems involving the volumes and surface areas of cylinders

Volume = $\pi r^2 h$
= $\pi \times 8^2 \times 25$
= 5027 (cm^3)
≈ 5 (L)

8 cm

25 cm

His water bottle can hold about 5 L of water.

Complete the formula for finding the volume of a cylinder. Then find the volume of each cylinder.

1.

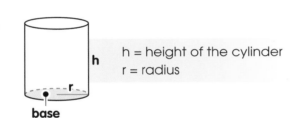

h = height of the cylinder
r = radius

Volume of a Cylinder

= base area x height

= _____ x _____

2. **r = 5, h = 4**

V =

3. **r = 3.5, h = 6**

V =

4. **r = 9.2, h = 5.5**

V =

5.

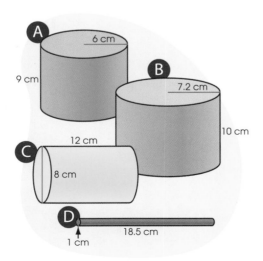

A   6 cm

9 cm

B   7.2 cm

12 cm   10 cm

C

8 cm

D

18.5 cm

1 cm

A

B

C

D

ISBN: 978-1-77149-036-8

Find the capacity of each container in litres. Then answer the questions.

6.

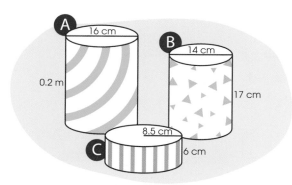

A

B

C

7. Jason poured some water into **B** and the water level reached 12 cm. How much water did Jason pour? _____

8. How much water can **C** hold if it is half full? _____

9. One cup holds 450 mL of water. How many cups are needed to fill **A** and **C**? _____

10. Philip filled up **B** with water and poured it into **C**. After filling up **C**, there is some water left in **B**. What is its water level? _____

11.

I poured 3500 mL of water into **A**. *What is its water level?*

_____

Look at the net of a cylinder. Record the measurements. Then complete the formula for finding the surface area of a cylinder.

12.

Surface Area of a Cylinder

$$= 2 \bigcirc + 1 \boxed{}$$

$$= 2\pi \underline{}^2 + \underline{} \times h$$

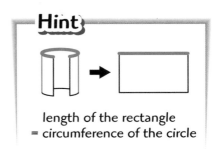

Hint

length of the rectangle
= circumference of the circle

Find the surface area of each cylinder.

13.

8 cm

25 cm

surface area =

14.

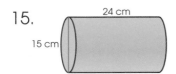

14 cm

9 cm

15.

24 cm

15 cm

16.

8 cm

0.5 cm longer
than its radius

ISBN: 978-1-77149-036-8

Given the volume or surface area, find the height of the solids.

17. V = 706.5 cm³

18. V = 1692.46 cm³

19. S.A. = 979.68 cm²

8 cm

20.

Its surface area is 1215.18 cm².

254.34 cm²

Solve the problems.

21.

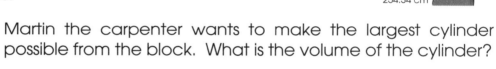

0.5 m   0.5 m

1.2 m

Martin the carpenter wants to make the largest cylinder possible from the block. What is the volume of the cylinder?

_____

22. A can of paint covers 0.56 m². If Martin puts 2 coats of paint on the cylinder, how many cans of paint will he need?

_____

23. If he cuts this cylinder into 3 identical small cylinders, what will be the surface area of each small cylinder?

_____

Volume and Surface Area of Solids (1)

- find the volume of solids
- find the surface area of solids
- solve problems involving the volumes and surface areas of solids

Volume = base x height
= (9 x 8 ÷ 2) x 4
= 144 (cm³)

I'm taller than you!

9 cm

8 cm

4 cm

Volume = s³
= 6 x 6 x 6
= 216 (cm³)

6 cm

Cube

But I have a greater volume.

Find the volume and surface area of each prism.

1.

4 cm   7.5 cm
12 cm

2.
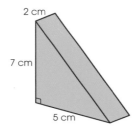
2 cm
7 cm
5 cm

Hint

Pythagorean Theorem

$$c^2 = a^2 + b^2$$

3.
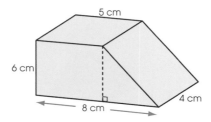
5 cm
6 cm
8 cm
4 cm

4.
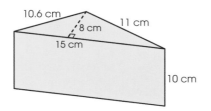
10.6 cm   11 cm
8 cm
15 cm
10 cm

ISBN: 978-1-77149-036-8

Find the volume and surface area of each solid.

5.

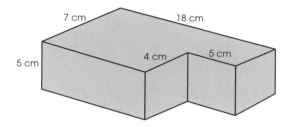

6.

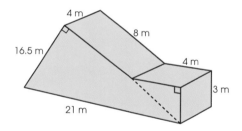

7.

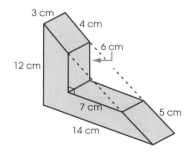

ISBN: 978-1-77149-036-8

Look at the dimensions of the blocks that Justin uses to build the solids. Find the volume and surface area of each solid. Then fill in the blanks.

8.

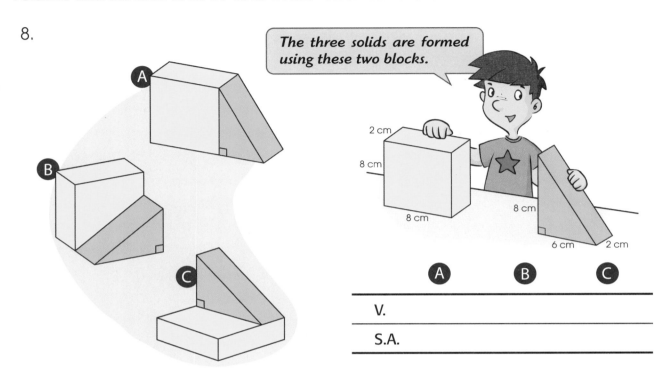

The three solids are formed using these two blocks.

	A	B	C
V.			
S.A.			

9. The volumes of the solids in different arrangement are _____ .

different/the same

10. The surface areas of the solids in different arrangement are _____ .

different/the same

11. Justin stacks up some rectangular blocks to make the smallest possible cube. What is the volume of the cube? _____

12. Justin makes a rectangular prism using 2 triangular blocks. What is the surface area of the rectangular prism? _____

13. A rectangular prism that has a volume of 1024 cm^3 is made with some rectangular blocks. How many blocks were used? _____

    ISBN: 978-1-77149-036-8

Solve the problems.

14. Connie paints the rectangular prism.

    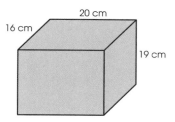

    a. What is the total surface area to be painted?

    _____

    b. If Connie removes a cube with the side length of 4 cm from each corner of the solid, what will be the volume of the solid?

    _____

15. A shoe box can hold 32 identical rectangular blocks. What is the total surface area of each block?

    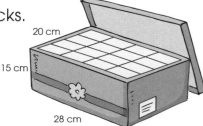

    _____

16.

    > I'm going to cut this loaf of cake into 10 equal pieces and coat each piece with icing.

    a. What is the volume of each piece?

    _____

    b. One bag of icing covers an area of 980 cm². How many bags of icing does she need?

    _____

Volume and Surface Area of Solids (2)

- find the volumes and surface areas of solids that have circular parts
- solve word problems involving volume and surface area
- identify the relationship between a change of radius or height to volume

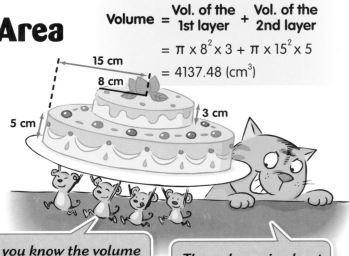

$$\text{Volume} = \frac{\text{Vol. of the}}{\text{1st layer}} + \frac{\text{Vol. of the}}{\text{2nd layer}}$$

$$= \pi \times 8^2 \times 3 + \pi \times 15^2 \times 5$$

$$= 4137.48 \ (\text{cm}^3)$$

15 cm
8 cm
5 cm
3 cm

Do you know the volume of this cake?

The volume is about 4000 cm³.

Find the volume and surface area of each solid.

1.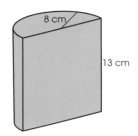

   8 cm

   13 cm

2.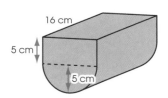

   16 cm

   5 cm

   5 cm

3.

   6 cm

   9 cm

   14 cm

   ISBN: 978-1-77149-036-8

Solve the problems.

4. Find the volumes and surface areas of the cylinder and the cube. Which one has a greater volume? Which one has a greater surface area?

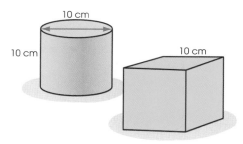

_____

5. Kenneth cuts out a cylinder with the greatest volume from a block of modelling clay. How much clay will be left?

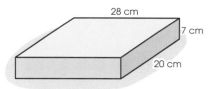

_____

6.
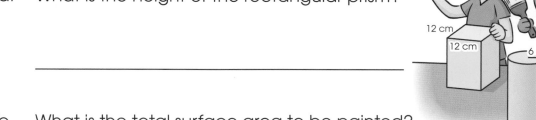

I want to paint two wooden blocks. Both have the same volume.

a. What is the height of the rectangular prism?

_____

b. What is the total surface area to be painted?

_____

Draw cylinders to match the descriptions. Then find the volumes of the solids and answer the questions.

7. **cylinder** 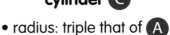 **A**
    - radius: 3 cm
    - height: 5 cm

    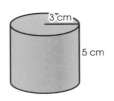
    3 cm
    5 cm

    $V = \pi r^2 h$

    =

    cylinder **B**
    - radius: double of **A**
    - height: 5 cm

    cylinder **C**
    - radius: triple that of **A**
    - height: 5 cm

8. If the heights of two cylinders are the same and the radius of the big cylinder doubles that of the small one, the volume of the big cylinder is _____ times that of the small one.

9. If the heights of two cylinders are the same and the radius of the big cylinder triples that of the smaller one, the volume of the big cylinder is _____ times that of the small one.

10.

    The heights of the cylinders are the same. The smallest cylinder has a volume of 450 cm^3.

    - The radius of the medium-sized cylinder is 2 times that of the smallest one. Its volume is _____ .

    - The radius of the largest cylinder is 3 times that of the smallest one. Its volume is _____ .

ISBN: 978-1-77149-036-8

Draw cylinders to match the descriptions. Then find the volumes of the cylinders and answer the questions.

11.   **cylinder** P
   - radius: 5 cm
   - height: 2 cm

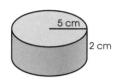

$V = \pi r^2 h$

=

cylinder Q
   - radius: 5 cm
   - height: 4 cm

cylinder R
   - radius: 5 cm
   - height: 6 cm

12.   If the radii of two cylinders are the same and the height of the tall cylinder doubles that of the short one, the volume of the tall cylinder is _____ times that of the short one.

13.   If the radii of two cylinders are the same and the height of the tall cylinder triples that of the short one, the volume of the tall cylinder is _____ times that of the short one.

14.

Our cylindrical containers have the same radius, but the height of my container is double that of yours. The volume of my container is 5400 cm³. What is the volume of your container?

_____

Angle Properties of Intersecting Lines

- Identify complementary angles, supplementary angles, and opposite angles
- Find measures of angles using angle properties

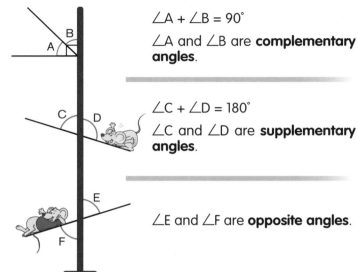

∠A + ∠B = 90°

∠A and ∠B are **complementary angles**.

∠C + ∠D = 180°

∠C and ∠D are **supplementary angles**.

∠E and ∠F are **opposite angles**.

Circle the correct answer. Then use the given word to describe the relationship between each pair of angles.

complementary   supplementary   opposite

1.  The sum of ∠a and ∠b is   90° / 180°   .

   ∠a and ∠b are _____ angles.

2. 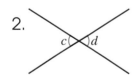 The measures of ∠c and ∠d are   the same / not the same   .

   ∠c and ∠d are _____ angles.

3. The sum of ∠AOB and ∠BOC is   90° / 180°   .

   ∠AOB and ∠BOC are _____ angles.

4. 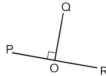 The sum of ∠POQ and ∠QOR is   90° / 180°   .

   ∠POQ and ∠QOR are _____ angles.

   ISBN: 978-1-77149-036-8

Name each pair of angles as "complementary", "supplementary", or "opposite".

5.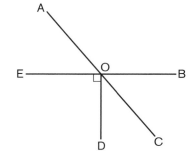

a. ∠BOC and ∠COD: _____ angles

b. ∠AOE and ∠AOB: _____ angles

c. ∠AOE and ∠BOC: _____ angles

d. ∠DOE and ∠DOB: _____ angles

6.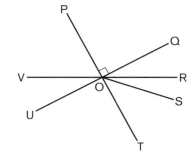

a. ∠VOP and ∠POR: _____ angles

b. ∠QOR and ∠ROT: _____ angles

c. ∠VOU and ∠QOR: _____ angles

d. ∠POV and ∠ROT: _____ angles

Name the angles.

7.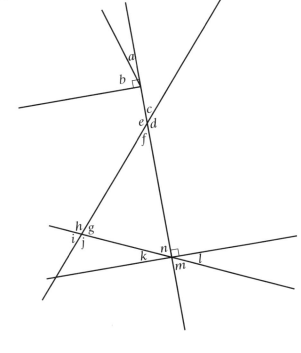

Complementary Angles

- ∠a and _____
- ∠n and _____
- ∠l and _____

Supplementary Angles

- ∠c and _____
- ∠i and _____
- ∠h and _____

Opposite Angles

- ∠d and _____
- ∠g and _____
- ∠k and _____
- ∠h and _____

ISBN: 978-1-77149-036-8

Name the relationship between the angles. Then find the measure of each angle.

8. ∠AOB and ∠BOC are _____ angles.

So, ∠AOB + ∠BOC = _____

∠BOC = _____ – ∠AOB

= _____

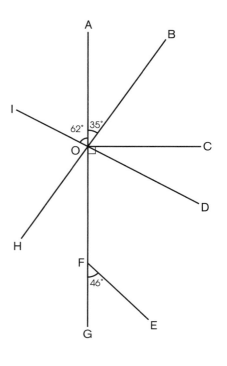

9. ∠DOF and ∠AOI are _____ angles.

So, ∠DOF = ∠AOI

= _____

10. ∠EFG and ∠OFE are _____ angles.

So, ∠EFG and ∠OFE = _____

∠OFE = _____ – ∠EFG

= _____

Look at the above diagram again. Find the measures of the angles. Show your work.

11. ∠FOH

12. ∠HOI

13. ∠DOF

14. ∠COD

ISBN: 978-1-77149-036-8

Draw a pair of angles that match each of the following descriptions.

15. opposite angles each having an angle of 35°

16. supplementary angles that are congruent

17. complementary angles that are congruent

18. supplementary angles with the measure of one angle being 30°

Find the measures of the coloured angles. Give reasons and show your work.

19.

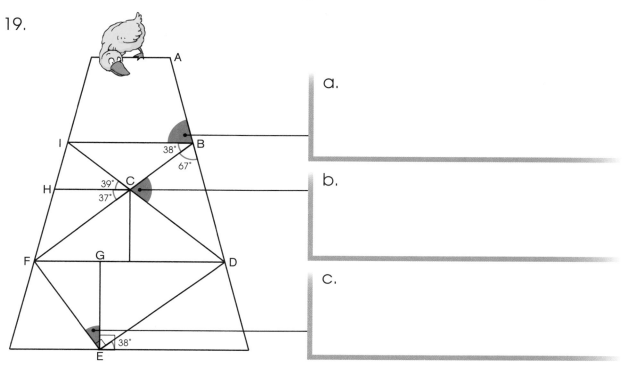

a.

b.

c.

Angle Properties in Parallel Lines

- identify corresponding, alternate, and interior angles
- find the angles in parallel lines
- find the measure of angles and state reasons

Joe, I have to climb up to find the measure of that angle.

62°

You don't need to do that, Sam. Since the ladder is a transversal of the two parallel horizontal lines, ∠a and the angle formed by the ladder to the ground are corresponding angles. So, the measure of ∠a is 62°.

Read the descriptions and draw the missing angles. Then fill in the blanks with the given words.

| Interior | Corresponding | Alternate |

1. _____ **angles**
   - two equal angles that are in matching corners

2. _____ **angles**
   - the two angles are inside the parallel lines and on the same side of the transversal where their sum is 180°

3. _____ **angles**
   - two equal angles that are either both inside or outside the parallel lines and on the opposite side of the transversal

4.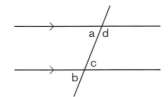

   ∠a and ∠b are _____ angles.

   ∠a and ∠c are _____ angles.

   ∠c and ∠d are _____ angles.

5.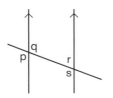

   ∠p and ∠s are _____ angles.

   ∠q and ∠s are _____ angles.

   ∠q and ∠r are _____ angles.

ISBN: 978-1-77149-036-8

Fill in the blanks. Then find one more pair of angles of each kind from each diagram.

| | alternate angles | corresponding angles | interior angles |

6.

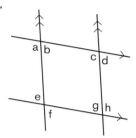

∠b and _____   ∠a and _____   ∠a and _____

∠c and _____   ∠b and _____   ∠b and _____

_____   _____   _____

7.

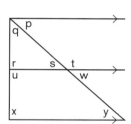

∠p and _____   ∠p and _____   ∠(p+q) and _____

∠w and _____   ∠r and _____   ∠u and _____

_____   _____   _____

Find the measures of the angles in each diagram.

8.

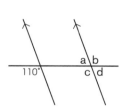

9.

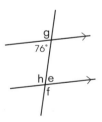

10.

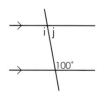

11.

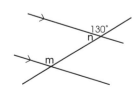

Find the measures of the angles in each diagram and state the reasons.

12.

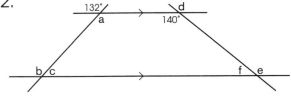

∠b = 132° (_____ angles)

∠a = ∠b (_____ angles)

= _____

∠c + ∠b = _____

(_____ angles)

∠c = 180° – ∠b

= _____

∠e = 140° (_____ angles)

∠d = ∠e (_____ angles)

∠f + ∠e = _____

(_____ angles)

∠f = 180° – ∠e

= _____

13.

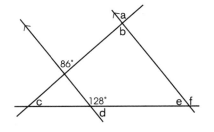

14.

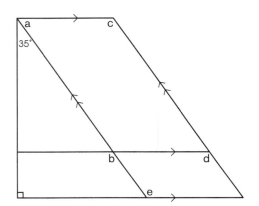

ISBN: 978-1-77149-036-8

Check the correct answers and state the reasons.

15. If ∠ABD = 65°, then

    (A) ∠CDG = 115° (_____ angles)

    (B) ∠CDG = 65° (_____ angles)

16. If ∠DEF = 115°, then

    (A) ∠CEF = 65° (_____ angles)

    (B) ∠EDG = 75° (_____ angles)

17. If ∠CDG = 65°, then

    (A) ∠ABD = 115° (_____ angles)

    (B) ∠DEF = 115° (_____ angles)

18.

Angle AHG is 150°.

    (A) ∠CIH = 30° (_____ angles)

    (B) ∠CIG = 30° (_____ angles)

Draw a diagram to match what Tony says. Answer his question.

19.

The small angle of a pair of interior angles is 10° less than the big one. What are the measures of the two angles?

Angle Properties in a Triangle

- find the measures of angles in triangles
- identify the appropriate set of measures of angles in triangles
- sketch triangles with the given information and find the measures of the angles
- solve problems

$\angle a + \angle b + \angle c = 180°$

Jack, no matter how hard you pull, the sum of the angles in the triangle will still be 180°.

Find the measure of the angle in each triangle.

1.

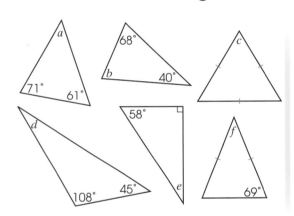

$\angle a =$ _____ $\angle b =$ _____

$\angle c =$ _____ $\angle d =$ _____

$\angle e =$ _____ $\angle f =$ _____

Check the appropriate set of measures of angles in each triangle.

2.

Ⓐ 90°, 35°, 55°

Ⓑ 90°, 40°, 60°

3.

Ⓐ 65°, 65°, 70°

Ⓑ 70°, 40°, 70°

4.

Ⓐ 38°, 90°, 38°

Ⓑ 45°, 90°, 45°

5.

Ⓐ 20°, 120°, 40°

Ⓑ 30°, 150°, 0°

Find the measures of the angles. Show your work.

6.

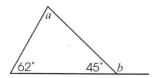

7.

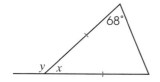

8.

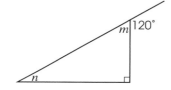

Find the measures of the coloured angles.

9.

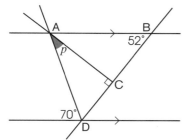

10.

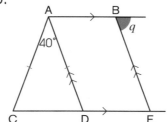

11.

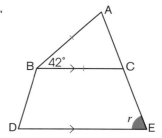

ISBN: 978-1-77149-036-8

Draw the lines and find the measures of the angles.

12. Draw line $\overline{BD}$ so that ∠ABD is 30°.

    • ∠ABC = _____

    • ∠ADB = _____

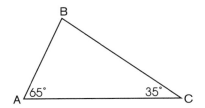

13. Draw line $\overline{FH}$ so that ∠EFH is 20°.

    • ∠GFH = _____

    • ∠EHF = _____

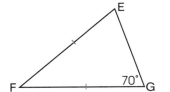

14. Connect points W and Y.

    • ∠WYZ = _____

    • ∠XYW = _____

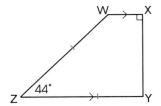

Sketch the diagrams and find the measures of the angles.

15. In △ABC,

    • ∠A = 35°
    • ∠B = 74°

    The measure of the supplementary angle of ∠C is _____ .

16. In isosceles △PQR,

    • ∠P is the vertex.
    • The supplementary angle of ∠Q is 110°.

    The measure of ∠P is _____ .

ISBN: 978-1-77149-036-8

Solve the problems.

17. Sarah wants to make a regular pentagon with isosceles triangles. What are the measures of the angles in each triangle?

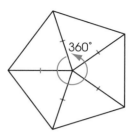

_____

18. The measures of the angles in a triangle are in the ratio of 1:3:6. Find the measures of the angles. (Hint: Let the measure of the smallest angle be x.)

_____

19. The vertex angle in an isosceles triangle is $y°$. If the measure of each base angle is 4 times that of the vertex, what are the measures of the angles?

_____

Prove that the sum of the angles in the trapezoid is 360°. Show your work.

20.

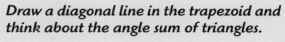

Draw a diagonal line in the trapezoid and think about the angle sum of triangles.

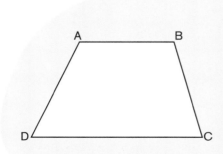

Constructing Bisectors

Let me have the compass. I'll show you how to bisect a slice of pizza.

- identify perpendicular bisectors and angle bisectors and their properties
- draw line bisectors and angle bisectors
- draw bisectors and find measures of the angles
- draw angles using only a ruler and a compass

Fill in the blanks to complete the sentences. Then highlight the perpendicular bisector of each line segment and the bisector of each angle.

1. The **perpendicular bisector** passes through the _____ of

   midpoint/endpoint

   the line segment. It meets the line segment at a/an _____

   acute/right

   angle.

   a.

   b.

   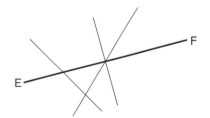

2. The **angle bisector** passes through the _____ of an angle.

   arms/vertex

   It divides the angle into _____ equal parts.

   two/three

   a.

   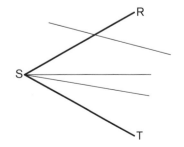

   b.

   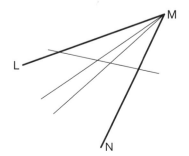

ISBN: 978-1-77149-036-8

Draw the bisectors.

3. Bisect the line segments.

4. Bisect the angles.

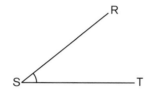 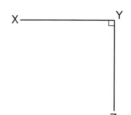 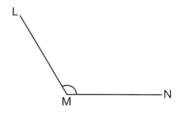

Draw the bisectors and find the measures of the angles without a protractor.

5. • Bisect the lines $\overline{AC}$ and $\overline{BC}$.

    • Mark the intersection of the bisectors as X.

    • Mark the intersection of the bisector and $\overline{AC}$ as Y.

    The measure of ∠AXY is _____ .

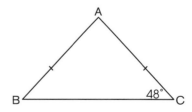

6. • Bisect ∠P and ∠R.

    • Mark the intersection of the bisectors as M.

    The measure of ∠PMR is _____ .

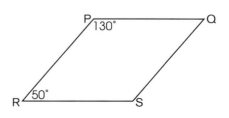

ISBN: 978-1-77149-036-8

Bisect the two line segments and answer the questions.

7.

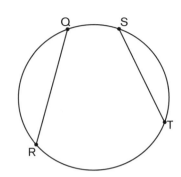

- Mark the intersection of the bisectors as X.
- Connect X to each point.

8. Find the lengths.

a. $\overline{QX} = $ _____   b. $\overline{RX} = $ _____

c. $\overline{SX} = $ _____   d. $\overline{TX} = $ _____

9.

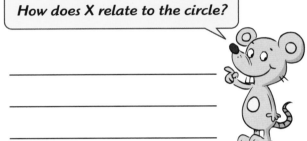

How does X relate to the circle?

_____

_____

_____

Follow the steps to construct a 45° angle from a 90° angle using only a ruler and a compass. Then fill in the blanks and do what the girl says.

10. ―――― **45° and 90° Angle** ――――

a. Steps to draw a 45° angle:

1st Draw a 90° angle by constructing a perpendicular bisector.

2nd Bisect the 90° angle.

b. To draw a 90° angle, construct a _____ bisector.

c. To draw a 45° angle, bisect a _____ angle.

11.

Describe how you would draw a 135° using only a ruler and a compass. Then draw it in the box and mark the angle.

―――― **135° Angle** ――――

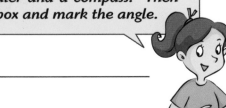

_____

_____

ISBN: 978-1-77149-036-8

Steps to Draw an Equilateral Triangle

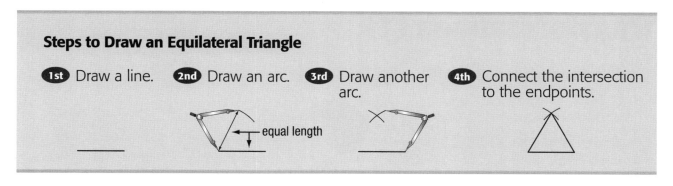

1st Draw a line. **2nd** Draw an arc. **3rd** Draw another arc. **4th** Connect the intersection to the endpoints.

equal length

Make the drawings with only a ruler and a compass. Then fill in the blanks and do what the puppy says.

12. Draw an equilateral triangle.

13. Draw a 30° angle by bisecting one of the 60° angles.

14. To draw a 60° angle, construct an _____ triangle.

15. To draw a 30° angle, bisect a _____ angle.

— 30° and 60° Angle —

16. *Describe how you would draw a 150° angle. Then draw it out and mark the angle.*

_____

_____

Draw the shape with the given information. Then answer the questions.

17. Parallelogram

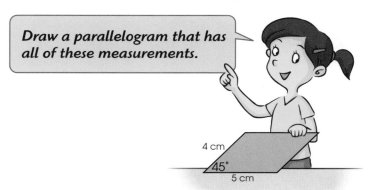

Draw a parallelogram that has all of these measurements.

4 cm
45°
5 cm

Transformations (1)

- identify which quadrant each point belongs to
- draw shapes on a grid
- find perimeters and areas of shapes on a grid
- identify translation images
- understand the change of the value of coordinates in translation

Julie's Translation
2 units right & 3 units up

Look! Julie is the fastest one to show a translation image of A.

Look at the points on the grid. Fill in the blanks.

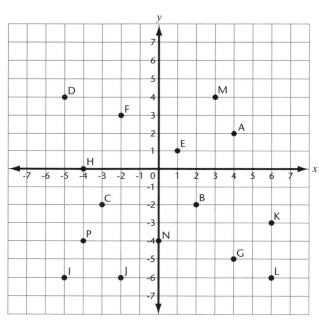

1. Points in each quadrant.

    Quadrant 1: _____

    Quadrant 2: _____

    Quadrant 3: _____

    Quadrant 4: _____

2. Points that do not belong to any quadrant:

    _____

3. Points that have the same x-coordinates: _____

4. Points that have the same y-coordinates: _____

5. Points that lie on the x-axis: _____

6. Points that have x-coordinate 0: _____

7. Points that have equal x- and y-coordinates: _____

8. Find the coordinates of each point.

A _____   B _____   C _____

D _____   E _____   F _____

G _____   H _____   I _____

J _____   K _____   L _____

M _____   N _____   P _____

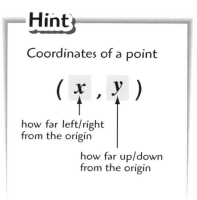

9. Draw a line to join the points D and M.

   a.   Is it a vertical or horizontal line?   _____

   b.   Write the coordinates of any three points on the line. _____

   c.   *Do the points on a horizontal line have something in common? What is it?*

   _____

10. Draw a line to join the points F and J.

   a.   Is it a vertical or horizontal line?   _____

   b.   Write the coordinates of any three points on the line. _____

   c.   *Do the points on a vertical line have something in common? What is it?*

   _____

11. The points (6,3), (-1,3), and (-4,3) are on a line. Is it a vertical or horizontal line?

   _____

Plot the points and find the missing vertex of each shape. Join the points in order. Then find the area and perimeter of each shape.

12.

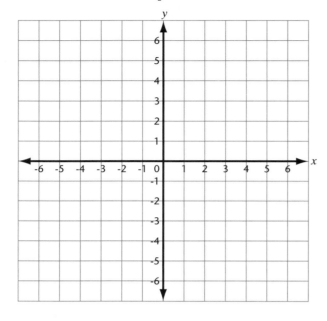

Square (1,3)   (3,5)
(5,3)   _____

Kite (-3,4)   (-1,2)
(-3,-2)   _____

Rectangle (-1,-2)   (4,-2)
(4,-4)   _____

13.

	Area (square units)	Perimeter (units)
Square		
Kite		
Rectangle		

Hint

Make use of Pythagorean Theorem to find the areas and perimeters.

$$a^2 + b^2 = c^2$$

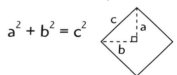

Find the translation images of each coloured figure. Write the letters.

14. **Translation Images**

triangle   _____

trapezoid   _____

L-shape   _____

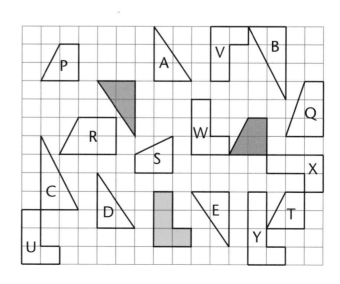

ISBN: 978-1-77149-036-8

Check the correct translation.

15. Translate 2 units left and 3 units up.

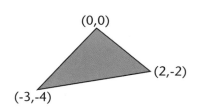

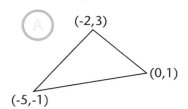

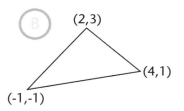

16. Translate 5 units right and 4 units down.

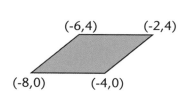

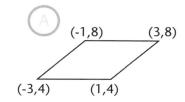

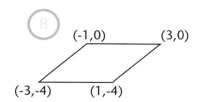

Write the coordinates of the vertices of the images after the translations. Then do what the boy says.

17. Translate trapezoid DEFG.

D(2,1)   D'(-4,5)

E(4,1)   →   E'(   )

F(4,-1)   F'(   )

G(1,-1)   G'(   )

18. Translate kite IJKL.

I(-3,0)   I'(3,-2)

J(-2,-1)   →   J'(   )

K(-3,-3)   K'(   )

L(-4,-1)   L'(   )

19. Trapezoid DEFG: _____

20. Kite IJKL: _____

Describe each translation.

Transformations (2)

- reflect the points and write their coordinates
- identify the change in the coordinates after reflections
- reflect shapes in the x- and y-axis
- rotate shapes
- identify the change in the coordinates after rotations

right eye (–2,2)
left eye (2,2)

Your left eye is reflected in the y-axis. Its y-coordinate stays the same and its x-coordinate changes in sign.

Reflect and label the points. Write their coordinates. Then fill in the blanks with the given words.

1. 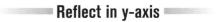 **Reflect in x-axis**

   A (-4,4)   A' _____

   B _____   B' _____

   C _____   C' _____

   Reflect in y-axis

   P _____   P' _____

   Q _____   Q' _____

   R _____   R' _____

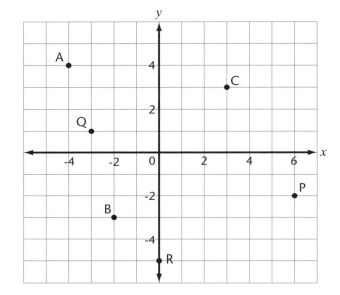

2. When a point is reflected in the x-axis,

   a. the x-coordinate _____ .

   b. the y-coordinate _____ .

3. When a point is reflected in the y-axis,

   a. the x-coordinate _____ .

   b. the y-coordinate _____ .

stays the same

changes in sign

ISBN: 978-1-77149-036-8

Reflect each figure and write the coordinates. Then answer the question.

4. Reflect △ABC in the x-axis

△ABC _____

△A'B'C' _____

5. Reflect △PQR in the y-axis

△PQR _____

△P'Q'R' _____

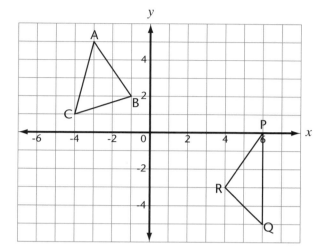

6. The vertices of a trapezoid are (15,3), (18,3), (18,-1), and (13,-1). Find the vertices of the reflection image if the trapezoid is reflected in the y-axis.

_____

Reflect the shapes.

7.

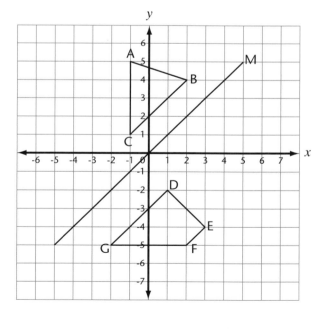

a. Reflect figure ABC in line M.

A( )   A'( )

B( ) ➝ B'( )

C( )   C'( )

b. Reflect figure DEFG in line M.

D( )   D'( )

E( )   E'( )

F( ) ➝ F'( )

G( )   G'( )

8. Describe what you observe in the coordinates of each point and its image.

_____

Draw the figure on the grid and do the rotations about the origin. Write the coordinates of the vertices of its image. Then read the descriptions to identify the rotations.

9.

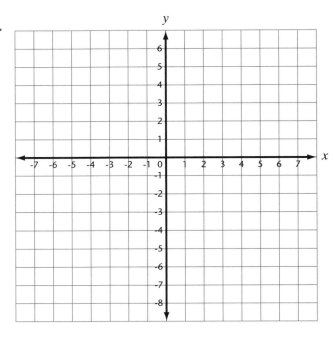

a. figure A

    (1,6)   (6,5)   (0,0)

b. rotate figure A 90° clockwise

    _____

c. rotate figure A 180°

    _____

d. rotate figure A 270° clockwise

    _____

10.

Rotation	Description
clockwise	Change the sign of the x-coordinate; then interchange the coordinates.
	Change the signs of both the x- and y-coordinates.
	Change the sign of the y-coordinate; then interchange the coordinates.

Write the coordinates of the vertices of the images after each rotation.

11.

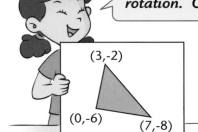

The negative sign denotes that it is a clockwise rotation. Otherwise, it is a counterclockwise turn.

(3,-2)

(0,-6)   (7,-8)

a. -270° turn   _____

b. -90° turn   _____

c. 180° turn   _____

Do the transformations and write the coordinates of the vertices of the images.

12. To get △I′J′K′

    • translate △IJK 2 units left and 1 unit up

    • reflect in x-axis

    Vertices: _____

13. To get △P′Q′R′

    • reflect △PQR in y-axis

    • make a 180° turn

    Vertices: _____

14. To get △A′B′C′

    • make △ABC a -90° turn

    • translate it 1 unit left and 2 units down

    Vertices: _____

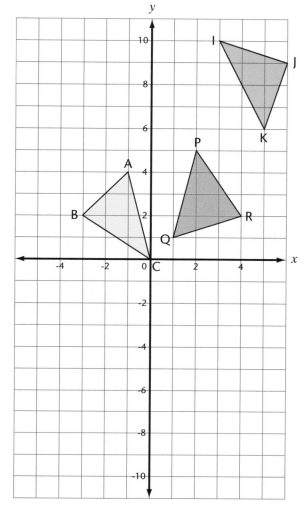

Find the vertices of the images.

15. a. *Translate the triangle 6 units right and 1 unit up.*

    _____

    b. Reflect the image in the y-axis.

    _____

16. a. Reflect the parallelogram in the x-axis.

    _____

    b. Make a 90° turn of the image.

    _____

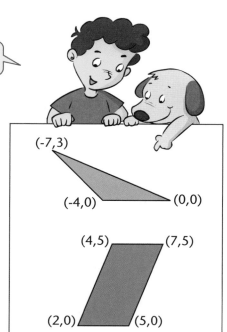

Number Patterns

- write algebraic expressions to describe patterns
- find the term value with the given term number
- find the term number with the given term value
- make graphs to represent patterns

Jacob, do you like my sombrero?

No. of Layers	No. of △
1	$1 (1^2)$
2	$4 (2^2)$
3	$9 (3^2)$
4	$16 (4^2)$

Look at the number pattern. Write an algebraic expression to describe the pattern. Then answer the questions.

Yes, I do. I want to make one with 5 layers. I think I need 25 triangles, right?

1.

Each term value increases by _____ . So, one of the terms in the pattern rule is _____ x n, where n is the term number. Compare the term values and the values of 3n.

Term No.	Term Value
1	4
2	7
3	10
4	13

Term No.	Term Value	$3n$	
1	4	3 x 1 = 3	← 1 less
2	7	3 x 2 = 6	← 1 less
3	10		
4	13		

An expression for the *n*th term:

_____ x *n* + _____

2.   Use the expression to find the value of each term.

   a.   the 10th term _____

   b.   the 14th term _____

   c.   the 26th term _____

   d.   the 35th term _____

ISBN: 978-1-77149-036-8

Write an algebraic expression to describe each pattern. Then find the value of each term.

3.

Term No.	Term Value
1	3
2	7
3	11
4	15

a. an expression for the nth term: _____

b. the 10th term: _____ the 16th term: _____

the 25th term: _____ the 30th term: _____

4.

Term No.	Term Value
1	1
2	4
3	7
4	10

a. an expression for the nth term: _____

b. the 9th term: _____ the 17th term: _____

the 20th term: _____ the 33th term: _____

Look at the diagram. Complete the table and write an algebraic expression to describe the number pattern. Then find the value of each term.

5. Figure 1

Figure 2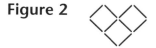

Figure 3

Figure 4

a.

Figure No.	1	2	3	4	5
No. of Lines					

b. an expression for the nth figure: _____

c. No. of lines in

• figure 8 _____

• figure 15 _____

• figure 20 _____

d. Which figure is it if it has

• 52 lines? _____

• 70 lines? _____

• 106 lines? _____

Complete the chart and the graph.

6.

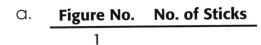

| Figure 1 | Figure 2 | Figure 3 | Figure 4 |

a.

Figure No.	No. of Sticks
1	
2	
3	
4	
5	
⋮	
k	
⋮	
30	

b.

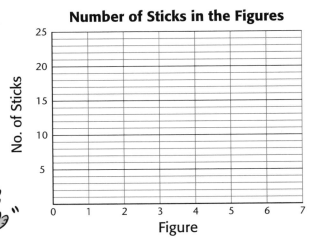

Number of Sticks in the Figures

7.

Figure 1

Figure 2

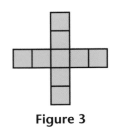

Figure 3

a.

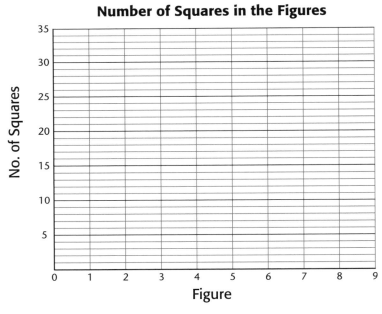

Number of Squares in the Figures

b. The number of squares in

- figure n: _____
- figure 33: _____

c. Which figure has 97 squares? _____

ISBN: 978-1-77149-036-8

Complete the chart. Then find the answers.

8.

Term No.	Term Value
1	1
2	4
3	9
4	
5	
⋮	
k	

9.   Find the term values.

   a.   the 8th term   _____

   b.   the 11th term   _____

   c.   the 15th term   _____

10.   Find the term number with the given term value.

   a.   400   _____

   b.   256   _____

   c.   361   _____

Complete the graph. Then answer the questions.

11.   a.

Figure 1

Figure 2

Figure 3

Figure 4

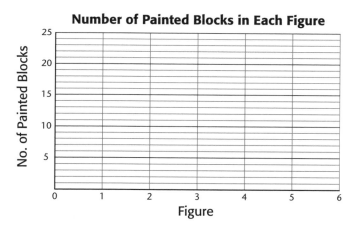

Number of Painted Blocks in Each Figure

b.   Expression: _____

c.   How many painted blocks are there in figure 20?

   _____

d.   A figure has between 75 and 85 painted blocks. What is the number of this figure?

   _____

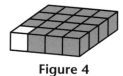

ISBN: 978-1-77149-036-8

Algebraic Expressions

- match algebraic expressions to the correct statements
- write algebraic expressions for the statements
- Use algebraic expressions to describe different situations
- evaluate algebraic expressions
- solve word problems

If you give me all your candies, I will have (4x + 2y) candies.

x candies x candies
x candies x candies
y candies y candies

$4x$ candies in all $2y$ candies in all

Match each algebraic expression with the correct statement.

1. subtract 7 from the sum of x and y •

    x divided by 7 plus y •

    subtract y from 6 times x •

    x multiplied by $\frac{1}{7}$ plus 6 times y •

    the difference between x and y times 7 •

    x increased by 7 and minus y •

- $6x - y$
- $x - 7y$
- $\frac{1}{7}x + 6y$
- $x + 7 - y$
- $x - 7 + y$
- $x \div 7 + y$

Write an algebraic expression for each statement.

2. add two different numbers   _____

3. the product of two different numbers   _____

4. subtract a number from 4 times another number   _____

5. multiply a number by 5 and add another number   _____

6.  *the sum of 2 times a number and $\frac{1}{3}$ of another number*

    _____

ISBN: 978-1-77149-036-8

Write the expressions and answer the questions.

7. Find the total amount of

    a. m toonies: _____

    b. n quarters: _____

    c. i toonies and j \$5 bills: _____

    d. x loonies and y pennies: _____

Hint

Each term in an expression must have the same unit.

8.      *I have \$c in toonies and \$d in quarters. How many coins do I have in all?*

     _____

9.   Find the costs.

     a.   8 cones   _____

     b. p sundaes   _____

     c.   5 cones and n sundaes   _____

     d.   9 cones and k sundaes   _____

Ice Cream Parlour   \$m   \$3

10. Lucy and her three sisters share the cost of 3 cones and r sundaes. How much does each child need to pay?   _____

11. Conrad spent \$32 on ice cream cones and \$d on sundaes. How many cones and sundaes did he buy in total?   _____

12. Alicia bought 9 cones and p sundaes and got \$12 for change. How much did Alicia pay for her treats?   _____

ISBN: 978-1-77149-036-8

Evaluate $2x + y$ where x is 5 and y is 3.

$$2x + y = 2(5) + 3 \leftarrow \text{Substitute 5 for } x \text{ and 3 for } y.$$
$$= 10 + 3 \leftarrow \text{Follow the order of operation to find the answer.}$$
$$= \underline{13}$$

Evaluate each expression using substitution.

13. **$m = 7$ $n = 6$**

   a. $4m + n$

   b. $m - \dfrac{1}{6}n$

14. **$x = 3$ $y = 8$**

   a. $5x - y \div 4$

   b. $3(x + y)$

15. **$i = 10$ $j = 5$**

   a. $50 - ij$

   b. $(i + 5) \div j$

Evaluate each expression.

$$a = 8 \quad b = 6 \quad c = 15 \quad d = 7 \quad e = 12 \quad f = 10$$

16. $8a + 2c$

17. $\dfrac{1}{5}c + d$

18. $2b - e \div 6$

19. $ab - f$ = _____

20. $7(c - d)$ = _____

21. $2a - 3b$ = _____

22. $2c \div f$ = _____

23. $e - 2b$ = _____

24. $(a + b) \div d$ = _____

25. $c - 2b + a$ = _____

26. $(e \div b) + f$ = _____

ISBN: 978-1-77149-036-8

Evaluate the expressions to complete the chart and answer the question.

27.

x	y	$2(x + y)$	$2x + y$	$2x + 2y$
-2	0			
-1	1			
0	2			
1	3			
2	4			

28. Which two expressions are equivalent? _____

Write the expression for each problem. Then evaluate to find the answers.

29. Kate has 5 bags of x candies and 1 box of y candies. Find the total number of candies.

 Ⓐ $5x + y$ Ⓑ $5x - y$

 For $x = 10$ and $y = 3$, Kate has _____ candies.

30. Joe gives his sister y of the x dozens marbles he has. What is the number of marbles that he has left?

 Ⓐ $12x - y$ Ⓑ $x - y$

 For $x = 3$ and $y = 8$, Joe has _____ marbles.

31.

> *The amount of frill that I needed to trim my pillow is y times that what you needed to trim yours, which is in the shape of an equilateral triangle.*

 Josie

 x cm

 x cm

 How much frill did Josie need to trim each side of her pillow?

 Ⓐ $\dfrac{4x + y}{3}$ Ⓑ $\dfrac{4x}{3y}$

 For $x = 12$ cm and $y = 2$, the side length is _____ cm.

Equations

- evaluate expressions using the distributive property of multiplication
- expand expressions
- write expressions to describe the perimeters and areas of shapes
- solve equations
- solve word problems with equations

The number of marbles that I have is 6 times that of yours.

Sue's marbles:

$6(5 + 30)$
$= 6 \times 5 + 6 \times 30$
$= 30 + 180$
$= 210$

I can't believe she has so many marbles!

Find the answers using the distributive property of multiplication.

1. $2(35 + 9)$

    $= 2(\quad) + 2(\quad)$

    $= \underline{\hspace{1.5cm}} + \underline{\hspace{1.5cm}}$

    $= \underline{\hspace{1.5cm}}$

2. $3(9 + 7)$

Hint

e.g. Evaluate $2(5 + 18)$ using distributive property of multiplication.

multiply

$2(5 + 18) = 2 \times 5 + 2 \times 18$

multiply $\quad = 10 + 36$

$\quad = 46$

3. $4(20 + 6 + 5)$

4. $6(5 + 5 + 5)$

Expand.

5. $4(3x + 2y)$

    $= 4(\quad) + 4(\quad)$

    $= \underline{\hspace{1.5cm}} + \underline{\hspace{1.5cm}}$

6. $4(5 + 4p)$

7. $9(2m + 3n)$

8. $2(3p + 5q) = \underline{\hspace{3cm}}$

9. $5(2a + 3b) = \underline{\hspace{3cm}}$

ISBN: 978-1-77149-036-8

Find the missing numbers.

10. $3(2a + \underline{\hspace{1.5cm}}) = 6a + 9b$

11. $6(a + \underline{\hspace{1.5cm}}) = 6a + 42$

12. $5(\underline{\hspace{1.5cm}} + 3n) = 20m + 15n$

13. $3(\underline{\hspace{1.5cm}} + q) = 3q + 21p$

14. $6(\underline{\hspace{1.5cm}} + y + 3z) = 12x + 6y + \underline{\hspace{1.5cm}}$

15. $7(i + \underline{\hspace{1.5cm}} + \underline{\hspace{1.5cm}}) = \underline{\hspace{1.5cm}} + 21j + 14k$

Write an expression for each situation. Then expand it.

16. 3 times the sum of 5 and $7a$

17. 2 times the sum of $4x$ and y

18. Find the perimeter of each shape.

a.
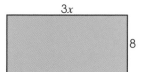
$3x$

8

b.

$(p + q)$

c.
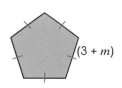
$(3 + m)$

19. Find the area of the whole figures.

a.
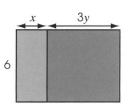
x $3y$

6

b.
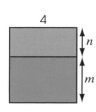
4

n

m

c.
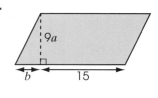
$9a$

b 15

ISBN: 978-1-77149-036-8

Solve the equations.

20. $x - 8 = 14$

21. $2y = 30$

22. $a \div 7 = 12$

23. $4y + 5 = 17$ $\qquad$ $y =$ _____

24. $3j - 4 = 14$ $\qquad$ $j =$ _____

25. $k \div 7 = 5 \times 3$ $\qquad$ $k =$ _____

26. $10 = 2(3x + 2)$ $\qquad$ $x =$ _____

27. $\dfrac{2b - 1}{7} = 9$ $\qquad$ $b =$ _____

28. $4 = \dfrac{a - 6}{3}$ $\qquad$ $a =$ _____

Solve each equation and check your answers.

29. $\qquad\qquad 5x = 16 + x$

$5x -$ _____ $= 16 + x -$ _____

$\dfrac{4x}{\rule{1.5em}{0.8em}} = \dfrac{16}{\rule{1.5em}{0.8em}}$

$x =$ _____

Left side: $\qquad$ **Right side:**

30. $2y - 4 = y + 8$

31. $4n - 5 = n + 13$

ISBN: 978-1-77149-036-8

Solve the problems and check your answers.

32. Joseph rented a car at $27/day and he paid a total of $182 including $74 of gasoline. How many days did Joseph rent the car for?

Let d be the number of days the car was rented.

$27(\quad) + \underline{\quad} = 182$

Joseph rented the car for _____ days.

33. Annie and Keith have a total of $(4n - 8)$ marbles. If Annie has n marbles and the number of Keith's marbles is 2 times that of Annie's, how many marbles does Annie have?

_____

34. The height of a plant is 21 cm. If its growth rate stays unchanged, it will be twice as tall after 3 years. What is the growth rate of the plant?

_____

35.

Jack has *m* marbles and the number of marbles that I have is 3 times that of Jack's. If we have a total of 2(*m* + 13) marbles, how many marbles does Jack have?

_____

Data Management (1)

- identify whether a situation is studied by census or sample
- make inferences about charts and graphs
- make a scatter plot and make inferences about it
- draw a circle graph and make inferences about it

> I'm the best salesperson, making an impressive $90 000 in the past two years.
>
> Judy

Determine whether each situation is studied by "census" or "sample". Then check the one that is appropriate.

1.

   > **Find the names of the students in my school that start with "A".**

   a. Obtain the name list of a Grade 8 class. _____ ◯

   b. Obtain the name lists of all classes. _____ ◯

   c. Find out the names of the students who got Grade A in English. _____ ◯

2.

   > **Find the highest temperature recorded this year.**

   a. Find all temperatures recorded this year. _____ ◯

   b. Find all temperatures recorded in the summer this year. _____ ◯

   c. Pick out several temperatures recorded in the summer randomly. _____ ◯

3.

   > **Find the approximated mean calories of 1000 lemons.**

   a. Find the amount of calories of a lemon. _____ ◯

   b. Find the mean calories of 50 lemons. _____ ◯

   c. Find the mean calories of all lemons. _____ ◯

ISBN: 978-1-77149-036-8

Look at the chart. Answer the question.

4. Julie said that most people like "fantasy" movies. Do you agree with what Julie said? Explain.

_____

_____

5. Make two inferences about the data.

_____

_____

Movie Genre	No. of Votes
Comedy	11
Action	7
Romance	3
Mystery	8
Fantasy	12

Look at the graph and answer the questions.

6. Check the sentence(s) that describe(s) the graph.

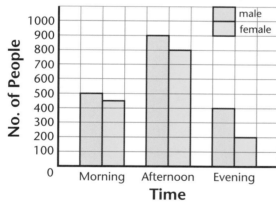

Number of People at Ski Resort Yesterday

No. of People — Time — Morning, Afternoon, Evening
male / female

(A) More people skied in the evening than in the morning.

(B) The greatest number of people skied in the afternoon.

(C) There are more male skiers.

7. Make two inferences about the graph.

_____

_____

_____

Look at the double line graph. Answer the questions.

8. What does the graph show?

_____

_____

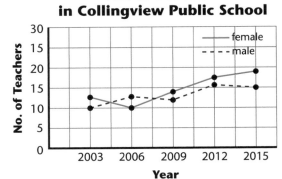

No. of Teachers in Collingview Public School

9. Predict the number of teachers in 2018.

_____

10. Make two inferences about the graph.

_____

_____

_____

Make a scatter plot to show the data. Then answer the questions.

11.

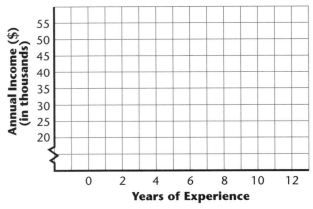

Years of Experience vs Annual Income

Fashion Industry

Years of Experience vs. Annual Income

0 yr – $21k	0 yr – $20k
1 yr – $25k	2 yr – $29k
4 yr – $34k	4 yr – $35k
4 yr – $30k	5 yr – $38k
6 yr – $39k	6 yr – $38k
7 yr – $39k	7 yr – $40k
7 yr – $42k	8 yr – $41k
9 yr – $42k	10 yr – $44k
10 yr – $45k	10 yr – $46k

"k" stands for 1000.

12. What relationship does the scatter plot show?

_____

13. Estimate the income of a person who has 12 years of experience.

_____

Look at the data that records a group of children's favourite superheroes. Complete the chart and make use of the data to draw a circle graph. Then answer the questions.

14.

Superhero	No. of Children	Sector Angle	Percent
Batman	17	$\frac{17}{65}$ x 360° ≈	$\frac{17}{65}$ x 100% =
Spiderman	15		
Superman	13		
X-Men	9		
Ironman	11		
Total	_____	_____	_____

15. Draw a circle graph in the space provided to show the result.

16. There are 3500 children in the community of Tellington. Use the circle graph to predict how many children have Batman as their superhero.

_____

17.

Make two inferences about the circle graph.

_____

_____

Data Management (2)

- draw a histogram
- draw a circle graph
- make inferences about graphs
- determine which graph is suitable to represent a set of data
- identify outliers in a set of data

The children recorded the heights of the plants they planted in their school garden. Make a histogram to show the data and answer the question.

mean score without the outliers (13 and 24):

(92 + 80 + 86) ÷ 3 = 86

1.

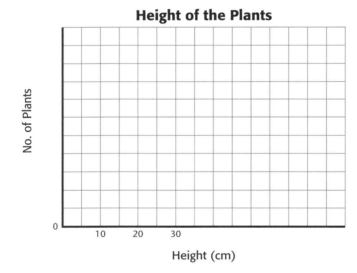

Height of the Plants

Height of the Plants

Height (cm)	No. of Plants
0-9	1
10-19	5
20-29	6
30-39	9
40-49	10
50-59	7
60-69	4

2. Make two inferences about the graph.

_____

_____

_____

ISBN: 978-1-77149-036-8

Types of Graphs

Circle graph:
to display part to whole relationship

Double bar graph:
to display 2 sets of discrete data

Double line graph:
to display 2 sets of continuous data

Scatter plot:
to represent 2 sets of related data

Histogram:
to display a set of data that can be grouped and arranged in numerical order

A histogram looks like a bar graph except that a histogram has no space between the bars.

Determine the most suitable graph for each situation.

3.   A sales manager wants to

a.   find out whether or not there is a relationship between the cost of an item and the quantity sold.

_____

b.   find the number of two kinds of items sold from 12:00 p.m. to 4:00 p.m.

_____

c.   find out the popularity of different colours of an item.

_____

d.   compare the number of male and female customers who made purchases on Friday, Saturday, and Sunday.

_____

e.   find the number of customers waiting to check-out from 10:00 a.m. to 8:00 p.m.

_____

f.   find out the relationship between the amount of a discount on an item and the quantity sold.

_____

Mrs. Winter is planning a ski trip for the students. Look at the number of participants who skied before. Present the data using the most suitable graph. Then answer the questions.

4.

Number of Participants at Each Age

Age	Skied Before	Never Skied
10	4	20
11	6	17
12	6	15
13	8	16
14	10	12

5. Which type of graph did you choose? Explain.

   _____

   _____

6. Make two inferences about the graph.

   _____

   _____

   _____

7.

   I want to compare the number of participants of each age to the whole group.

   Which graph should Mrs. Winter use to display the data? Explain.

   _____

   _____

   _____

Circle the outlier(s) in each set of data if applicable.

8. 2   28   29   29   32   33

9. 5   48   48   56   64   97

10. 3   7   32   43   47   53   59

11. 16   18   18   20   20   23   27   28

12. 5   33   39   40   45   46   102   180

Hint

An outlier is a number that is very different from other numbers in a set of data.

e.g. ② 15   16   16   ㉝

2 and 33 are the outliers.

Circle the outliers and find the central tendency. Then answer the questions.

13.

Distances (km) Covered by 10 Cyclists
6   37   38
39   40   41
41   41
96   96

14.   **the central tendency**

with the outliers   without the outliers

mean: _____   mean: _____

median: _____   median: _____

mode: _____   mode: _____

15.

In general, would you use the mean to represent the data if ...

a. there are some outliers in the data?

_____

_____

b. there are no outliers in the data?

_____

_____

Probability

- complete the formula for theoretical probability
- draw a tree diagram
- find probability from a tree diagram
- identify the suitable model to do simulation
- find the odds in favour and odds against

Draw one ball, Sue. If the ball you picked is red, you'll do the dishes. Otherwise, I'll do them.

2 favourable outcomes; 10 unfavourable outcomes

odds against drawing a red ball:

10 to 2 = 5 to 1

10 red
1 blue
1 yellow

This is not fair. The probability that I need to do the dishes is 5 times yours.

Complete the formula for theoretical probability. Then fill in the blanks.

1. Probability = $\dfrac{\text{No. of } \rule{2cm}{0.4pt} \text{ outcomes}}{\text{No. of } \rule{2cm}{0.4pt} \text{ outcomes}}$

numerator		equal
favourable		possible
0	1	5

e.g.  Draw a red ball from this box.

P(red ball) = $\dfrac{}{3}$

2. When all the outcomes of an event are favourable, the numerator and denominator are _____ , and the probability is _____ .

e.g.  Draw a red ball from a box of 5 red balls.

P(red ball) = $\dfrac{}{5}$ = ____

3. When no outcomes of an event are favourable, the _____ equals 0, and the probability is _____ .

e.g.  Draw a blue ball from a box of 5 red balls.

P(blue ball) = $\dfrac{}{5}$ = ____

ISBN: 978-1-77149-036-8

Draw a tree diagram to show all the possible combinations. Then answer the questions.

4.

Blouse

- plain
- with ruffles
- with lace

Skirt

- black
- grey

Mrs. Nelly's Boutique

5. Find the probability that a customer will choose each of the following.

a. P(a blouse with ruffles and a black skirt) _____

b. P(a plain blouse or a blouse with lace and a grey skirt) _____

c. P(not a plain blouse) _____

d. P(not a black skirt) _____

6. Which simulation model below could Mrs. Nelly use to simulate the combinations that her customers could buy?

(A) a number cube labelled from 1 to 6 and a coin

(B) a spinner divided into 3 equal parts and a coin

(C) a spinner divided into 5 equal parts

Find the probability of each event in percent.

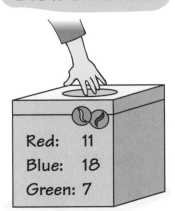

Draw a Marble

Red: 11
Blue: 18
Green: 7

7.   P(red marble) = _____

8.   P(brown marble) = _____

9.   P(green or blue marble) = _____

10. P(red or blue marble) = _____

11. P(red, blue, or green marble) = _____

Loretta spins a wheel and tosses a dice. Find the probability and answer the question.

12. **Spin the wheel.**

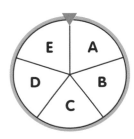

a.   P(getting "A") = _____

b.   P(getting "C" or "D") = _____

c.   P(not getting "A") = _____

d.   P(not getting "E") = _____

Hint

Find the probability of not getting a "2" in a toss.

$P(\text{not } 2) = 1 - P(2)$
$= 1 - \dfrac{1}{6}$
$= \dfrac{5}{6}$

13. **Toss a dice.**

a.   P(getting "1") = _____

b.   P(not getting "3") = _____

c.   P(not getting an odd number) = _____

d.   P(not getting a prime number) = _____

14.

Is there a higher probability of not getting a vowel in a spin than not getting a composite number in a toss?

_____

 ISBN: 978-1-77149-036-8

Odds For and Against:

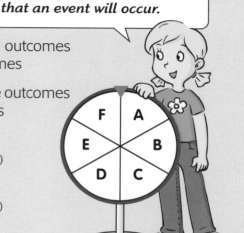

"*Odds" refers to the likelihood that an event will occur.*

odds in favour – the ratio of the number of favourable outcomes to the number of unfavourable outcomes

odds against – the ratio of the number of unfavourable outcomes to the number of favourable outcomes

e.g.   The odds in favour of spinning "C": **1 to 5**
(no. of favourable outcomes: 1 ; no. of unfavourable outcomes: 5)

The odds against spinning a vowel: **4 to 2**
(no. of unfavourable outcomes: 4 ; no. of favourable outcomes: 2)

Joshua draws a card from his deck. Find the answers.

15.

Joshua's Cards

3	4	U	11
C	7	B	▲
5	E	2	A
	★	E	♥

Picking a ...	Odds in Favour	Odds Against
a. "5"	_____	_____
b. a number	_____	_____
c. vowel	_____	_____
d. letter	_____	_____
e. prime number or vowel	_____	_____

16. Find the odds in favour of the "Toronto Tigers" winning.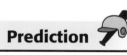

• probability of favourable outcomes: _____

• probability of unfavourable outcomes: _____

• odds in favour: _____
(write as a ratio in simplest form)

Prediction

Team	Toronto Tigers	Rangers
win	45%	36%
lose	18%	24%
tie	37%	40%

17. What are the odds against the "Rangers" losing?   _____

ISBN: 978-1-77149-036-8

Polar Bears –
Did You Know?

Have you ever wondered what the most dangerous animal on Earth really is? It is generally agreed that bears are the most dangerous animals known to humans, and of all bear species, it is the large grizzly that inspires the most fear in us. However, it is the polar bear, and not the grizzly, that is in fact the most dangerous animal known to humans. The polar bear is as aggressive as the grizzly, but what makes it more dangerous is that it is more curious and less fearful of humans. This is partly due to the fact that most polar bears have had little interaction with humans, as the northern regions where they live are sparsely populated. Also, the polar bear's diet is almost entirely meat-based; they exist primarily on a diet of fish, seal, and walrus. However, these sea-borne food sources are becoming increasingly difficult to hunt down in northern climes, making the polar bear more prone to hunger.

Despite the fact that the polar bear has gained the title of "most dangerous animal", it has a lot to fear from people. Hunters are the polar bear's only predator, and other human activity threatens its existence to the same degree. This activity has led to global climate change, which is now believed to be a cause of significant shrinkage of the arctic ice cap. By now you have probably seen sad images of polar bears trapped on tiny ice floes as they try to hunt for food, or swimming in the sea up to 50 kilometres from land. Because of this, the polar bear has become a symbol of the reality of global climate change. They are an endangered species and may possibly become extinct within our lifetime.

Polar bears actually descended from the brown bear species. During the Pleistocene epoch (when large swathes of Canada were covered in glaciers) some brown bears were isolated in northern regions. In order to adapt to the environment, these brown bears underwent a striking, and relatively rapid, evolutionary change. For example, a polar bear's fur differs from other bear species in an interesting way. The hairs on the outer coat of polar bears are actually hollow! These tube-like hairs, unique to polar bears, increase buoyancy and improve insulation. Polar bears also have thick coats of blubber. A polar bear's skin colour is black, another difference from other bear species, believed to be an adaptation to increase heat retention. The relatively

    ISBN: 978-1-77149-036-8

long necks of polar bears make swimming easier, and their remarkably large stomachs can hold as much as 80 kilograms of food.

The habitat of the polar bear is the entire arctic polar region, covering Russia, Norway, Sweden, Greenland, Alaska, and Canada. Most polar bears live in Canada, in the arctic areas along the sea. But because of Hudson Bay, their habitat dips into the provinces of Manitoba, Ontario, and Quebec. It is not uncommon now for hungry polar bears to be found scavenging trash cans in the northern Manitoba town of Churchill. It seems a sad decline for the now endangered polar bear, the true "King of the Beasts".

A. Check the best answer for each of the following questions.

1. Which of the following is not true about the polar bear?

   A. It is more curious about humans than the grizzly.

   B. It is a carnivore.

   ✓ C. It avoids humans whenever possible.

2. Polar bears are an endangered species because __B__ .

   A. there are fewer and fewer sea-borne food sources for them

   B. global climate change has threatened their survival

   C. there is an increase in human activity in the northern regions

3. Which two of the following statements are true?

   ✓ A. The arctic ice cap has almost vanished.

   ✓ B. Some brown bears evolved during the Pleistocene epoch to become polar bears.

   C. Canada was mostly covered in glaciers during the Pleistocene epoch.

4. Which of the following is true about the polar bear?

   ✓ A. The hollow, tube-like hairs of the polar bear help it float.

   B. The underlayer of short, fine black hair traps the heat.

   ✓ C. The polar bear's blubber helps conserve energy for the long winter.

Finite and Non-Finite Verbs

A **finite verb** is a verb that agrees with its subject, that is, it changes with the person or number of the subject. A **non-finite verb** or **verbal** is a verb that does not have to agree with the subject.

Examples: Polar bears <u>exist</u> primarily on a diet of fish, seal, and walrus. (finite)

The polar bear has a lot <u>to fear</u> from people. (non-finite)

There are three types of non-finite verbs:

- **Gerunds**:   gerunds look like present participles but they function as nouns.
- **Participles**: both present and past participles function as adjectives.
- **Infinitives**: to-infinitives can function as nouns, adjectives, or adverbs. In some cases, an infinitive without "to" (**bare infinitive**) should be used.

B.   Look at the underlined verbs. Write "F" for finite verbs, "PRP" for present participles, "PP" for past participles, "G" for gerunds, "TI" for to-infinitives, and "BI" for bare infinitives.

1.   The shrinkage of the arctic ice cap makes people <u>realize</u> the destructive consequence of global warming.   _____

2.   A polar bear's fur differs from other bear species in an <u>interesting</u> way.   _____

3.   The relatively long neck of a polar bear makes <u>swimming</u> easier.   _____

4.   The polar bear <u>has</u> a keen sense of smell, so it can easily detect prey on land.   _____

5.   <u>To outrun</u> a polar bear is impossible as it can reach a speed of 40 kilometres per hour.   _____

6.   The polar bear is now on the long list of <u>endangered</u> animal species.   _____

7.   Let us all <u>do</u> something to help stop global warming so the polar bear will not become extinct.   _____

C. Make sentences of your own using the verb types given in parentheses.

1. represent (finite verb)

    _____

    _____

2. conserve (gerund)

    _____

    _____

3. result (present participle)

    _____

    _____

4. intensify (past participle)

    _____

    _____

5. solve (to-infinitive as noun)

    _____

    _____

6. trap (to-infinitive as adjective)

    _____

    _____

7. understand (to-infinitive as adverb)

    _____

    _____

8. help (bare infinitive)

    _____

    _____

Cambodia's **Angkor Wat:**
Endangered by **Tourism**

Angkor Wat is an ancient temple located just a few kilometres north of the town of Siem Reap in Cambodia. It was built in the early 12ᵗʰ century as a Hindu place of worship, but evolved into a revered Buddhist temple as the religion and inhabitants changed. In fact, it is part of a much larger complex of temples, which comprise the Angkor World Heritage Site under the auspices of UNESCO. Some of the structures and the grounds surrounding them are larger. Other temples are smaller and hidden away among the remarkable ancient trees that have grown in and around the ruins. (   )

The temples of Angkor were in ruin long before the first western explorers laid eyes on them, and it is a mystery as to why the ancient Khmer culture that built them allowed them to go to ruin. (   ) In more recent times, rural poverty and demands in the illegal market for ancient Khmer artifacts meant that Cambodians themselves were participating in the destruction of the sites.

From 1976 to 1979, the country was under the control of Pol Pot, head of an organization called Khmer Rouge. He renamed the country Democratic Kampuchea and began a brutal campaign to force city-dwellers to live and work in the countryside. (   ) For this reason, while other countries in the region, such as Thailand and Malaysia, began to prosper and invite foreign tourists on a large scale, Cambodia, with little infrastructure, was still a place that outsiders knew little about.

However, over the last 20 years, international tourism in Cambodia has trickled in and is now, one could say, a torrent. (   ) Consequently, destruction of Cambodia's cultural heritage has increased. For example, the rapid urbanization of the Siem Reap area has led to a drop in the water table, resulting in the instability of the Angkor monuments. Moreover, the number of impoverished parents removing their children from school so that they can sell postcards and souvenirs to tourists has been increasing.

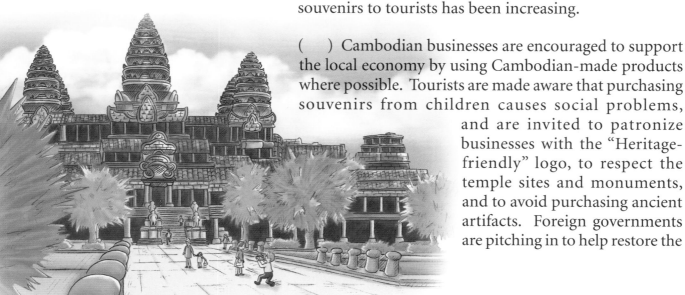

(   ) Cambodian businesses are encouraged to support the local economy by using Cambodian-made products where possible. Tourists are made aware that purchasing souvenirs from children causes social problems, and are invited to patronize businesses with the "Heritage-friendly" logo, to respect the temple sites and monuments, and to avoid purchasing ancient artifacts. Foreign governments are pitching in to help restore the

ISBN: 978-1-77149-036-8

Angkor site. These changes show that concerted efforts are finally being made to restore the ancient wonders of Angkor – and Cambodian society.

A. Each of the following statements goes with a paragraph of the preceding passage. Decide on the matching statements and paragraphs. Write the letters in the parentheses where the statements should go.

a. As a result, measures are now being taken to ensure that Cambodia's tourism industry is "heritage-friendly".

b. But of all the ruins, it is Angkor Wat that has become the symbol of Cambodia, appearing on that country's flag.

c. A few years ago (2004) over a million foreigners came to Cambodia, and more than half said they had come to visit Angkor Wat.

d. Ever since then, looting has persisted, as treasure-hunters excavated ancient burial grounds, or simply walked off with chunks of the extraordinary architecture and stone carvings as souvenirs.

e. A state of anarchy ensued and up to 1.7 million Cambodians died.

B. Answer the following questions.

1. Which sentence in the passage explains the evolution of Angkor Wat over the years?

   _____

   _____

2. Which sentence in the passage shows that there was little progress in Cambodia between 1976 and 1979?

   _____

   _____

3. Which sentence in the passage illustrates that international tourism in Angkor Wat has increased tremendously?

   _____

   _____

Non-Progressive Verbs

Some verbs are not normally used in progressive tenses. They are called **non-progressive verbs** or **non-action verbs**. They are verbs that describe sense perceptions, mental, emotional, or existing states, and possession. However, some of these verbs can be used in progressive tenses when they have meanings other than those mentioned above.

Examples: Many people <u>think</u> that the Cambodian government should put effort in restoring the Angkor site.
("think" here describes a mental state – non-progressive)

Foreign governments <u>are thinking</u> of ways to help restore the Angkor site.
("think" here means "consider" – can be progressive)

C.   Put the following non-progressive verbs under the correct headings. Think of two more verbs that can be put under each heading if there are any.

appear   be   believe   belong   contain   fear   feel
hate   have   hear   know   like   mind   own
possess   remember   see   seem   taste   want

Sense	Mental State	Emotional State	Existence	Possession
_____	_____	_____	_____	_____
_____	_____	_____	_____	_____
_____	_____	_____	_____	_____
_____	_____	_____	_____	_____

ISBN: 978-1-77149-036-8

D. **Each of the verbs below can be used as both progressive and non-progressive verbs. Make a sentence with the verb in each form.**

1. look

   Progressive _____

   Non-progressive _____

2. feel

   Progressive _____

   Non-progressive _____

3. have

   Progressive _____

   Non-progressive _____

4. be

   Progressive _____

   Non-progressive _____

5. smell

   Progressive _____

   Non-progressive _____

6. appear

   Progressive _____

   Non-progressive _____

7. weigh

   Progressive _____

   Non-progressive _____

8. see

   Progressive _____

   Non-progressive _____

The naming of the Nobel Prize winners is among the most eagerly anticipated awards ceremonies in the world. The Nobel Prizes were established at the bequest of Alfred Nobel (the inventor of dynamite) and first awarded in 1901, in the subject areas of physics, chemistry, physiology or medicine, literature, and peace. Sweden's central bank instituted a Prize in economics, first awarded in 1969, which is now identified with the Nobel Prizes. The "Nobels" are regarded as the most prestigious awards in the world. They consist of a medal, a personal diploma, and a money award (which increases in value annually and is more than a million dollars now). But the true value lies in the social prestige and worldwide attention brought to the subject associated with the winners.

Canada is well-placed among the countries that have Nobel laureates. There are 18 Canadian Nobel laureates, which is an impressive record. Most of our laureates are scientists: Bertram Brockhouse won the Prize in Physics in 1994 for his work on condensed matter; Michael Smith won the Prize in Chemistry in 1993 for site-directed mutagenesis; Rudolph Marcus won the Prize in Chemistry in 1992 for electron transfer reactions; Richard Taylor won the Prize in Physics in 1990 for verifying Quark Theory; Sidney Altman, a molecular biologist, won the Prize in Chemistry in 1989, sharing it with his colleague Thomas R. Cech, for their research into the catalytic properties of RNA; John Polanyi won the Prize in Chemistry in 1986 for chemi-luminescence; Henry Taube won the Prize in Chemistry in 1983 for electron transfer reactions; David Hubel won the Prize in Medicine in 1981 for mapping the visual cortex; Gerhard Herzberg won the Prize in Chemistry in 1971 for his contributions to the knowledge of free radicals; William Giauque won the Prize in Chemistry in 1949 for research into the properties of matter at temperatures close to absolute zero; Sir Frederick Banting won the Prize in Medicine in 1923 for discovering insulin. He shared the prize with fellow-Canadian (Scottish-born) John Macleod.

Canadian
Nobel Prize Laureates

The following Canadian Nobel laureates won in the field of economics: Robert Mundell won in 1999 for his work on currency areas and exchange rates; Myron Scholes won in 1997 for his work on a new method to determine the value of derivatives; William Spencer Vickrey won the Nobel Memorial Prize in Economics in 1996, sharing the prize with James Mirrlees for research into an economic theory of incentives under asymmetric information. Sadly, Vickrey passed away three days after the announcement.

ISBN: 978-1-77149-036-8

Canada can also lay claim to two Nobel Peace Prize laureates – well...almost. Lester Pearson was a diplomat who won the Nobel Peace Prize in 1957 for his role in diffusing the Suez Crisis. He later became Prime Minister. And in 1995, a Nova Scotia-founded organization, The Pugwash Conferences on Science and World Affairs, shared the Nobel Peace Prize in 1995 with Polish physicist Joseph Rotblat (who co-founded the organization) for their efforts toward nuclear disarmament. Lastly, Saul Bellow, a Canadian-born American writer, won the Nobel Prize in Literature in 1976.

There are almost 800 Nobel Prize laureates now. They come from all over the world, are from various walks of life, and represent all faiths, social classes, and educational backgrounds. The stories of these people, and the 18 Canadians among them, are a testament to what can be achieved if you believe.

A. Complete the following with words from the passage.

Revered as the most 1._____ awards in the world, the Nobel Prizes

were 2._____ in 1901 at the 3._____ of Alfred Nobel, who was

the 4._____ of dynamite. The Nobel Prizes are awarded in these

areas: physics, chemistry, physiology or medicine, literature, peace, and

5._____ . Apart from a medal, a 6._____ diploma, and a sum

of money, a Nobel laureate enjoys social 7._____ and worldwide

8._____ .

Canada has an 9._____ record of 18 laureates, most of whom are

distinguished 10._____ . The award of Nobel prizes is not confined to

individuals; organizations can be recipients of Nobel Prizes too. In 1995, for

example, the Pugwash Conferences on Science and World Affairs, which

was 11._____ in Nova Scotia, 12._____ the Nobel 13._____

Prize with Polish physicist Joseph Rotblat for their 14._____ toward

nuclear disarmament.

Phrasal Verbs

A **phrasal verb** is a verb used with a preposition or an adverb. It usually has a meaning that is completely different from the verb itself.

Example: Vickrey <u>passed away</u> three days after the announcement.
(died)

B. **Fill in the blanks with the suitable phrasal verbs to complete the sentences. Use the correct form of the verbs.**

go through   break in   take down   keep to

die down   carry on   get over   come about

1.   The interviewer asked the Nobel laureate in Literature how the idea for her winning book _____ .

2.   When the Nobel laureate was interviewed by the magazine, somebody _____ and asked for her autograph.

3.   The Nobel laureate's speech _____ for hours, but it was so amusing that no one wanted to leave. Some students even _____ what he said.

4.   The controversy about whether the Nobel Peace Prize laureate was justified in getting the award _____ as time went by.

5.   The candidate for the Nobel Prize found it hard to _____ his disappointment.

6.   The Nobel laureate in Physics _____ many ups and downs in his career.

7.   No matter how hard and impossible it may seem to achieve your dream, _____ it and one day it will be realized.

C. **Look up the definition of each phrasal verb below in the dictionary and write it on the given line. Then make a sentence with the phrasal verb.**

1. wear off

   Definition: _____

   Sentence: _____

2. draw up

   Definition: _____

   Sentence: _____

3. call on

   Definition: _____

   Sentence: _____

4. put off

   Definition: _____

   Sentence: _____

5. take after

   Definition: _____

   Sentence: _____

6. hand over

   Definition: _____

   Sentence: _____

7. iron out

   Definition: _____

   Sentence: _____

8. look into

   Definition: _____

   Sentence: _____

Naming a
Public Holiday

Winters are long and cold in Manitoba. And, what's more, February is one of the months in that province without a statutory public holiday. Slowly, the idea to pressure the Manitoba government to give Manitobans a holiday to help get rid of those "February Blahs" took hold in the local media. At first, the government officials scoffed at the idea, but eventually, after public pressure "snowballed", they began to give the idea serious consideration. And why not? After all, before the new holiday was proclaimed, Manitobans had only seven statutory holidays, less than Canada's national average. Moreover, Alberta has been enjoying a February holiday – called Family Day – since 1990, and Saskatchewan inaugurated its own Family Day on February 19, 2007.

But when you're a government leader, you need to be careful about how you do things. Of course, government leaders would be happy to give people this "gift", knowing that it could generate goodwill among the general public. But then you have to decide what to call it! A savvy political leader does not want to be seen spending precious time deciding on the name of a holiday when there are other important matters to discuss in the legislative assembly. So what do you do? You delegate. The government decided to give this important task to...Manitoba's young people! Certainly no one would argue with the decision to let the youth of the province have a role in government affairs – not even the Official Opposition!

And so it was that the students of the province decided on the name of Manitoba's newest statutory holiday. Schools were invited to submit names in a contest, and the MB4Youth Advisory Council (a committee of 15 young people between the ages of 15 and 24 selected on the basis of their community involvement, reporting to the Minister of Education, Citizenship and Youth) chose the winner from a shortlist. Some of the names offered up by schoolchildren included: Nellie McClung Day, Duff Roblin Day, Bison Break, Winnipeg Jets Day, and Spirited Energy Day. What was it going to be?

"It's very, very tough to make all of the people happy all of the time, but at the end of the day, this is the name that was chosen, and I think Manitobans will be happy with it," said Labour Minister Nancy Allan on September 25, 2007, when the winning name was announced. Manitoba's newest holiday was going to be called Louis Riel Day, in honour of the legendary – and controversial – Métis leader who led the Red River and Northwest Rebellions in a fight for Aboriginal rights. He

ISBN: 978-1-77149-036-8

was hanged for treason in 1885, but is considered by many to be the founder of Manitoba. Eleven schools had put his name forward and were each given a $1000 grant to buy library materials.

The Labour Minister was right; not everyone was pleased. Some felt it should have been called Family Day (since February is so cold you really can't do anything except stay at home with your family). Many business people did not want a holiday at all, saying that it was unfair to expect businesses to pay for another public holiday for their staff. But many others also felt that these young people had done the adults proud by following their own lead, showing an appreciation for history and heritage, and being unafraid of the inevitable controversy. Manitobans celebrate Louis Riel Day on the third Monday of February.

A. Check the best answer for each of the following questions.

1. Which of the following statements is true?

    A. Manitobans pressured their government for a Family Day in February.

    B. Both Alberta and Saskatchewan have a holiday in February.

    C. Canadians on average enjoy seven statutory holidays.

2. A savvy political leader is one who _____ .

    A. sticks to his or her principles

    B. is practical-minded

    C. is smart

3. Which of the following is not true?

    A. Louis Riel was hanged for treason in 1885.

    B. Eleven schools took part in the naming contest.

    C. Louis Riel played a crucial role in fighting for Aboriginal rights.

B. If you were asked to name a new holiday in June, what name would you give it? Why?

_____

_____

_____

Prepositional Verbs

Some verbs need to be used with particular prepositions. They are called **prepositional verbs**. A prepositional verb is different from a phrasal verb in that the adding of the preposition to the verb does not result in a complete change of its meaning.

Example: The students of the province <u>decided on</u> the name of Manitoba's newest statutory holiday.

C.   Write the preposition that goes with each of the following verbs.

1.   insist   _____

2.   account _____

3.   borrow   _____

4.   delight _____

5.   recover _____

6.   believe   _____

7.   worry   _____

8.   approve _____

9.   consent _____

10.   vote   _____

11.   wrestle   _____

12.   substitute _____

D.   Fill in the blanks with the correct prepositions.

1.   The government officials of Manitoba scoffed _____ the idea of adding a statutory public holiday at first.

2.   The MB4Youth Advisory Council consists _____ 15 members between 15 and 24 years old.

3.   The committee members of MB4Youth Advisory Council agreed _____ naming the new holiday Louis Riel Day.

4.   Some businesses objected _____ adding one more public holiday. They were not happy about having to pay _____ another public holiday for their employees.

5.   Compared _____ some Canadian provinces or territories, Manitoba has fewer statutory holidays.

6.   Louis Riel was a Métis leader who fought _____ Aboriginal rights.

Prepositional Adjectives

There are some adjectives that must be used with prepositions, too. They are called **prepositional adjectives**.

Example: When you're a government leader, you need to be <u>careful about</u> how you do things.

E.   Write the preposition that goes with each of the following adjectives.

1. infamous _____

2. crazy _____

3. worried _____

4. curious _____

5. proud _____

6. popular _____

7. confident _____

8. guilty _____

9. capable _____

10. interested _____

11. fond _____

12. serious _____

F.   Make sentences of your own with the following prepositional adjectives.

1. angry with

_____

2. cautious about

_____

3. unafraid of

_____

4. quick at

_____

5. hesitant about

_____

6. competent in

_____

The Christmas tradition probably began in and around what is now Germany as far back as the 4th century! A man named Nicholas gave his inherited wealth to the poor and became a monk, travelling the countryside and helping those in need. Over the years, he became known as the protector of children and sailors, and was made a saint. By the 1500s, Saint Nick was the most popular saint in Europe. He would give gifts of fruits, nuts, and candies to good children and lumps of coal to naughty children, reminding us that even way back then children needed some help deciding whether to be "naughty or nice". The Christmas stocking tradition also seems to have stemmed from Saint Nick: attempting to help a poor girl who needed a wedding dowry, he threw a sack of gold coins through her window. The coins landed in one of her stockings, which had been hanging up to dry.

But the idea of gift-giving at Christmas stems from the Bible. The Book of Matthew tells us the story of the three wise men bringing gifts of gold, frankincense, and myrrh to baby Jesus. German advances in printing technology during the Middle Ages meant that the Bible was becoming more widely read, and this helps to explain how Santa became a central figure in the Christmas tradition.

The Christmas tree tradition also came from Germany. During the Middle Ages, to celebrate the feast day of Adam and Eve on December 24, German families would set up a "Paradise Tree" in their homes representing the Garden of Eden. Originally, they hung wafers on the tree to symbolize the Holy Communion, but over time these were replaced by more delicious things: biscuits, sweets, nuts, fruits, and even popcorn strings. As years went by, the decorations became more ornamental: roses, barley sugar twists, gingerbread shapes, pretzels, paper flowers, and waxen figurines.

The History of
Christmas Giving

Victorian England took the Christmas tree custom to new heights. By the time it caught on in the mid-19th century, there were other decorations, including tinsel, silver wire ornaments, beads, and candles. But the British added their own touches from their Victorian-style crafts: finely embroidered pouches with secret gifts, delicate lace snowflakes, miniature paper baskets with sugared almonds, and glittery, beaded garlands. They also hung small toys on the tree. By the late 19th century, Christmas trees were jam-packed with ornaments, sweets, and toys! As the toys got bigger, they were placed under the tree. At the time, Victorian England was fascinated with moving things. In addition to wooden rocking horses, doll houses, and flip-books (the first motion pictures), mechanical toys such as kaleidoscopes, spinning tops, and jack-in-the-boxes were popular items.

Before the 1860s, Christmas was not widely celebrated in the United States, but by the close of the 19th century, Christmas had really taken off. The inventive Americans patented ornament hooks and the first electric Christmas tree lights. But this may not have come about if the big American department store Macy's had not seen the value of commercializing the holiday back in 1867. At that time, Macy's kept its doors open until midnight on Christmas Eve. In 1874, Macy's began enticing shoppers with Christmas-themed window displays. And so began Christmas as we know it. From teddy bears, board games (especially Monopoly), crayons, through to Barbie dolls, hula hoops, and G.I. Joe – these were just a few of our favourite toys of the last century. Toys are a reflection of the times and a reflection of our values, reminding us of who we once were, and what we are becoming.

A. Answer the following questions.

1. Who was Santa Claus?

   _____

   _____

2. "...even way back then children needed some help deciding whether to be 'naughty or nice'." How did Nicholas help children in that regard?

   _____

3. Describe how the stocking tradition came about.

   _____

   _____

4. How did Macy's commercialize Christmas?

   _____

   _____

5. Do you agree with the writer that "toys are a reflection of the times and a reflection of our values"? Why or why not?

   _____

   _____

Order of Adjectives

When we use more than one adjective before a noun, we need to put them in the right order according to the type of each adjective. Adjectives are usually put in this order: opinion, size, age, shape, colour, origin, material, purpose.

Opinion	great, terrifying, unforgettable
Size	tiny, big, enormous
Age	old, young
Shape	oval, square, triangular
Colour	green, beige, maroon
Origin	Canadian, American, French
Material	plastic, woollen, glass
Purpose	<u>dancing</u> shoes, <u>car</u> engine, <u>washing</u> machine

Example: Mom has bought a Christmas glittery beaded garland. (✘)
Mom has bought a glittery beaded Christmas garland. (✔)

B. Put each of the following groups of adjectives in order before the noun they describe.

1. a _____ tree
(tall, gorgeous, Christmas, green)

2. the _____ saint
(European, most, popular)

3. the _____ coins
(heavy, precious, gold)

4. a/an _____ tradition
(special, German, old)

5. the _____ ornaments
(long, wire, beautiful, silver)

6. the _____ baskets
(colourful, paper, miniature, interesting)

7. a/an _____ house
(expensive, doll, new, big)

8. the _____ store
(American, old, department, famous, big)

C. Rewrite each sentence by using at least three adjectives to describe the underlined noun.

1. We have put lots of <u>presents</u> under the Christmas tree.

   _____

   _____

2. All shopping malls around the country swarmed with <u>shoppers</u>.

   _____

   _____

3. Carl found a <u>jack-in-the-box</u> in the attic.

   _____

   _____

4. Wendy hung lots of <u>ornaments</u> on the Christmas tree.

   _____

   _____

5. We have <u>dinner</u> at Grandpa and Grandma's house every Christmas.

   _____

   _____

6. Grandma likes telling us a <u>story</u> after Christmas dinner.

   _____

   _____

7. My best friend Lisa bought me a <u>scarf</u> as a present.

   _____

   _____

8. Mom showed us the <u>toys</u> she had kept since she was a girl.

   _____

   _____

The Remarkable Journey of Al Gore

Albert Gore, Jr. was born in Washington, D.C. in 1948. He enjoyed his life in Washington, especially his summers working on the family farm in Tennessee. When he graduated from college, he enlisted to serve his country in Vietnam, even though he did not agree with the war. On his return, he began a career in journalism and later in politics. Just like his father, Gore became the congressional representative and later, the senator of Tennessee. He eventually became the Vice President of the United States under Bill Clinton, a Democrat. In 2000, when Bill Clinton's eight-year term was complete, Gore ran for the presidency against the Republican candidate George W. Bush. People agreed it would be a close race, but no one ever expected what happened next.

Al Gore received about 500 000 more votes than George W. Bush, but those votes needed to be converted into delegates for the Electoral College, which decides the winner in this unique American system. The state of Florida was a close race, and there were reported irregularities in the way the election had been administered there. In the end, it was decided that all the delegates from that state were to come from the George W. Bush camp, effectively making him the next U.S. President. Many people wanted Al Gore to fight this outcome through legal action (and in fact legal action had already been started by both sides). After a lot of thought, Al Gore decided not to continue the legal battle. He did not want the country to be divided throughout a long court case. He pledged to support the new president, George W. Bush.

Shortly after, Al Gore and his wife, Tipper, went away to Europe to re-evaluate their lives. When Gore returned, people asked if he would return to politics. Gore replied that he had "fallen out of love with politics". This response did not satisfy some people. The media did not treat him kindly; they made fun of his new beard and the fact that he had gained weight. Some said that being the U.S. vice president, not a particularly important job, would be his greatest achievement. But Gore continued to work quietly toward his long-held goals and beliefs. Long before Gore became U.S. vice president, he had created a slideshow about global warming. Now, with Tipper's encouragement, he dusted off the old slideshow. His children told him he needed to turn it into a PowerPoint presentation. Al Gore went back to the grassroots, imparting his message to small groups in places like schools and town halls. It was very different from the days when he could fill banquet halls with wealthy, powerful people and plenty of reporters to cover the event.

One day, a documentary filmmaker saw Gore's presentation and asked if he could turn it into a film. The result was *An Inconvenient Truth*. Not only was this documentary turned into a

ISBN: 978-1-77149-036-8

bestselling book (with a bestselling children's version following), but the film also won an Academy Award for Davis Guggenheim, the director. The film was shown around the world, making people everywhere take notice of the problem of global warming and climate change. As a result of this remarkable achievement, and along with all his other efforts, Gore was given the 2007 Nobel Peace Prize, sharing it with the scientists of the Intergovernmental Panel on Climate Change. People still ask Gore if he will ever run for the presidency again. Many hope that he will, as history has shown us that the best leaders are humble, wise, compassionate, and steadfast.

A. Read the following statements. Rewrite the ones that are not true.

1. George W. Bush beat Al Gore by 500 000 votes in the 2000 presidential race.

   _____

2. Tipper encouraged Gore to make good use of his slideshow about global warming.

   _____

3. The documentary *An Inconvenient Truth* was based on a bestselling book with the same title.

   _____

4. Al Gore shared the 2007 Nobel Peace Prize with Davis Guggenheim for their efforts in addressing the problem of global warming and climate change.

   _____

   _____

B. Would you say that Al Gore's defeat in the 2000 presidential race was in fact a blessing in disguise? Why or why not?

_____

_____

_____

_____

Interrogative Adverbs

"When", "why", "where", and "how" are **interrogative adverbs**. They are usually placed at the beginning of a question.

Examples: <u>When</u> was Albert Gore born?

<u>Why</u> did Al Gore serve the United States in Vietnam if he did not agree with the war?

<u>Where</u> did Al Gore and his wife go to re-evaluate their lives?

<u>How</u> was his slideshow about global warming turned into a film?

C. Write questions that elicit the given responses with interrogative adverbs.

1. _____

_____

Al Gore ran for the presidency against the Republican candidate George W. Bush in 2000.

2. _____

_____

Al Gore received about 500 000 more votes than George W. Bush.

3. _____

_____

Al Gore presented his message about global warming using PowerPoint.

4. _____

_____

The film *An Inconvenient Truth* was shown around the world.

5. _____

_____

Many people hope that Al Gore will run for the presidency again because he is humble, wise, compassionate, and steadfast.

ISBN: 978-1-77149-036-8

Relative Adverbs

"When", "why", and "where" can also be used to join clauses as **relative adverbs**. They are often used to replace the more formal structure of "preposition + which" in a relative clause.

Examples: It was very different from the days <u>when</u> he could fill banquet halls with wealthy and powerful people.
("when" is used in place of "in which")

The media wanted to know <u>why</u> Gore gave up his pursuit of the presidency.
("why" is used in place of "the reason for")

Tennessee is the place <u>where</u> the Gores' family farm is located.
("where" is used in place of "at which")

D. Join the sentences with the appropriate relative adverbs. Make any other necessary changes.

1. Al Gore went to schools and town halls. He imparted his message about global warming.

_____

2. 1965 was the year. Gore enrolled in Harvard University in that year.

_____

3. Gore enlisted in the U.S. military. The media wanted to know the reason.

_____

4. There was a time. Gore struggled to make a decision about joining the U.S. military at that time.

_____

5. This is the cathedral. Gore married Tipper here.

_____

6. Gore gave a speech. He gave his reason for supporting the use of green energy in his speech.

_____

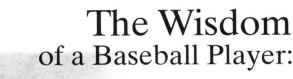

The Wisdom
of a Baseball Player:
Yogi Berra's
Quotes

The ability to amuse someone with clever witticisms is always appreciated, but not easy to do. Some people, such as stand-up comedians and writers of humour, make a career out of it – if they're good enough. But one of the English language's most quoted "humorists" is neither of those – but rather a retired professional baseball player who goes by the name of Yogi Berra.

Yogi was born Lawrence Peter Berra in St. Louis, Missouri in 1925. He quit school in the eighth grade and soon after served in the U.S. Navy during World War II. On his return to the United States, he began playing minor league baseball. In 1946, he began his remarkable career as a major league baseball player (with the New York Yankees) and later as a manager. He is known to many as the best baseball catcher of all time, was named the Most Valuable Player of the American League three times, and was one of only a handful of managers to lead teams from both the American and National Leagues to the World Series. He was inducted into the Baseball Hall of Fame in 1972.

Throughout his remarkable career, Yogi Berra was also well known for his unique sense of humour. He liked to offer his observations, often deceptively and cleverly simplistic on the one hand, yet quite meaningful, even profound, on the other. Some of his most quoted sayings are malapropisms. A malapropism is defined as an accidental misuse of a word in a sentence, usually with a comic effect – although in the case of Yogi Berra, one could easily assume he did it on purpose.

If this is not enough, Yogi is also a humanitarian. Throughout his life, he has given generously to worthy causes, in particular to organizations that support young people. His annual golf tournament has raised more than a million dollars for youth scholarships and educational programming. He founded the Yogi Berra Museum and Learning Centre in Little Falls, New Jersey, with the following mission statement: "...to preserve and promote the values of respect, sportsmanship, social justice and excellence through inclusive, culturally diverse, sports-based educational programs and exhibits."

For his many talents, Yogi Berra is a much-loved person. By now you are perhaps eager to read some of these great "one-liners". As you go down the list, think of how many you have already heard – and try not to smile!

ISBN: 978-1-77149-036-8

- *When you come to a fork in the road, take it.*
- *Never answer an anonymous letter.*
- *I didn't really say everything I said.*
- *You can observe a lot by watching.*
- *We made too many wrong mistakes. (on why his team lost the 1960 World Series)*
- *I usually take a two-hour nap from one to four.*
- *It ain't over till it's over.*
- *If the world were perfect, it wouldn't be.*

A. Answer the following questions.

1. "But one of the English language's most quoted 'hurmorists' is neither of those..." What does "those" refer to?

   _____

2. Why is Yogi Berra revered as a humorist?

   _____

3. "...to preserve and promote the values of respect, sportsmanship, social justice and excellence through inclusive, culturally diverse, sports-based educational programs and exhibits." What does "inclusive" imply?

   _____

4. Which one of Yogi's quotes in the passage amuses you most? Why?

   _____

   _____

5. Search the Internet and find more of Yogi Berra's quotes. List them below, and share them with your friends.

   _____

   _____

   _____

   _____

Position of Adverbs

Adverbs can be placed at different positions in a sentence: at the beginning, in the middle, or at the end.

Generally, adverbs that modify adjectives or other adverbs go in the middle, right before the words they modify, with the exception of "enough" and "ago".

Examples: He liked to offer his observations, often <u>cleverly</u> simplistic on the one hand, yet quite meaningful on the other.

Some people can make a career out of their ability to amuse people – if they're good <u>enough</u>.

Adverbs of frequency go after the verb "to be" in both active and passive voice sentences, but with other verbs, they are put before them. However, if the main verb is preceded by a modal verb or an auxiliary verb, an adverb of frequency goes between them.

Examples: The ability to amuse someone with clever witticisms is <u>usually</u> appreciated.

In the case of Yogi Berra, one could <u>easily</u> assume he did it on purpose.

B.   Check if the adverbs in the following sentences are put in the appropriate places. If not, rewrite the sentences to make them correct.

1.   Stand-up comedy shows started to be popular ago long.

_____

2.   Yogi Berra is always ready to amuse others with his wit.

_____

3.   I find it never easy to be a person of humour.

_____

4.   It is amusing certainly to read Yogi Berra's one-liners.

_____

5.   Being humorous is different completely from being silly.

_____

C. **Add the given adverbs in the appropriate places in the following sentences. Make any other necessary changes.**

1. never

    My brother finds it hard to make me laugh.

    _____

2. extremely

    The comedian is so famous that he drew a large audience to his show.

    _____

3. enough

    His performance is humorous to bring laughter to everyone throughout the two-hour show.

    _____

4. quite

    Lester commented casually on the controversial issue.

    _____

5. widely

    Yogi Berra is known for his sense of humour.

    _____

6. always

    He is quick at coming up with new one-liners.

    _____

7. usually

    You can discover great philosophy in what he says.

    _____

Too Much of a Good Thing: the "Law of Unintended Consequences"

Government leaders try hard to make the best decisions. Sometimes they canvass the general public or get expert advice, hold meetings, and set up committees and panels of inquiry. Of course, we already know the following from Aesop's fable "The Man, the Boy, and the Donkey": "Please all, and you will please none." These days, no policymaker – or member of the public – needs to be told that pleasing everyone is going to be impossible. But there are, perhaps more importantly, times when decisions made in good faith and with the best of intentions result in outcomes that are not what anyone could have foreseen. Good examples of this can be considered serendipitous, but sadly, there are cases where public policy decisions have resulted in injurious outcomes difficult to remedy.

In Australia – A large toad, known as the Giant Neotropical Toad or cane toad, native to the southern United States and Brazil, was introduced into Australia and certain countries in the South Pacific as a way to control the greyback cane beetle pests, which were devastating the sugar cane crops – those countries' main commodity crops at the time. This introduction of a foreign species was done after examining the case of the toad's introduction into several Caribbean islands, particularly into Puerto Rico, to curb the white grub population there. At that time, it was believed that the introduction of the toad had served its purpose. However, later studies concluded that it was wrong to attribute the reduction in the white grub population to the toad. The cane toad policy in Australia has obviously been a mistake: from 102 toads introduced in 1935 into northern Queensland, the population has now extended as far as the Northern Territory and New South Wales and numbers over 200 million. The cane toad's voracious appetite has caused considerable damage to the native Australian ecosystem, as well as to fauna and domestic animals that have been in contact with its poisonous skin. Concerted efforts are being made to eradicate what is now one of the country's biggest nuisances.

In Iceland – A lovely purple flower, the Alaskan Lupin (Lupinus nootkatensis) is a contentious issue in Iceland. The species was introduced into Iceland as a conservation measure to stabilize soil erosion. But it grew and spread like a weed, threatened the natural flora of the country, and slowed down, or got in the way of, forest rejuvenation. Iceland does not have much flora to begin with, and reforestation is a major undertaking there. But now the government of Iceland is embarking on a concerted effort to eradicate the Lupin. Summertime work projects have students from Iceland and abroad moving in to cut down the Lupin and, if possible, remove its seeds from the ground.

In Canada – Canadian Forest Service has become "too successful" with its fire-prevention initiatives. Fire is a natural part of the life cycle of forests, and the reduction of forest fires created new problems when, for example, large stands of mature trees, susceptible to pests and disease, were not killed off by fire. Moreover, accumulated matter on the forest floor remained longer, preventing new seedlings from sprouting and new trees from growing. The resulting forests of older trees are now seriously threatened by pests such as the pine beetle. They are now threatening to destroy the forests of British Columbia and Alberta.

A. Complete the following with reference to the passage.

1. Fact: 102 Giant Neotropical Toads were brought into Australia in 1935.

   Purpose: _____

   Consequence: _____

   _____

2. Fact: The Alaskan Lupin was introduced into Iceland around 2000.

   Purpose: _____

   Consequence: _____

   _____

3. Fact: Canadian Forest Service has launched many fire-prevention initiatives.

   Purpose: _____

   Consequence: _____

   _____

4. Describe another case of the "law of unintended consequences".

   _____

   _____

   _____

Viewpoint Adverbs

Viewpoint adverbs are used to help express our viewpoint or opinion about an action. They are placed at the beginning of a sentence.

Example: I feel sad that there are many cases where public policy decisions have resulted in injurious outcomes difficult to remedy.

Sadly, there are many cases where public policy decisions have resulted in injurious outcomes difficult to remedy.

B.   Rewrite each of the following sentences by starting it with a viewpoint adverb. Make any other necessary changes.

1.   I was surprised that the government did not do any research before introducing the species to the country.

_____

_____

2.   According to theory, the cane toad can control the damage done by greyback cane beetles to the sugar cane.

_____

_____

3.   In an ideal situation, the whole population of cane beetles could be wiped out from Australia.

_____

_____

4.   To be honest with you, I don't think this policy will work without causing other problems.

_____

_____

5.   It is now clear that the Australian government is facing another serious pest problem – the cane toad.

_____

_____

Commenting Adverbs

Commenting adverbs are similar to viewpoint adverbs. In many cases, they are the same words, but they go in a different position in the sentence – after the verb "to be" or before the main verb.

Example: The cane toad policy in Australia is a mistake.
The cane toad policy in Australia is <u>obviously</u> a mistake.

C. Add an appropriate commenting adverb to each of the following sentences.

1. Soil erosion has been a serious problem in Iceland.

   _____

2. Reforestation is a major undertaking there, too.

   _____

3. Cutting down the Lupin or removing its seeds from the ground is not an easy job.

   _____

4. It is unwise to make public policy decisions hastily.

   _____

5. It is not a problem that can be solved within the next decade.

   _____

6. Matter accumulated on the forest floor prevents new seedlings from sprouting.

   _____

   _____

7. Pine beetles will destroy all forests if the government takes no measures to control them.

   _____

   _____

N o one wants to be out of style. The world of fashion changes all the time. What you say, as well as what you wear, tells people whether you are "in style" or not! So, let's look at the glossary of current style trends. There's plenty for you to dig (like) or dis (dislike, disdain, disregard).

Punk rock: The punk rock style usually consists of ripped jeans and T-shirts with the sleeves cut off and leather or denim jackets with punk rock band decals. For a more feminine look, girls wear fishnet stockings (with holes), black boots, and black leather miniskirts.

How to Talk Like a
Fashion Trendsetter

Goth glam: This is a dark, gothic style with a touch of glamour. For the gothic look, anything black works. Lots of makeup makes things more "glam", but the main colours are a pale face and large black-rimmed eyes. The goth glam look must include dyed black hair too, if it isn't black already.

Boho chic: Boho chic is a mix of nice, old clothing updated by more fancy and trendy glamorous items. Boho is short for Bohemia, a place in Europe famous for the unique clothing of the gypsies that live there. Wide print skirts, especially with flower patterns, combined with neat T-shirts and string vests or denim and leather jackets, are good Boho chic choices. Lots of jewellery is important too.

Bollywood: Bollywood is India's equivalent of Hollywood. In fact, more movies are made each year in Bollywood! This look borrows from the traditional Indian sari, a six-metre long piece of cotton or silk that women wrap around themselves to create a particular kind of dress. Bollywood fans wrap themselves in bright colours to be beautiful!

Preppy chic: First found in American preparatory schools, this style consists of khaki pants or shorts, pastel-coloured polo shirts, and leather deck shoes. Sweater sets (short-sleeved sweater with matching knit jacket), pencil-skirts, and strings of pearls are what the girls wear when they want to dress up.

Hipster cool: This trend is about what the peace-loving hippies wore in the 1960s – bell-bottom trousers (striped is best!) and T-shirts with 1960s rockers like Joan Baez, the Beatles, or

ISBN: 978-1-77149-036-8

Bob Dylan on them. The peace-sign necklace is also an important part of the look. It's a look that borrows from the hippie saying, "Feeling Groovy!"

Classic: Some clothes are timeless. Sweater sets have been a favoured piece for more than 50 years. Regular blue jeans of almost any leg width can safely be called a "classic" item. A nice, simple woollen blazer can also last for ages, as long as it isn't in last season's "must-have" far-out print or doesn't have shoulder pads (that's so 1980s!). Neutral colours (tan, brown, black, navy) and simple lines are the key to buying classic pieces that outlast trends.

Remember that fashionistas (people who are passionate about clothes and keeping their own up-to-date) do not want to be out of style. If you like what you see, you can say to the person, "That's so fly!" But, if you need to tell your friend that what he or she has on is looking dated, you might want to whisper in his or her ear, "That's so last season!"

A. Name the styles that the following people are dressed in.

1. a man in his 30s in a T-shirt and a pair of striped bell-bottom pants _____

2. a teenage girl wearing black boots and a black leather miniskirt _____

3. a teenage boy in a polo shirt and a pair of khaki shorts _____

4. a young woman with a long piece of floral fabric wrapped around her _____

5. a girl wearing lots of makeup: black-rimmed eyes on her pale face _____

6. a woman in her 30s wearing a string vest and a wide print skirt _____

B. Which style mentioned in the passage is your favourite? Why?

_____

_____

_____

_____

Conjunctions

A **coordinating conjunction** (and, or, but) is used to link independent clauses to form a compound sentence.

A **subordinating conjunction** is used to link a dependent clause to an independent clause to form a complex sentence.

Note that coordinating conjunctions and subordinating conjunctions are also used to join words and phrases in parallel structures.

Correlative conjunctions are used in pairs. Some common correlative conjunctions are "either...or", "neither...nor", "both...and", "whether...or", and "not only...but also".

C. **Circle the conjunctions in the sentences below. Write "C" for coordinating conjunctions, "S" for subordinating conjunctions, and "CR" for correlative conjunctions.**

1. A string of pearls is what the girls wear when they want to dress up. _____

2. Wide print skirts combined with neat T-shirts and string vests, or denim and leather jackets are some good Boho chic choices. _____

3. What you say, as well as what you wear, tells people whether you are "in style" or not. _____

4. If you find Boho chic too glamorous, you can try preppy chic. _____

5. Kate is a great follower of goth glam, and she stocks up her wardrobe with black clothing. _____

6. Both khaki pants and pastel-coloured polo shirts are the basics of preppy chic. _____

7. Would you like to buy this beige sweater, or would you like to get something brighter in colour? _____

8. Although this leather skirt looks great, it is way too expensive. _____

D. **Rewrite each group of sentences below as one using the appropriate conjunctions.**

1. You can buy the belt. You can buy the necklace. You can't have both.

   _____

   _____

2. Try both jackets on. Then you decide which one to buy.

   _____

   _____

3. My friend, Sean, likes the punk rock style. I prefer the classic style.

   _____

   _____

4. Sharon has decided to wear something purple to the prom. Angela has decided to wear something purple to the prom, too.

   _____

   _____

5. Kenneth is saving up his allowance. He wants to buy a pair of leather gloves for his mom's birthday.

   _____

   _____

6. Jeans are a favourite for many young people. They have been popular since the 1950s.

   _____

   _____

Watch Out for Those
Language Bloopers!

Everyone knows that public speaking is scary. However, even when speaking with friends, we can say the funniest things! And if you have some language "howlers", you are not alone. Former American president George W. Bush is well known for language bloopers in his speeches. There are all sorts of language errors that we may make from time to time. A few are listed below:

Metathesis – Have you ever transposed letters, sounds, or syllables within a word, such as in the case of "ossifer" for "officer" or "iern" instead of "iron"? Actually, metathesis is a common mistake, and many examples (like "aks" for "ask") have their roots in the evolution of the word: the word "ask" was pronounced as "aks" in Old English.

Spoonerisms – Have you ever said something like "keys and parrots" instead of "peas and carrots"? Such slips of the tongue are called spoonerisms – when the order of sounds is mixed up within a phrase. They are named after Reverend William Archibald Spooner, who lived at the turn of last century and apparently made these errors often. While some spoonerisms are unintentional, others are conscious plays on words, such as "Go and shake a tower" ("Go and take a shower"). Children's book author Shel Silverstein wrote a book called *Runny Babbit: a Billy Sook*, which is full of spoonerisms.

Mondegreens are mistakes of hearing, which happens often, particularly with song lyrics. For example, in the Christmas song "Rudolph the Red-Nosed Reindeer", some people heard the words "...All of the other reindeer..." as "Olive, the other reindeer". Eventually, a book was written about a dog named Olive who fills in for one of the reindeer. The word mondegreen was invented by a writer named Sylvia Wright who misheard a line from an old Scottish song: "They have slain the Earl of Murray, and laid him on the green." Wright thought she'd heard, "They have slain the Earl of Murray and Lady Mondegreen"!

Eggcorns are examples of people saying new words because they are what they thought they heard, such as "eggcorn" for acorn and "duck tape" for duct tape. They are, in fact, homonyms of sorts.

A **malapropism** comes from the French phrase meaning "badly for the purpose". If you have heard someone accidentally substituting a

ISBN: 978-1-77149-036-8

similar-sounding word for an obvious "other" word, you've heard a malapropism. These are named after Mrs. Malaprop, a character in Richard Sheridan's play *The Rivals*, who had a habit of mixing up her words. (In the play, Mrs. Malaprop says "He's the very pineapple of politeness", instead of "He's the very pinnacle of politeness".) George W. Bush said "nuclear power pants" instead of "nuclear power plants" in a 2003 speech.

Speaking of this former American president, there is another type of language blooper coined to categorize his unique gaffes – **Bushisms**. Of course, it's not nice to make fun of people's mistakes, but this is part and parcel of a public profile nowadays. Here are just a few of the many statements classified as Bushisms: "We need an energy bill that encourages consumption"; "Rarely is the question asked: is our children learning?"; "I know the human being and fish can coexist peacefully."

So, what does this tell us? No one ever needs to be afraid of public speaking! If you make a spoonerism, or a malapropism, or some other silly mistakes, you will be in good company – or, perhaps, "could gumpany"!

A. Make up an example or two for each of the following language errors.

1. metathesis: _____

2. spoonerism: _____

3. mondegreen: _____

4. eggcorn: _____

5. malapropism: _____

B. Write the statements that the former U.S. President George W. Bush wanted to say.

1. "We need an energy bill that encourages consumption."

_____

2. "Rarely is the question asked: is our children learning?"

_____

Noun Phrases

A **noun phrase** is a group of words that functions as a single noun in a sentence. It can therefore be the subject, the object of a verb, the object of a preposition, a subject complement, an object complement, or an appositive in a sentence.

Examples: Such slips of the tongue are called spoonerisms. (subject)

When we speak with friends, we can say the funniest things. (object of the verb "say")

A malapropism comes from the French phrase meaning "badly for the purpose". (object of the preposition "from")

Mondegreens are mistakes of hearing. (subject complement)

I consider this spoonerism of his an intentional one. (object complement)

Mrs. Malaprop, a character in the play The Rivals, has a habit of mixing up her words. (appositive)

C. **Determine whether each underlined noun phrase is the subject (S), object of a verb (OV), object of a preposition (OP), subject complement (SC), object complement (OC), or appositive (A) in the sentence.**

1. *Runny Babbit: a Billy Sook* is a book full of spoonerisms.   _____

2. Rudolph, the red-nosed reindeer, had a very shiny nose.   _____

3. She considered him the very pinnacle of politeness.   _____

4. Sometimes, spoonerisms are conscious plays on words.   _____

5. Many examples of metathesis have roots in the evolution of the word.   _____

6. A writer named Sylvia Wright invented the word "mondegreen".   _____

7. "Keys and parrots" and "Go and shake a tower" are examples of spoonerisms.   _____

8. Reverend William Archibald Spooner lived at the turn of last century.   _____

Other Phrases as Nouns

A **gerund phrase** or an **infinitive phrase** can also function as a noun and take the place of a noun in a sentence as a noun phrase does.

Examples: <u>Speaking with metathesis</u> is a common mistake.
(gerund phrase as subject)

A malapropism is <u>substituting a similar-sounding word for an obvious "other" word</u>.
(gerund phrase as subject complement)

<u>To make fun of people's mistakes</u> is not nice.
(infinitive phrase as subject)

Spoonerisms – <u>to mix up the order of sounds within a phrase</u> – are named after Reverend William Archibald Spooner.
(infinitive phrase as appositive)

D. Make sentences of your own with the given phrases.

1. making a silly mistake

_____
(Subject)

_____
(Object of Preposition)

_____
(Subject Complement)

_____
(Appositive)

2. to speak publicly

_____
(Subject)

_____
(Subject Complement)

_____
(Appositive)

Don't Be a Dope:
Drugs
in Sports

Drugs are dangerous, and they are being abused more than ever these days. Decades ago, cigarettes (the main delivery system of nicotine, one of the world's most powerful and commonly used addictive drugs) used to be considered healthy and chic! They were often shown being smoked by beautiful women in films. They were given to soldiers during World War I and World War II as part of their government rations. Some doctors even appeared in cigarette advertisements claiming that cigarettes had health benefits, such as providing extra protection against colds and boosting concentration. Of course, we all know now that smoking kills and that "second-hand" smoking can also kill by causing cancer, debilitating emphysema, and other terrible conditions. It is also, for many, the first step on the rough road to drug abuse.

Given these facts, it is surprising that drug abuse still goes on in the world of sports. The use of performance-enhancing drugs has been around for a long time and, in fact, during the earliest days of competitive sport, was not altogether frowned upon, in much the same way that cigarettes were thought to be "helpful". For example, it is alleged that the winner of the 1904 Olympic marathon was given an injection of strychnine and a dram of brandy to keep him going. An official race report noted, according to sports historian Dr. Jean-Pierre de Mondenard, that "The marathon has shown from a medical point of view how drugs can be very useful to athletes in long-distance races."

Doping in sports continued and was pushed into the realm of secret and illicit activity with both known and unknown risks and consequences. Soviet weightlifters were injected with the male hormone testosterone as early on as the 1950s. East Germany was notorious for plying its athletes with performance-enhancing drugs and illicit protocols. Females began to grow facial hair, and their voices became lower. Eventually, their menstrual cycles stopped. In some cases, they were told that the pills and injections were vitamins. Years later, when these women tried to have children, they suffered complications.

Doping in sports has ruined many promising athletic careers and reputations. Canadian Ben Johnson became the "World's Fastest Man" – the world-record holder and gold medalist for the 100-metre sprint at the 1988 Seoul Summer Olympics. But those accolades were taken away within days when he tested positive for anabolic steroid, and he admitted to using human growth hormone as well. Baseball star Barry Bonds and 2006 Tour de France winner Floyd Landis are some of the many other sporting "heroes" under the cloud of doping.

The formation of regulatory bodies and "watchdogs", such as the World Anti-Doping Agency (WADA – founded in 1999 in Switzerland and now headquartered in Montreal) helps keep a vigilant watch on sports cheats. Lists of banned substances are in place, making it very clear to all concerned which drugs will not be tolerated, and testing has become precise, as well as more frequent. However, new forms of illegal performance enhancement are being developed. The newest method of such illegal activity is called "gene doping". As the name suggests, it does not involve the use of drugs, but is something that many consider equally sinister. Gene doping activity involves the alteration of cells, genes, and other genetic material for the purpose of improving athletic performance. WADA has called on scientists and geneticists around the world to prevent gene doping from gaining ground.

A. Read the following statements. Check the true ones and rewrite the false ones, based on the information from the passage.

1. During the two World Wars, soldiers were given cigarettes because cigarettes were said to be able to relieve pain.

_____

_____

2. Cigarettes are regarded as one of the world's most powerful and commonly used addictive drugs.

_____

_____

3. Performance-enhancing drugs have been banned from use in competitive sports right from the start.

_____

_____

4. Gene doping refers to the activity of stimulating cells, genes, and other genetic material for the purpose of improving health conditions and muscle strength.

_____

_____

Active Voice and Passive Voice

In the **active voice**, the subject performs the action of the verb; in the **passive voice**, the subject receives the action of the verb. While it is usually better to use the active voice since it is clearer and more forceful, the passive voice provides a shift of emphasis – from the doer to the thing or person being acted upon. We can leave out the "doer" if it is obvious, unimportant, or unknown.

Examples: Doping in sports has ruined many promising athletic careers and reputations. (active voice)

Many promising athletic careers and reputations have been ruined by doping in sports. (passive voice)

During the earliest days of competitive sport, the use of performance-enhancing drugs was not altogether frowned upon.
(passive voice with the "doer" left out)

B.   Rewrite the following sentences using the passive voice.

1.   The World Anti-Doping Agency has introduced some new drug-testing policies.

_____

_____

2.   You can obtain the WADA Athlete Guide from their website.

_____

_____

3.   One cannot dispute the hard evidence that some performance-enhancing drugs have resulted in long-term harmful consequences for those who took them.

_____

_____

4.   Many people consider "gene doping" to be as sinister as drug doping.

_____

_____

ISBN: 978-1-77149-036-8

Other Passive Forms

We can use "**get/have something done**" to focus on the result of an activity rather than the person or object that performs the activity.

Example: The International Olympic Committee banned the use of performance-enhancing drugs in Olympic Games.

The International Olympic Committee <u>had the use of performance-enhancing drugs banned</u> in Olympic Games.

We can also use "**need + v-ing**" to focus on the person or thing that will experience the action.

Example: The World Anti-Doping Code needed to be revised.

The World Anti-Doping Code <u>needed revising</u>.

C. Rewrite the following sentences using "get/have something done" or "need + v-ing".

1. The organizing committee needed to test all athletes for performance-enhancing drugs before the commencement of the competitions.

    _____

    _____

2. They want someone to examine the samples as soon as possible.

    _____

    _____

3. Methods of detecting various performance-enhancing drugs need to be improved.

    _____

    _____

4. People need to be educated about the harmful effects of doping.

    _____

    _____

One of the World's Most
Published Editorials

Over one hundred years ago, an eight-year-old girl named Virginia O'Hanlon wrote a letter to the editor of *The New York Sun*. A response was printed as an unsigned editorial on September 21, 1897, and has become one of the most reprinted newspaper editorials in history.

TUESDAY, SEPTEMBER 21, 1897.

DEAR EDITOR: I am 8 years old. Some of my little friends say there is no Santa Claus. Papa says, "If you see it in THE SUN it's so." Please tell me the truth; is there a Santa Claus? – Virginia O'Hanlon

VIRGINIA, your little friends are wrong. They have been affected by the skepticism of a skeptical age. They do not believe except they see. They think that nothing can be which is not comprehensible by their little minds. All minds, VIRGINIA, whether they be men's or children's, are little. In this great universe of ours man is a mere insect, an ant, in his intellect, as compared with the boundless world about him, as measured by the intelligence capable of grasping the whole of truth and knowledge.

Yes, VIRGINIA, there is a Santa Claus. He exists as certainly as love and generosity and devotion exist, and you know that they abound and give to your life its highest beauty and joy. Alas! How dreary would be the world if there were no Santa Claus. It would be as dreary as if there were no VIRGINIAS. There would be no childlike faith then, no poetry, no romance to make tolerable this existence. We should have no enjoyment, except in sense and sight. The eternal light with which childhood fills the world would be extinguished.

Not believe in Santa Claus! You might as well not believe in fairies! You might get your papa to hire men to watch in all the chimneys on Christmas Eve to catch Santa Claus, but even if they did not see Santa Claus coming down, what would that prove? Nobody sees Santa Claus, but that is no sign that there is no Santa Claus. The most real things in the world are those that neither children nor men can see. Did you ever see fairies dancing on the lawn? Of course not, but that's no proof that they are not there. Nobody can conceive or imagine all the wonders there are unseen and unseeable in the world.

ISBN: 978-1-77149-036-8

You may tear apart the baby's rattle and see what makes the noise inside, but there is a veil covering the unseen world which not the strongest man, nor even the united strength of all the strongest men that ever lived, could tear apart. Only faith, fancy, poetry, love, romance, can push aside that curtain and view and picture the supernal beauty and glory beyond. Is it all real? Ah, VIRGINIA, in all this world there is nothing else real and abiding.

No Santa Claus! Thank GOD! He lives, and he lives forever. A thousand years from now, VIRGINIA, nay, ten times ten thousand years from now, he will continue to make glad the heart of childhood.

A. Explain in your own words what the following statements from the editorial imply.

1. They think that nothing can be which is not comprehensible by their little minds.

   _____

2. The eternal light with which childhood fills the world would be extinguished.

   _____

3. Only faith, fancy, poetry, love, romance, can push aside that curtain and view and picture the supernal beauty and glory beyond.

   _____

B. Answer the following questions.

1. How did the editorial explain the existence of Santa Claus to Virginia?

   _____

   _____

2. Why do you think The Sun's response to Virginia's letter to the editor has become one of the most reprinted newspaper editorials in history?

   _____

   _____

Mood

A verb can be in one of these moods: indicative, imperative, or subjunctive.

The **indicative mood** is the most common type used. It is used to make an objective statement.

Example: The response has become one of the most reprinted newspaper editorials in history.

A verb in the **imperative mood** expresses commands or requests.

Example: Please tell me the truth.

A verb in the **subjunctive mood** expresses a wish or something that is not true. The past or perfect tense is used.

Example: I wish I could see Santa Claus (but I cannot see him).

If Virginia's friends had seen Santa Claus (but they had not), they would have believed in his existence (they did not believe in it).

C. Determine the mood in the following sentences. Write "IND" for indicative, "IMP" for imperative, and "SUB" for subjunctive.

1. Nobody sees Santa Claus, but that is no sign that there is no Santa Claus. _____

2. If I were Virginia, I would not have doubted the existence of Santa Claus. _____

3. How I wish I could see fairies in my backyard. _____

4. Don't forget to hang a Christmas stocking by your bed on Christmas Eve. _____

5. Children who believe in fairies and Santa Claus are more creative and imaginative than those who do not. _____

6. Please show this editorial to your friends who think there is no Santa Claus. _____

7. I would have told you if I knew the truth. _____

8. There are many things in the world that are beyond our imagination. _____

ISBN: 978-1-77149-036-8

D. Rewrite the following sentences in the subjunctive mood.

1. Cindy has asked the silly question. She regrets that she has done so.

     _____

     _____

2. I don't think Keith should have turned down the offer.

     _____

     _____

3. Jan wanted to see fairies. Then she could take pictures of them.

     _____

     _____

4. Timothy thinks that Molly should not have believed in that story.

     _____

     _____

E. Make sentences of your own using the three types of mood.

1. Indicative Mood

     _____

     _____

2. Imperative Mood

     _____

     _____

3. Subjunctive Mood

     _____

     _____

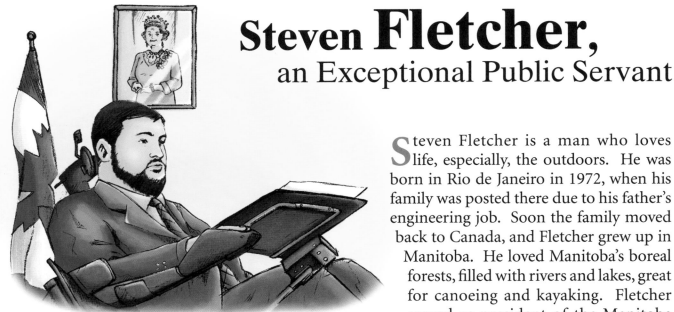

Steven **Fletcher,**
an Exceptional Public Servant

Steven Fletcher is a man who loves life, especially, the outdoors. He was born in Rio de Janeiro in 1972, when his family was posted there due to his father's engineering job. Soon the family moved back to Canada, and Fletcher grew up in Manitoba. He loved Manitoba's boreal forests, filled with rivers and lakes, great for canoeing and kayaking. Fletcher served as president of the Manitoba Recreational Canoeing Association, and was twice the Manitoba kayak champion. He also decided to follow in his father's footsteps, earning a Bachelor of Science Degree in Geological Engineering from the University of Manitoba in 1995. He soon found work in his chosen profession in the environment he loved, and life was good.

A year later, while Fletcher was driving to a job site in northern Manitoba, his vehicle hit a moose. As a result of the collision, Fletcher became paralyzed from the neck down. Doctors told him he would be spending the rest of his life in an institution, but Fletcher decided things would be otherwise, and after a long and painful period of rehabilitation, during which time Fletcher regained the ability to speak, he returned to university to obtain a Master of Business Administration Degree. During this time, Fletcher got involved in student politics. He was twice elected president of the University of Manitoba Students' Union. He also served on the university's board of governors and the Canadian Alliance of Student Associations. It was only natural that Fletcher would want to continue this type of public service once his student career was completed.

Fletcher became involved in federal politics and was elected President of the Progressive Conservative Party of Manitoba. In 2004, he ran as a candidate for the Winnipeg riding of Charleswood–St. James–Assiniboia and won, becoming the first permanently disabled member of the House of Commons. He wasted no time becoming a busy Member of Parliament, taking up responsibilities as Official Opposition Critic for Health and member of the Standing Committee on Health, in addition to his duties to his constituents and his other community involvement. After his re-election in 2006, Fletcher was appointed Parliamentary Secretary to the Minister of Health.

Fletcher has worked hard to help people affected by Hepatitis C, mental illness, heart disease, and cancer, and has won numerous awards for his tireless endeavours, including the inaugural Award

ISBN: 978-1-77149-036-8

for Outstanding Individual Leadership, the Courage and Leadership Award from the Canadian Cancer Society, and the Champions of Mental Health Award. He was recently inducted into the Terry Fox Hall of Fame. Steven Fletcher's success shows us not only that mobility impairment does not mean an inactive and unsatisfying life, but also that a "catastrophic injury" does not have to define a person.

Fletcher still loves the outdoors. When his busy schedule allows, he likes visiting the Fort Whyte Centre. It is an environmental, educational, and recreational facility located at the edge of Winnipeg, on a man-made lake among aspen groves and nature trails, and it contains a 28-hectare prairie meadow supporting a herd of roaming bison.

A. Check the best answer for each of the following questions.

1. Steven Fletcher's father _____ .
   A. worked as an engineer in Rio de Janeiro
   B. moved to Rio de Janeiro before Steven Fletcher was born
   C. returned to Canada and took a job at the University of Manitoba

2. What made Fletcher consider going into public service?
   A. his long and painful period of rehabilitation after a serious accident
   B. his involvement in student politics while doing his MBA
   C. the influence of the board of governors at the University of Manitoba

3. Fletcher was _____ .
   A. the first President of the Progressive Conservative Party of Manitoba
   B. the parliamentary secretary to the Minister of Health
   C. the chairman of the Standing Committee on Health

4. Which one below was not one of Fletcher's achievements?
   A. He won the inaugural Award for Outstanding Individual Leadership.
   B. He was inducted into the Terry Fox Hall of Fame.
   C. He received an award from the Canadian Mental Health Society.

Types of Sentences by Structure

Sentences can be classified according to their structure.

- A **simple sentence** consists of a single independent clause with no dependent clauses.

- A **compound sentence** consists of two or more independent clauses with no dependent clauses. These independent clauses are joined together by coordinating conjunctions (and, or, but), punctuation, or both.

- A **complex sentence** consists of one independent clause with at least one dependent clause joined together by subordinating conjunctions like "if" and "although".

- A **compound-complex sentence** consists of two or more independent clauses, one of which has at least one dependent clause.

B. **Find examples of the following types of sentences from the passage "Steven Fletcher, an Exceptional Public Servant".**

Simple Sentence

1. _____

2. _____

Compound Sentence

3. _____

4. _____

Complex Sentence

5. _____

6. _____

Compound-Complex Sentence

7. _____

_____

C. Rewrite the following groups of sentences.

1. Fletcher has been inducted into the Terry Fox Hall of Fame. He has received the King Clancy Award. (Compound Sentence)

   _____

   _____

2. Fletcher won the Manitoba kayak competition two times. That was before the accident happened. (Complex Sentence)

   _____

   _____

3. Maybe you like the outdoors. You can visit the Fort Whyte Centre. You can hike along the pond. You can listen to the sounds of water foul there. (Compound-Complex Sentence)

   _____

   _____

D. Compose a paragraph that consists of the four types of sentences.

   _____

   _____

   _____

   _____

   _____

   _____

   _____

   _____

How can we become better people? From all the wisdom we can gather, there appears to be a strong overlap between cultures regarding certain ideas. Below is a list of what we consider the "Seven Sacred Teachings". This list is based on First Nations cultures and spirituality, but the concepts are found throughout other cultures around the world, seen in their stories, actions, and beliefs. These seven sacred teachings are, in fact, what unify us, as they give us hope for the possibility of a better world, primarily through the betterment of ourselves. They can guide us in our relations with people, the natural world, and – more important now than ever – the planet itself.

Wisdom: Do you understand that your actions have consequences? If you took the time to think through the possible outcomes of your actions, would it change the way you do things? We all need to think before we act, and have a clearer idea in our minds about what is good and bad, or right and wrong. Wisdom is understanding that what we do and say is important because everything we do leads us to the next moment.

Love: Can you love someone unconditionally – give kindness without asking for or expecting anything in return? Try to understand that the best kind of love is the love given when it is needed the most, even though it may seem difficult to give our care and concern at the time.

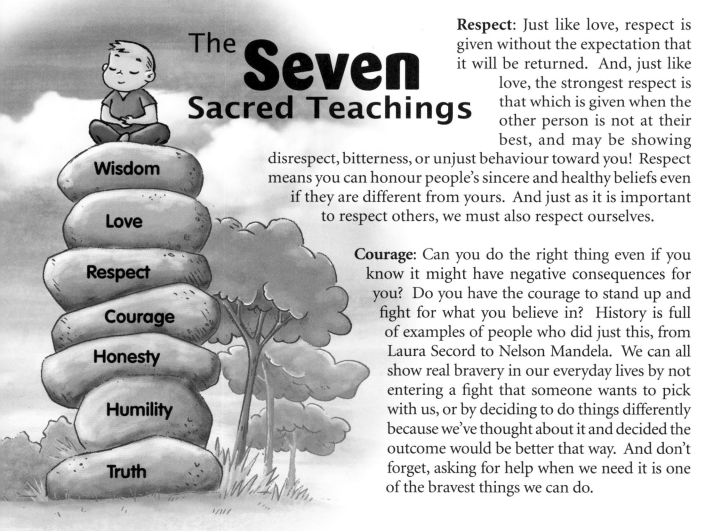

The Seven Sacred Teachings

Wisdom
Love
Respect
Courage
Honesty
Humility
Truth

Respect: Just like love, respect is given without the expectation that it will be returned. And, just like love, the strongest respect is that which is given when the other person is not at their best, and may be showing disrespect, bitterness, or unjust behaviour toward you! Respect means you can honour people's sincere and healthy beliefs even if they are different from yours. And just as it is important to respect others, we must also respect ourselves.

Courage: Can you do the right thing even if you know it might have negative consequences for you? Do you have the courage to stand up and fight for what you believe in? History is full of examples of people who did just this, from Laura Secord to Nelson Mandela. We can all show real bravery in our everyday lives by not entering a fight that someone wants to pick with us, or by deciding to do things differently because we've thought about it and decided the outcome would be better that way. And don't forget, asking for help when we need it is one of the bravest things we can do.

   ISBN: 978-1-77149-036-8

Honesty: Honesty comes in many forms, but it begins and ends with you, considering and formulating ideas about who you are, what you do, and why you do it. It is one thing to answer someone's question honestly, which we should always do, but that's the "easy" honesty. The more difficult kind is in trying to be honest with ourselves, about who we really are. Sometimes it may be easier to fool ourselves than others because we just don't want to know the honest answer! Try to say, think, and do only the things you really mean.

Humility: Can you admit you don't know everything? Can you show penitence when necessary, admitting mistakes? Can you accept success with pride and avoid slipping into arrogance? Can you step back and allow others the limelight, even if you could do just as well? Do you believe that it is a measure of your self worth to set aside what you want for the needs of another? If you say "yes" to all these questions, then you will do well in life, because life is full of times when personal setbacks will knock us down. People that have consciously practised humility in their lives will be better able to show resilience at such times.

Truth: Do you tell the truth even when you don't want to? Can you walk through life being truthful about yourself and others? Living with truth involves not only an ability to tell the truth, but a desire to be truthful because you believe that the truth is best no matter what.

What a wonderful world it would be if everyone followed the Seven Sacred Teachings!

A. Define in your own words the Seven Sacred Teachings described in the passage.

Sacred Teaching	How You Define It
Wisdom	
Love	
Respect	
Courage	
Honesty	
Humility	
Truth	

Types of Sentences by Purpose

Sentences can also be classified according to their purpose.

- A **declarative sentence** makes a statement.

  Example: The "Seven Sacred Teachings" is a list based on First Nations cultures and spirituality.

- An **interrogative sentence** requests information.

  Example: What are the common concepts found throughout the cultures around the world?

- An **exclamatory sentence** shows surprise and strong emotions.

  Example: How honest you are in admitting your weakness!

- An **imperative sentence** gives a command or makes a request.

  Example: Let's find more information about the "Seven Sacred Teachings" from the library.

B. Find an example of each type of sentence from the passage, "The Seven Sacred Teachings".

1. Declarative Sentence

   _____

   _____

2. Interrogative Sentence

   _____

   _____

3. Exclamatory Sentence

   _____

   _____

4. Imperative Sentence

   _____

   _____

C. Write sentences in the types specified based on the given situations.

1. Christine wants to know how she can improve herself.

   Interrogative: _____

   _____

2. The teacher explains what the "Seven Sacred Teachings" include.

   Declarative: _____

   _____

3. Ms. Deswell tells the class to hand in their project ideas on First Nations culture next Friday.

   Imperative: _____

   _____

4. Matthew's sister, Christine, will take part in a play at school. He wants to know what the play is about.

   Interrogative: _____

   _____

5. Christine asks Matthew to see her performance.

   Imperative: _____

   _____

6. Matthew is at Christine's school. He is asking someone where the school hall is.

   Interrogative: _____

   _____

7. Matthew exclaims that it is a great show.

   Exclamatory: _____

   _____

Twenty Thousand "Oskar Schindlers": the Holocaust Rescuers

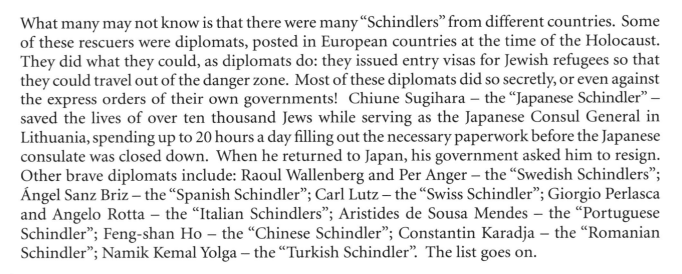

Most Canadian students know who Oskar Schindler was, thanks in part to the movie *Schindler's List* directed by Steven Spielberg. Schindler was a German industrialist who saved the lives of over one thousand Jews during Hitler's era of Nazi atrocities in Europe. Schindler did this by persuading Nazi authorities to allow him to hire Jews for work in his enamelware and munitions factories, sparing them from the Nazi death camps.

What many may not know is that there were many "Schindlers" from different countries. Some of these rescuers were diplomats, posted in European countries at the time of the Holocaust. They did what they could, as diplomats do: they issued entry visas for Jewish refugees so that they could travel out of the danger zone. Most of these diplomats did so secretly, or even against the express orders of their own governments! Chiune Sugihara – the "Japanese Schindler" – saved the lives of over ten thousand Jews while serving as the Japanese Consul General in Lithuania, spending up to 20 hours a day filling out the necessary paperwork before the Japanese consulate was closed down. When he returned to Japan, his government asked him to resign. Other brave diplomats include: Raoul Wallenberg and Per Anger – the "Swedish Schindlers"; Ángel Sanz Briz – the "Spanish Schindler"; Carl Lutz – the "Swiss Schindler"; Giorgio Perlasca and Angelo Rotta – the "Italian Schindlers"; Aristides de Sousa Mendes – the "Portuguese Schindler"; Feng-shan Ho – the "Chinese Schindler"; Constantin Karadja – the "Romanian Schindler"; Namik Kemal Yolga – the "Turkish Schindler". The list goes on.

Others rescuers, like journalist Varian Fry, the "American Schindler", risked their lives to run secret rescue networks. Jaap Penraat, the "Dutch Schindler", an architect, was able to save Jews by convincing the Nazis that the 406 people he was harbouring were slave labourers. He was later tortured for the ruse. Some rescuers were children, such as the German schoolgirl Sophie Scholl and her brother Hans, who started the "White Rose" resistance movement. It can also be said that the entire population of Denmark was a Holocaust "rescuer", a collective resistance, and it included an organized effort among Danish civil servants to evacuate about 8000 Danish Jews to Sweden. As a result, 99% of Danish Jews survived.

These are only a few of the more than 20 000 people on the List of Righteous Among the Nations, dedicated to those non-Jewish "rescuers" of the Holocaust, located at the Yad Vashem Holocaust

ISBN: 978-1-77149-036-8

memorial in Israel. But there are no native-Canadians on it. Is there a "Canadian Schindler"? Well, one couple Pauline and Georges Vanier can perhaps be so considered. Georges Vanier was Canada's top diplomat in France when World War II began, and he entreated his government to allow immigration for Jewish refugees, pointing out that "Canada has a wonderful opportunity to be generous and yet profit by accepting some of these people." The Vaniers returned to Canada in 1941 and spoke out about the plight of the Jews in Europe, but were often met with indifference and hostility. Immediately after the war's end in 1945, Georges Vanier and his wife returned to France. After viewing the Buchenwald concentration camp for himself, Georges said in a CBC radio broadcast: "How deaf we were then to cruelty and the cries of pain which came to our ears, grim forerunners of the mass torture and murders which were to follow." Pauline and Georges continued their efforts to help change Canadian immigration policy. Due in part to their efforts, along with those of humanitarian organizations, more than 186 000 European refugees settled in Canada between 1947 and 1953. Georges Vanier served as Governor General of Canada from 1959 to 1967, the year he died. Pauline then moved to France to live and work with their eldest son, Jean, who founded a humanitarian organization called "L'Arche" (The Ark), a worldwide movement to help people with mental handicaps live productive lives.

A. Answer the following questions.

1. What does the name "Schindler" stand for today?

   _____

   _____

2. Find a sentence that shows that some countries did not want to take in Jewish refugees in Paragraph Two.

   _____

   _____

3. What made the writer consider Georges Vanier a "Schindler"?

   _____

   _____

4. Georges Vanier pointed out that "Canada has a wonderful opportunity to be generous and yet profit by accepting some of these people." How do you think Canada might have benefited from accepting Jewish refugees?

   _____

   _____

Dependent Clauses

Some clauses cannot stand on their own as sentences. They are called **dependent clauses**. A dependent clause has to be attached to an independent clause to add information to that clause.

A **noun clause** is a dependent clause that acts as the subject or object of a verb or the object of a preposition.

Example: <u>What many may not know</u> is <u>that there were many "Schindlers"</u>.

An **adjective clause** modifies a noun or a pronoun.

Example: Schindler was a German industrialist <u>who saved the lives of over one thousand Jews</u>.

An **adverb clause** functions like an adverb and gives information about "when", "where", "why", and "how".

Example: Georges Vanier was Canada's top diplomat in France <u>when World War II began</u>.

B. **Underline the dependent clauses in the following sentences. Then write "N" for noun clauses, "ADJ" for adjective clauses, and "ADV" for adverb clauses.**

1. Some diplomats issued visas for Jewish refugees so that they could travel out of the danger zone. _____

2. Many Jews whom Schindler rescued were hired to work in his factories. _____

3. Chiune Sugihara saved over ten thousand Jews while he served as the Japanese Consul General in Lithuania. _____

4. He was asked by his government to resign when he returned to Japan. _____

5. "L'Arche" is a humanitarian organization which Georges Vanier's son, Jean, founded. _____

6. Exactly how many "Schindlers" there were is unknown. _____

7. Many people may not understand why someone risked his or her life to save others. _____

C. Complete the following sentences with the dependent clauses specified.

Noun Clause

1. _____

   _____ is still a mystery.

2. Many people believe _____

   _____ .

3. The students were sad to learn _____

   _____ .

Adjective Clause

4. The fact _____

   _____ is incontrovertible.

5. The journalist _____

   _____ was sent to the country to cover the event.

6. The story _____

   _____ is really touching.

Adverb Clause

7. A memorial has been put up _____

   _____ .

8. The students put the story on stage _____

   _____ .

9. *Schindler's List* is a great film _____

   _____ .

An Ancient Story about the Sun and the Moon

Every country and every culture has its own myths, legends, and folktales. For those who have spent time reading or researching these ageless stories, one thing becomes quite clear – there are a lot of similarities and "overlaps" among the legends and folktales around the world. For example, a great many folktales the world over have to do with the story of how the elements of the universe, our Earth, humans, and animals were created. Of course, versions of this story is also in the Bible and other religious texts. Below is a folktale about the Sun and the Moon from the Philippines. Do you know which physical phenomena are being alluded to in this ancient folk story?

"The Sun and the Moon were happily married for a great many years. The Sun was always a little bit grouchy, but the gentle Moon was always there to cool down and placate the hot and fiery Sun. Even so, the Sun, over time, became ugly and quarrelsome in a way that not even the Moon could do anything about. One day, the hot-tempered Sun became enraged at the Moon and started to chase her around in circles. The Moon ran and ran, very fast, until she had created some distance between herself and the Sun, although there were times when she had grown tired and the Sun had almost caught her up. Ever since then, the hot and fiery Sun has been chasing the gentle, silvery Moon, at times almost reaching her, only to fall behind again and again.

The Sun and the Moon had a child, a large bright Star, and the object of the Moon's boundless maternal love. Over time, the Star grew larger and brighter, and became so large and bright that the Sun became jealous. Other heavenly bodies were attracted to the Star, and the Star returned their admiration with pure love. Finally, one day, the hot-tempered Sun could take no more. He cut the Star up into small pieces and scattered the Star's body across the universe, just like a woman scatters rice in a field. Since that time, there have been many stars across the night sky, all pieces of the child borne of the Sun and the Moon.

The Sun and the Moon had another child, in the form of a giant Crab. The Crab lives with us still, and is such a powerful being here on Earth that he sends us flashes of lightning every time he opens and closes his eyes. He is the creator of the storms that roil the seas. This giant Crab lives at the bottom of the sea, in a huge dungeon-like lair. He spends half of his life in the lair and half out of it, prowling the seas. When he is in his lair, the waters are high; when he leaves his lair, the seas rush into the

ISBN: 978-1-77149-036-8

empty space he leaves behind, and the waters become low. His every move creates great waves – and dangers – for people on or near the water.

This giant Crab has inherited some of his father's traits; he is quarrelsome and bad-tempered. He sometimes becomes so angry with his mother, the Moon, that he tries to eat her up. The people on Earth love their gentle silver Lady Moon, and so when they see the Crab going near her, they run out of their huts to shout and beat on their gongs until the giant Crab is frightened away, and the gentle Lady Moon is thus saved, until next time."

A. **Write about the physical phenomena described in the folktale *The Sun and the Moon*.**

_____

_____

_____

_____

B. **Write your own folktale to illustrate the relationships among the sun, the moon, and the stars.**

_____

_____

_____

_____

_____

_____

_____

_____

Reported Speech

In **reported speech** or **indirect speech**, we report what someone said without using the speaker's exact words.

Changing a sentence from direct speech to reported speech involves changes in verb tenses when the reporting verb (like "said") is in the past tense. Usually, the verb form is one step back into the past from the original. Note that pronouns need to be changed too.

Example: "You <u>will</u> be doing a project on folktales from around the world," Mrs. Wright said to the class.

Mrs. Wright told the class that <u>they</u> <u>would</u> be doing a project on folktales from around the world.

However, when the reporting verb is in the present tense, or when the reported subject is a general truth, the present tense is retained.

Examples: "Reading legends is my favourite pastime," Ida <u>says</u>.
Ida <u>says</u> that reading legends <u>is</u> her favourite pastime.
Tim said, "Different cultures <u>have</u> their own folktales."
Tim said that different cultures <u>have</u> their own folktales.

C. Rewrite the following sentences in reported speech.

1. Linda said to Julie, "The Star and the Crab are children of the Sun and the Moon."

   _____

2. "There are a lot of similarities among the folktales of different countries around the world," Timothy says.

   _____

3. Ginny said to Kingsley, "My mom has bought me a set of books on Greek mythology."

   _____

4. "I will tell you an interesting folktale before you go to bed," Mom said.

   _____

   ISBN: 978-1-77149-036-8

Reported Questions and Commands

When we report a yes/no question, "whether" or "if" is used. If the question begins with a question word, the question word is retained.

Examples: Lily asked me, "Have you read the legend before?"

Lily asked me <u>whether</u> I had read the legend before.

The students asked Mrs. Wright, "When do we have to hand in the project?"

The students asked Mrs. Wright <u>when</u> they had to hand in the project.

When we report a command, we simply add "to" before the verb if it is positive; add "not to" if it is negative.

Examples: "Do some research in the library," the teacher told us.

The teacher told us <u>to do</u> some research in the library.

"Don't hand in your work late," she told the class.

She told the class <u>not to hand</u> in their work late.

D. Rewrite the following as reported questions or commands.

1. Jerry asked Shirley, "Who told you that there were ten suns in the past?"

_____

2. The teacher asked the children, "Do you want to learn more about our country's legends?"

_____

3. "Where can I find the illustrations of ancient heroes?" Cedric asked.

_____

4. "Don't write or draw in the books," the librarian reminded us.

_____

5. Mr. Willis told me, "Create another story about the sun and the moon."

_____

Do Aliens Exist?

Do you think alien beings exist somewhere in the universe? The idea has inspired the whole genre of science fiction – in the form of film, literature, and even radio drama. Perhaps you have heard of *The War of the Worlds*. Orson Welles directed a radio drama adapted from a classic novel by the same name written by famed writer H. G. Wells and published in 1898. This novel was one of the first examples of science fiction, and was a story about aliens from Mars invading England. When Orson Welles adapted it for radio in 1938, it was said to have caused mass hysteria because some people, who had switched on their radios during the broadcast, actually believed that Earth was being invaded by aliens from Mars! It is believed that some people committed suicide over this.

It seems like Mars, our closest neighbour, has inspired the most science fiction as the place where aliens are most likely to come from. But *The War of the Worlds* is fiction, and recent Mars probes have shown us that there is no life on that planet – at least not now. But that does not mean that life does not exist elsewhere – after all, the universe is really big. A lot of scientific research is going on in the search for "extraterrestrial life" – life originating outside of Earth.

Think about it – why should the six billion people on this little planet be the only sentient beings in the universe? It would, in fact, seem logical that this is not the case. So scientific research in this matter is based around the idea of finding other planets that have environments that can support life – environments similar to Earth. The search is on for the evidence of the existence, or prior existence, of life: from sapient beings (beings with judgment) to simple organisms, such as bacteria.

So far, there have been a number of theories as to which planetary bodies may have an atmosphere that can support such life and therefore warrant closer attention. As for places within our own Milky Way Galaxy, it has been hypothesized over the decades that Mars and Venus, as well as some of the moons of Jupiter and Saturn, may have been hosts for life (or may continue to be!). Now, as technologies have improved and we can obtain measurements of the composition of the atmosphere on extra-solar planets (planets outside of our own Milky Way Galaxy, also called "exoplanets"), the chances of finding "alien" life forms are increasing.

ISBN: 978-1-77149-036-8

Recently, there has been speculation that some of the planets in the habitable zone of the red dwarf star Gliese 581, the brightest star in the constellation Libra, may be able to support life as we know it to be. In 2007, scientists discovered exoplanet Gliese 581c – and felt that its atmosphere was most amenable to supporting life. But further research revealed that it would not. Now, attention has been turned to Gliese 581d, at the outer edge of the star's habitable zone. The main criteria for deciding whether a planetary body can be life-supporting are atmospheric conditions which allow the existence of water. Gliese 581 is about 20.4 light years away from Earth, so even if life does exist there, the distance would mean that communication would be unlikely.

Having said this – who says alien life forms (if they exist) need water?

A. Check the best answer for each question.

1. *The War of the Worlds* was _____ .

   A. written by Orson Welles

   B. adapted from a radio drama

   C. a novel published in 1898

2. Some people committed suicide because _____ .

   A. they believed that aliens from Mars were invading Earth

   B. they had been tortured by aliens

   C. they were worried that aliens would attack Earth

3. Scientists believe that _____ .

   A. the six billion people on Earth are the only living organisms in the universe

   B. simple organisms can be found on other planets

   C. there may be forms of life on other planets in the universe

4. Which of the following statements is not true?

   A. Gliese 581c was discovered in 2007.

   B. Gliese 581d is far away from Earth.

   C. Libra is the brightest star that is about 20.4 light years away from Earth.

More on Reported Speech

Changing sentences from direct speech to reported speech requires changes in place and time expressions too. Even certain verbs need to be changed.

Examples: "Did you see the DVD of *The War of the Worlds* I left <u>here</u> <u>yesterday</u>?" David asked Sue.

David asked Sue if she had seen the DVD of *The War of the Worlds* he had left <u>there</u> <u>the day before</u>.

Mr. Jamieson told Eric, "<u>Come</u> over <u>here</u> and take a look at <u>this</u> picture of Mars."

Mr. Jamieson told Eric to <u>go</u> over <u>there</u> and take a look at <u>that</u> picture of Mars.

B. Change the given words or phrases to the reported form.

Direct Speech   **Indirect Speech**

1. now   _____

2. today   _____

3. tonight   _____

4. tomorrow   _____

5. last year   _____

6. next Monday _____

7. eight years ago _____

8. in five days _____

9. next month   _____

10. three weeks ago _____

11. last weekend _____

12. next Christmas _____

13. this afternoon _____

C. Rewrite the following sentences in reported speech.

1. "I borrowed this book from the library last week," said Jenny.

_____

2. Sandra asked Dave, "Do you believe there really are aliens now?"

_____

3. Mr. and Mrs. Hayes said, "We saw a UFO hover over our house six years ago."

_____

4. "We can go to the Ontario Science Centre next weekend," Anna said.

_____

5. "A seminar about the existence of life on other planets will be held here next Friday," Emily told Sam.

_____

D. Rewrite the following sentences in direct speech.

1. Nelson asked me if I would watch the program about aliens on the Discovery Channel the following day.

_____

2. The astronomer explained to us that research into the atmospheric conditions of different planetary bodies had started some years before.

_____

3. Tammy said her uncle had bought her those cute alien dolls the previous summer when he had gone to visit.

_____

4. Ricky's sister told him that she had to hand in a book report on a science fiction book two weeks from then.

_____

Saving Lake **Winnipeg**

ALGAE BLOOMS! STOP

- Avoid swimming or other contact with the water.
- Prevent pets or livestock from drinking the water.
- Do not eat fish from this lake that appear unhealthy.

If you look at a satellite image of Canada, you will see that the natural physical landscape is quite distinctive; different parts of the country look very different from one another. The Canadian Shield is comprised of millions of waterways and lakes – most are referred to as "finger" lakes, but some are large, such as the Great Lakes of Southern Ontario and the USA, and Lakes Winnipeg and Manitoba in the province of Manitoba.

Lake Winnipeg has often been referred to as one of Canada's "Great Lakes". In fact, it is the 10th largest freshwater body in the world. Because of this lake and its neighbouring lakes, along with all the rivers that connect them to the sea, Manitoba can lay claim to the highest concentration of cottage owners in the world! Yes, Manitoba, with its lakes and rivers, its boreal forests, its gentle grassy prairie, and vast prairie skies, is a lovely place to live and play.

But Lake Winnipeg is now in deep trouble. Large blue-green algae blooms are occurring in the lake with increasing frequency, covering hundreds of square kilometres with a thick goo. They have occurred in summer almost every year for a decade now. The toxins in them can kill livestock, and they have caused the closures of many beaches in recent years as well. And what is perhaps most disturbing is that most of these algae blooms are happening in Lake Winnipeg's large, north basin, where there is considerably less human activity. This means that the whole body of water is on the verge of becoming a "dead" lake because the algae blooms can deplete the oxygen in the water and kill off plankton – the main food source of lake fish.

These algae blooms form when the water contains much more phosphorous than nitrogen. The phosphorous comes from different sources. Lake Winnipeg is a drainage basin for many of the rivers that cross the prairie. Fertilizers, rich in phosphates, are used by farmers growing crops in the watershed area. The phosphates leach into the soil and eventually into these rivers. Animal and municipal waste (sewage) is another source in the phosphate cycle.

Yet another source of the phosphates that end up in Lake Winnipeg is the wastewater effluent from the Red River. The Red River is an important waterway originating in the United States. It runs through, or alongside, many cities, such as Fargo, Grand Forks, Moorhead, and of course, Winnipeg. Water laden with phosphates, primarily from household detergents, is discharged into the river, exacerbating an already dangerous situation.

ISBN: 978-1-77149-036-8

In 2003, the Government of Manitoba set up the Lake Winnipeg Stewardship Board to assist the government in formulating an action plan to save Lake Winnipeg. Positive steps are being taken, including campaigns to urge households to use phosphate-free detergents. Let's hope it is not too late!

A. Check the main idea of each paragraph.

Paragraph 1

A. Canada is a country with a distinctive natural physical landscape.

B. The Canadian Shield comprises millions of waterways and lakes.

Paragraph 2

A. Manitoba is a great place to live and play.

B. Lake Winnipeg is one of Canada's "Great Lakes" and the 10th largest freshwater body in the world.

Paragraph 3

A. There is little human activity in Lake Winnipeg's large, north basin.

B. Large blue-green algae blooms may cause Lake Winnipeg to become a "dead" lake.

Paragraph 4

A. Phosphorous is the main cause for the blue-green algae blooms.

B. Animal and municipal waste is the main source of phosphate.

Paragraph 5

A. The use of household detergents is a primary cause for the blue-green algae blooms.

B. Water laden with phosphates from the Red River flows into Lake Winnipeg.

Paragraph 6

A. The Government of Manitoba has been taking steps to save Lake Winnipeg.

B. Lake Winnipeg Stewardship Board is responsible for formulating an action plan to save Lake Winnipeg.

Conditional Clauses

Conditional clauses are clauses with "if" that are used to talk about a possible situation and its results. There are three types of conditional clauses.

- For something that may happen in the future, we use the present or present perfect tense in the conditional clause and the simple future tense in the main clause.

  Example: If you <u>look</u> at a satellite image of Canada, you <u>will see</u> that the natural physical landscape is quite distinctive.

- For something that is unlikely to happen, we use the past tense in the conditional clause and "would" in the main clause. Note the use of "were" instead of "was" in the conditional clause.

  Example: If I <u>were</u> a farmer, I <u>would not use</u> fertilizers rich in phosphates.

- For something that could have happened in the past but did not actually happen, we use the past perfect tense in the conditional clause and "would have" with a past participle in the main clause.

  Example: The problem <u>would not have become</u> that serious if farmers <u>had used</u> phosphate-free fertilizers.

B.   Complete the following conditional sentences.

1.   If you ask me why I like Manitoba, _____

_____ .

2.   If George were a government official, _____

_____ .

3.   If the Red River did not run through so many cities, _____

_____ .

4.   Lake Winnipeg will become a "dead" lake if _____

_____ .

5.   Large algae blooms would not have formed if _____

_____ .

ISBN: 978-1-77149-036-8

C. Check the correct sentences and rewrite the wrong ones.

1. If I owned a cottage in Manitoba, I will spend every summer there. ☐

_____

2. You will see the beautiful prairie, lakes, and forests if you go to Manitoba. ☐

_____

3. If Macy had been to Winnipeg before, she would know more about the city. ☐

_____

4. If the pollution problem of Lake Winnipeg continues, all wildlife would have been adversely affected. ☐

_____

5. Lake Winnipeg will recover if everyone started using phosphate-free detergents today. ☐

_____

6. If you swallow the lake water accidentally, you will probably suffer from gastrointestinal illnesses. ☐

_____

7. I would teach everyone how to make phosphate-free detergent if I have the formula. ☐

_____

8. If I was a citizen of Manitoba, I would do everything I could to help save Lake Winnipeg. ☐

_____

Depression
in Teenagers: a Very Treatable Condition

Depression is more common than many people think. Each year, about one in ten adults experience a major bout of depression. In the past, not much was said about this common ailment, and sufferers were reluctant to talk about it or even to seek help, and this took a toll on families as well. Thankfully, people, and society in general, are more open about depression and other mental illnesses today. We know more about them and no longer attach a stigma to the conditions. And depression is not just a condition affecting adults. About one out of every 25 teens are affected by depression each year. Studies in other countries, such as Japan, have figures that are higher. In fact, studies there reveal that as many as one in 10 students have experienced a bout of depression within the previous year.

So what exactly is depression? Of course, everyone gets upset and sad and down-in-the-dumps from time to time – life is full of all kinds of problems, some of which we can control and some we cannot. But for some people, these sad feelings last longer and affect them in serious ways. Depression can occur for many reasons. It can come about as a reaction to a stressful situation, a big disappointment, or a loss of a loved one. Sometimes it may appear to come about for no particular reason. Depression can also be the result of a chemical imbalance in the brain, and there is a hereditary link in some cases. Depression, if left untreated, can be very disruptive, affecting relationships with family and friends, work and school life, as well as physical well-being. The good news is that a variety of things can be done to treat the condition, ranging from a change in diet and exercise, to counselling, to group therapy, to medication – or a combination of these methods.

The Canadian Mental Health Association has advice for parents who are worried that their children may be experiencing a form of depression. If you think you may be depressed, ask yourself if any of these apply to you:

- *Changes in feelings – showing signs of being unhappy, worried, guilty, angry, fearful, helpless, hopeless, lonely, or rejected*

- *Physical changes – complaining of headaches or general aches and pains; having a lack of energy; sleeping or eating problems; feeling tired all the time*

- *Changes in thinking – saying things that indicate low self-esteem, self-dislike, or self-blame; having difficulty concentrating; frequently experiencing negative thoughts; thinking about suicide*

- *Changes in behaviour – withdrawing from others; crying easily or showing less interest in sports, games, or other fun activities that you normally like; over-reacting and having sudden outbursts of anger or tears over fairly small incidents*

People who are dealing with depression may try to hide it and may not want to talk about it, thinking, perhaps, that no one will understand them. But it is very important to talk about it. If the lines of communication in your family are not open, professional help is available. Your school guidance counsellor can refer you to an appropriate caregiver. You can also visit your family doctor in the first instance. Other community organizations, such as the Canadian Mental Health Association, can also offer assistance. The most important thing to remember is that you are not alone, and that there are people waiting to help you. Depression is a treatable condition.

A. Read the statements below. Check the ones that are true and rewrite those that are not true.

1. Depression is a common ailment affecting 25% of teens each year.

   _____

2. People suffering from depression did not want to talk about it or seek help.

   _____

3. Depression can be caused by an imbalance in hormones.

   _____

4. Depression cannot be treated with medication.

   _____

5. If you show changes in thinking, such as disliking yourself and having difficulty concentrating, you may be suffering from depression.

   _____

6. People suffering from depression may be saddened by fairly small incidents.

   _____

Use of Modals in Conditional Clauses

Modals like "can", "may", and "must" can sometimes be used in conditional clauses or main clauses.

Examples: If you <u>can</u> let people help you, depression will not be a problem.

If depression is left untreated, it <u>can</u> be very disruptive.

B.   Complete the following conditional sentences that involve the use of modals.

1.   You may give me a call anytime _____

_____ .

2.   Depression can be easily treated _____

_____ .

3.   We should always think positively _____

_____ .

4.   You must pay attention to mental health _____

_____ .

5.   If Sarah could talk more with her friends, _____

_____ .

6.   If a change in diet can help, _____

_____ .

7.   If you think you may be depressed, _____

_____ .

8.   If you cannot solve the problem on your own, _____

_____ .

ISBN: 978-1-77149-036-8

Omitting "If" in Conditional Clauses

Some other expressions, such as "unless", "only if", and "as long as" can be used to begin conditional clauses to indicate that one event only happens or is true if another event happens or is true.

Example: We can be healthy both physically and mentally <u>as long as</u> we work out regularly.

C. Make conditional sentences using the following expressions.

1. unless

_____

_____

2. only if

_____

_____

3. even if

_____

_____

4. provided that

_____

_____

5. so long as

_____

_____

6. as long as

_____

_____

Norway is a small country with a small population – and a long history. There are many myths and legends about the people and the place itself, and some of these stories constitute some of the world's oldest written legends – the sagas. The word "saga" originates from the Icelandic language, and is the word from which the English word "say" is derived. Present day Icelandic is actually a version of Old Norse. After all, it was the Vikings, from the region that we now call Norway, who made their way to Iceland and settled it about a thousand years ago. From that time on, the language of the people who lived on that island remained the same, while the language of the people back on the European continent continued to evolve.

Most sagas are long sweeping tales of fantastical adventures and heroic acts, and the litany of characters includes Scandinavian kings, an assortment of gods, strong women (the Valkyries), and mortals with human qualities and frailties. Many of the stories chronicle family feuds, Viking voyages, and even romance, and most were written in long prose, often with poems and stanzas included within the text. Alliterative verse was also a common literary device used in sagas.

One of the greatest writers of these sagas was the Icelandic poet and historian Snorri Sturluson. He wrote some of the best-known sagas, including the Prose Edda (meaning Younger Edda) and the King's Sagas (Heimskringla) about the lives of Norwegian kings. He is also believed to be the author of another most popular work, Egils Saga. The Laxdœla Saga is another of the most popular sagas and is still widely read today; it is believed to have been written by a woman.

The Start of the Sagas

There are numerous sagas, and the cast of characters is large. They contain a pantheon of gods in much the same manner as the legendary stories from the ancient Greek civilization. The chief god in Norse mythology is Odin – the god of wisdom, war, and death. Loki is another popular god, or giant, and a member of Odin's family. Dagur was the god of the daylight. Delling was the god of dawn. But who begot them all? The progenitor of all gods in Norse Mythology is Búri. He did not have a mother or father but was borne, in effect, from a giant frozen cow. The cow, named Audhumla, licked a salt block in a place called Ginnungagap, between the barren land of snow and ice called Niflheim and a fiery vastness called Múspell. From the salt block Búri emerged. Búri means "the producer". He married an ice giantess and had a son named Borr. Borr started a family with a woman named Bestla and had three sons: Odin, Vili, and Ve. And from them, one could say, the adventures of Norse Mythology begin.

ISBN: 978-1-77149-036-8

Much of the written record of these sagas originated in Iceland, but the original manuscripts were, over the ages, taken back to Norway and Denmark, which took turns ruling over the island until the mid-20th century. Now, however, the ancient written records of these legends are being returned, placed in special museums under special, sealed display cases.

A. Read the descriptions and match them with the names of the sagas, characters, or places.

Laxdœla   Niflheim   Odin   Loki   Dagur   Delling

Búri   Bestla   Heimskringla   Borr   Valkyries   Múspell

Name of saga/character/place	Description
1.	god of the daylight
2.	son of Búri and a giantess
3.	believed to be a saga written by a woman
4.	strong women
5.	about the lives of Norwegian kings
6.	god of wisdom, war, and death
7.	a giant god and a member of Odin's family
8.	a barren land of snow and ice
9.	mother of Odin, Vili, and Ve
10.	borne from a giant frozen cow
11.	god of dawn
12.	a vast land of fire

Paraphrasing

To **paraphrase** is to express someone's ideas in your own words.

Example: The sagas contain a pantheon of gods in much the same manner as the legendary stories from the Greek civilization. (original)

Like the legendary stories from the Greek civilization, the sagas have a pantheon of gods. (paraphrase)

B. Paraphrase the following statements from the passage.

1. There are many myths and legends about the people and the place itself, and some of these stories constitute some of the world's oldest written legends – the sagas.

_____

_____

_____

_____

2. It was the Vikings, from the region that we now call Norway, who made their way to Iceland and settled it about a thousand years ago.

_____

_____

_____

_____

3. From that time on, the language of the people who lived on that island remained the same, while the language of the people back on the European continent continued to evolve.

_____

_____

_____

_____

ISBN: 978-1-77149-036-8

Summarizing

To **summarize** is to reduce a text to its bare essentials: the gist, the key ideas, and the main points that are worth noting and remembering.

In summarizing, we:

- read the original and understand the main subject
- pull out the main ideas
- focus on key details
- use key words and phrases
- break down the larger ideas
- leave out examples and illustrations

C. **Write a summary of "The Start of the Sagas" in no more than 100 words.**

_____

_____

_____

_____

_____

_____

_____

_____

_____

_____

_____

_____

_____

_____

_____

_____

_____

Green Iceland:
a Letter from Uncle Josh

Dear Sammy,

You have probably learned about Vikings in school. These rough and tough men travelled from Norway over 1000 years ago – stopped off in Ireland for some wives – then landed in Iceland. Later they travelled farther. In order to get more people to follow them and settle in these faraway places, they called the iciest places "Greenland" and "Vineland" (which is today's USA northeast seaboard). When I was a kid, my teacher told me to remember the place names by thinking: "Greenland is ice and Iceland is green". After coming here to Iceland this summer, I can tell you it's true: Iceland is green in more ways than one!

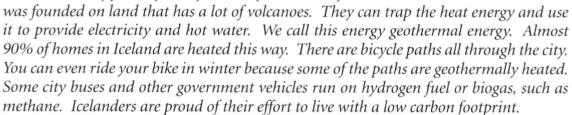

The capital city, Reykjavik, is filled with parks and gardens, and the air smells like flowers at the moment – honeysuckles and violets especially! The people of Iceland are very environmentally friendly. They are lucky: the country was founded on land that has a lot of volcanoes. They can trap the heat energy and use it to provide electricity and hot water. We call this energy geothermal energy. Almost 90% of homes in Iceland are heated this way. There are bicycle paths all through the city. You can even ride your bike in winter because some of the paths are geothermally heated. Some city buses and other government vehicles run on hydrogen fuel or biogas, such as methane. Icelanders are proud of their effort to live with a low carbon footprint.

Swimming is the national sport of Iceland, and there are seven geothermally heated outdoor pools in the capital city. The most famous "pool" of all is The Blue Lagoon. It is located in the middle of an old lava field, next to a geothermal power plant, about 50 kilometres from the city. The water is hot and full of minerals that are supposed to be good for the skin. Some people will tell you it smells like egg sandwiches because of the sulfur in it. You can also dig up white silica sand from the bottom of this outdoor pool and put it on your face. It really does make your skin feel smoother.

Tomorrow I plan to go on a special bus ride called "The Golden Circle Tour". It will take us to a great waterfall called Gulfoss, as important to Iceland as Niagara Falls is to Canada. We will also visit a place called Geysir, where there are a lot of colourful bubbling mud pots and steam vents and, of course, a few geysers. Then the bus will pass through Thingvellir National Park, to a place that is the site of the world's oldest parliament. Icelandic people call this the Althing, and it began more than 1000 years ago! We will also stop at the Nesjavellir geothermal plant nearby. I am really looking forward to it!

I am enjoying my visit to Iceland: the land of fire (volcanoes) and ice (glaciers). It's an interesting place for a geologist like me, but I know you would love it, too. You should ask your parents to bring you here someday – then I'll have an excuse to come back!

Take care,

Uncle Josh

A. Complete the chart based on the information from Uncle Josh's letter.

Place	How is it special?
Reykjavik	
The Blue Lagoon	
Gulfoss	
Geysir	
Thingvellir National Park	

B. Answer the following questions.

1. Give an example to illustrate that the people of Iceland are environmentally friendly.

   _____

   _____

2. Explain why Uncle Josh says that "Icelanders are proud of their effort to live with a low carbon footprint."

   _____

   _____

Adding Emphasis

We can **add emphasis** to someone or something in a sentence in a number of ways.

The **passive voice** can be used to draw the reader's attention to the person or thing affected by an action rather than who or what brings about the action.

Example: The minerals in the water are supposed to be good for the skin.

We can also use "**do**", "**does**", or "**did**" in a positive sentence to emphasize something we feel strongly about.

Example: It really <u>does</u> make your skin feel smoother.

C.   Rewrite the following sentences in the passive voice to shift the emphasis.

1.   The United Nations' Human Development Index ranked Iceland as the most developed country in the world in 2007.

   _____

2.   Many restaurants in Iceland serve ocean-fresh seafood.

   _____

3.   Icelanders still speak the ancient language of the Vikings.

   _____

D.   Add emphasis to the sentences with "do", "does", or "did".

1.   Many Icelanders believe in the existence of elves.

   _____

2.   The hotel provides free shuttle services to many attractions around the city.

   _____

3.   It's not usual to see polar bears in Iceland but I saw one on my trip there.

   _____

More on Adding Emphasis

Inversion is another way to add emphasis to a sentence. We can begin a sentence with expressions like "never", "seldom", "rarely", and "at no time", followed by inverted word order.

Example: <u>Never have I been</u> to a country where all citizens are so conscious about being environmentally friendly.

We can also use a clause introduced by "**what**" as the subject of a sentence to draw the reader's attention to this subject. This clause is followed by the verb "to be".

Example: <u>What Icelanders are proud of</u> is their effort to live with a low carbon footprint.

E. Rewrite the following sentences using inversion.

1. We did not expect to see the Northern Lights in Iceland.

    _____

2. Keith does not know much about Iceland.

    _____

3. Icelanders seldom add salt to their food.

    _____

4. The tourists had hardly arrived at the geyser when it erupted.

    _____

F. Rewrite the following sentences using "What" to begin them.

1. We all must try the Icelandic skyr.

    _____

2. Some tourists to Iceland want to see the Northern Lights.

    _____

3. Many people do not know that it is not that cold in Iceland.

    _____

Magnificent Trees

How many trees are there on Earth? No one would be able to give an exact answer, but trees surely number in the billions and they cover almost 30% of the Earth's land surface. With so many trees around the world, there are certainly some majestic and remarkable ones that are worthy of our attention.

You may know that trees have been on Earth for a very long time, but how long ago did they start to exist? Fossils have revealed that the earliest known tree, an eight-metre tall Wattieza resembling the modern palm tree or the tree fern, existed about 385 million years ago – much earlier than the dinosaur and any human civilization!

Did you know that some trees living today were already in existence when the first ancient Egyptian pyramid was built? These trees actually witnessed the rise and fall of various civilizations. The oldest among them is a Great Basin bristlecone pine in the White Mountains of California, and it is the oldest known non-clonal organism still living in the world. This tree, yet to be named, was 5062 years old when it was discovered in 2012! Imagine if these trees could talk, they would have been able to tell us incredible stories about why the Maya, the Indus, or other ancient civilizations declined or disappeared!

If you have a chance to visit Sequoia National Park in California, why not give a salute to General Sherman? It is a 2100-year-old Giant Sequoia that measures about 84 m in height and 31 m around the base, making it the largest non-clonal tree in the world by volume.

Being the biggest does not make General Sherman the stoutest. Located on the grounds of a church in Oaxaca, Mexico is the world's stoutest tree, the Tule Tree, a Montezuma cypress tree estimated to be at least 2000 years old. Compared to General Sherman, the Tule Tree is much shorter, at about 40 m in height, but it has a bigger base of about 50 m around. Its trunk is so thick that the Tule Tree was once thought to be several trees that masqueraded as one, but DNA analysis has proved that it is only one tree. The Tule Tree is also famous for the interesting images of animals like lions and elephants that are visible on its gnarled trunk.

Pando, or the Trembling Giant, which weighs over 6 000 000 kilograms, is the heaviest living organism on Earth. If you are thinking of

GENERAL SHERMAN

ISBN: 978-1-77149-036-8

Pando as a humongous tree, you are wrong. Spreading over 107 acres of land in Utah, USA, Pando is in fact a massive colony of approximately 47 000 "trees" that stem from one single quaking aspen tree. All the "trees" are genetically identical and share a giant underground root system. It is estimated that the entire organism is 80 000 years old!

There have been sad stories about some fascinating trees, like the Lonely Tree of Ténéré in the Sahara that was knocked down and killed when a drunk truck driver crashed into it, despite the fact that it was the only tree in the wide open desert, without any other trees for 400 kilometres around! Another sad story is that of Prometheus. It was only when this Great Basin bristlecone pine was unwittingly cut down for research purposes that scientists realized it was more than 5000 years old!

No one wants to see these precious and magnificent trees meet a similar fate, so the exact locations of many of them are kept secret so that they can be protected from inquisitive visitors who may trample their root systems and others who may perform acts of vandalism.

A. Complete the chart based on the information from the passage.

Name	——	——	General Sherman	The Tule Tree	Pando/ Trembling Giant
Species	Wattieza				
Location	——				
Age	——	about 5062 years old			
Measurement	Height:	——	Height: Base circumference:	Height: Base circumference:	Weight:
Record	the earliest known tree				

Paragraphs

Almost all types of writing are made up of an introductory paragraph, body paragraphs, and a concluding paragraph.

An **introductory paragraph** lets the reader know what the piece is about. It contains a thesis statement that introduces the main idea. A well-written introductory paragraph should capture the reader's attention.

Body paragraphs give supporting details to the main idea. In writing body paragraphs, we should first list the points that develop the main idea, and then expand each point into its own paragraph, each consisting of a topic sentence, supporting facts, details, examples, and a concluding sentence.

A **concluding paragraph** restates or summarizes the main idea. We can also give our personal opinion or call for action.

B. **Search for information about other magnificent trees in the world on the Internet. Compose an essay on this topic.**

Introductory Paragraph (thesis statement)

_____

_____

_____

_____

Body Paragraph 1 (topic sentence, supporting details, concluding sentence)

_____

_____

_____

_____

Body Paragraph 2 (topic sentence, supporting details, concluding sentence)

_____

_____

_____

_____

Body Paragraph 3 (topic sentence, supporting details, concluding sentence)

_____

_____

_____

_____

Body Paragraph 4 (topic sentence, supporting details, concluding sentence)

_____

_____

_____

_____

Concluding Paragraph (restate/summarize main idea, give personal opinion, etc.)

_____

_____

_____

_____

High Flight –
a Poem by John Gillespie Magee, Jr.

When the American shuttle spacecraft Challenger exploded shortly after takeoff on January 28, 1986, U.S. President Ronald Reagan offered a moving memorial. Of that speech, written by presidential speechwriter Peggy Noonan, it is perhaps the last words which are the most memorable and still remembered and quoted today:

> ...The crew of the space shuttle Challenger honored us by the manner in which they lived their lives. We will never forget them, nor the last time we saw them, this morning, as they prepared for their journey and waved goodbye and "slipped the surly bonds of Earth" to "touch the face of God".

What is not well known is that President Reagan was, in fact, quoting from a poem written by a pilot-officer of the Royal Canadian Air Force named John Gillespie Magee, Jr. Although born in China to an American missionary father and a British mother, Magee joined the Royal Canadian Air Force at the age of 18, in 1940, before the U.S. entered World War II. He received his flight training and became a fighter pilot in Canada. He died a year later while on a flying exercise in England. The poem entitled "High Flight" is very evocative, clearly displaying Magee's infatuation with flight and his chosen career as a pilot (although not necessarily as a fighter pilot). Here is the poem in its entirety:

High Flight

Oh! I have slipped the surly bonds of Earth
And danced the skies on laughter-silvered wings;
Sunward I've climbed, and joined the tumbling mirth
Of sun-split clouds, – and done a hundred things
You have not dreamed of – wheeled and soared and swung
High in the sunlit silence. Hov'ring there,
I've chased the shouting wind along, and flung
My eager craft through footless halls of air...

Up, up the long, delirious burning blue
I've topped the wind-swept heights with easy grace
Where never lark, or ever eagle flew –
And, while with silent, lifting mind I've trod
The high untrespassed sanctity of space,
Put out my hand, and touched the face of God.

ISBN: 978-1-77149-036-8

Peggy Noonan was a skilled speechwriter for President Reagan, penning some of his most memorable speeches. But she is actually a bestselling author, newspaper columnist, and essayist, writing mostly about politics, religion, and culture. One of the marks of a skilled writer is the ability to make references to other great works or issues and to reinterpret them to achieve a desired effect. The reference to "High Flight" in President Reagan's speech is a good example of this. Can you think of others?

A. Answer the following questions.

1. Why do you think the writer has such a high regard for Peggy Noonan apart from Noonan's strong credentials as a writer?

   _____

   _____

2. How would you interpret "...slipped the surly bonds of Earth to touch the face of God"?

   _____

   _____

3. Why does the writer say that "...The poem entitled 'High Flight' is very evocative, clearly displaying Magee's infatuation with flight..."?

   _____

   _____

4. "Sunward I've climbed, and joined the tumbling mirth of sun-split clouds..." Check the best alternative for "tumbling mirth" below.

   A. the thrilling journey

   B. the merry acrobatic fall

   C. the slow movements

   D. the speedy descent

5. Which lines in "High Flight" impress you most? Explain why.

   _____

   _____

Words for Paragraphs that Explain

In writing a paragraph to explain a certain issue, words like "since...thus", "due to...hence", "because...therefore", and "as a result" are used to explore the causes and effects of certain events.

B. **Compose short paragraphs with the following words and phrases.**

1. since...thus

_____

_____

_____

_____

_____

2. due to...hence

_____

_____

_____

_____

3. for this reason

_____

_____

_____

_____

Words for Paragraphs that Compare and Contrast

In writing a paragraph to show the similarities and differences between people, things, places, or ideas, words like "similar to", "differs from", "in contrast", and "on the other hand" are used to compare and contrast.

C. **Compose short paragraphs with the following words and phrases.**

1. similarly

_____

_____

_____

_____

2. in contrast

_____

_____

_____

_____

3. on the contrary

_____

_____

_____

_____

Hannah Taylor
and the Ladybug Foundation

Hannah Taylor is a schoolgirl from Manitoba. She was born in 1997. One day, when she was five years old, she was walking with her mother in downtown Winnipeg. They saw a man eating out of a garbage can. She asked her mother why he had to do that, and her mother said that the man was down on his luck, and was homeless and hungry. Hannah was very upset by this encounter. She could not understand why some people had to live their lives without shelter or enough food. Hannah started to think about how she could help, but – of course – there is not a lot one five-year-old can do to solve the large social problem of homelessness.

Later, when Hannah began attending school, she saw another homeless person on her way to school. It was a woman this time, shuffling along, pushing a battered, old shopping trolley. The trolley was piled with bags; it seemed that everything the woman owned was in those bags. This made Hannah very sad, and even more determined to do something. She had been talking to her mother about the lives of homeless people since that first time they saw the man eating out of the garbage can. Her mother told her that if she did something to change the problem that made her sad or worried, she would not feel as bad. And this was the beginning of Hannah's remarkable journey.

Hannah began to speak out about the problem of homelessness in Manitoba and then in other provinces, spreading her message of hope and awareness further afield. She started the Ladybug Foundation, a charity organization dedicated to eradicating homelessness. She began to host "Big Bosses" lunches, where she would try to persuade local business leaders to help contribute to the cause, reminding them that it is certainly in their best interests to make sure that homeless people are not living on the streets. At her very first Big Bosses lunch, she drew pictures to sell at an auction, and two businessmen had a bidding war for a picture of a ladybug, which resulted in a $10 000 donation! She and the volunteers of the Ladybug Foundation also organized a fundraising drive in "Ladybug Jars" – household jars painted red and black to look like ladybugs and dispensed to schools and businesses across Canada to collect everyone's spare change during "Make Change" month. More recently, the foundation began another campaign called National Red Scarf Day – a day when people donate $20 and wear red scarves in support of Canada's hungry and homeless. For the inaugural National Red Scarf Day on January 31, 2008, Hannah went to Ottawa to speak to Members of Parliament and was congratulated in the House of Commons by Ontario MP Ruby Dhalla.

ISBN: 978-1-77149-036-8

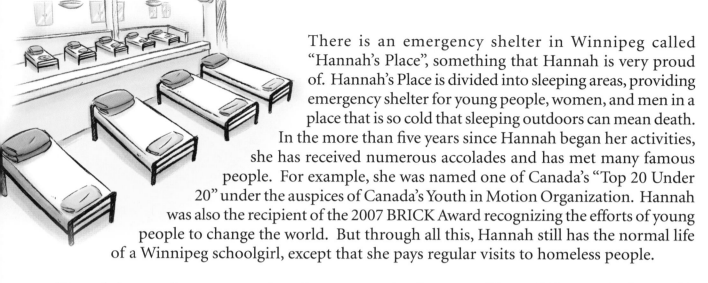

There is an emergency shelter in Winnipeg called "Hannah's Place", something that Hannah is very proud of. Hannah's Place is divided into sleeping areas, providing emergency shelter for young people, women, and men in a place that is so cold that sleeping outdoors can mean death. In the more than five years since Hannah began her activities, she has received numerous accolades and has met many famous people. For example, she was named one of Canada's "Top 20 Under 20" under the auspices of Canada's Youth in Motion Organization. Hannah was also the recipient of the 2007 BRICK Award recognizing the efforts of young people to change the world. But through all this, Hannah still has the normal life of a Winnipeg schoolgirl, except that she pays regular visits to homeless people.

Hannah is one of many examples of young people who are making a difference in the world. You can, too!

A. Answer the following questions.

1. "Hannah was very upset by this encounter." What incident does "this encounter" refer to?

_____

2. "And this was the beginning of Hannah's remarkable journey." What does "Hannah's remarkable journey" refer to?

_____

3. Why do you think Hannah met with Members of Parliament to kick-start National Red Scarf Day?

_____

_____

4. Hannah has been working for the welfare of the homeless. Describe another social problem that you think should be addressed, and how we can address it.

_____

_____

_____

_____

Transitional Words and Phrases

Transitional words and phrases serve as the glue that holds ideas together in a piece of writing. They help clarify the relationships between ideas and ensure that sentences and paragraphs flow smoothly, making them easy for the reader to follow. Below are examples of some common transitional words and phrases for different relationships between ideas:

- Addition: besides, moreover, in addition
- Similarity: similarly, likewise, in like manner
- Contrast: although, however, on the contrary
- Example: for example, for instance, as an illustration
- Emphasis: in fact, surely, above all
- Sequence: afterwards, meanwhile, eventually
- Generalizing: generally, in general, as a rule
- Cause: since, because of, for this reason
- Consequence: thus, hence, as a result
- Exception: excluding, other than, with the exception of
- Summary: in short, to summarize, in conclusion

B. Think of three more words or phrases for each of the relationships specified below.

1. Addition   _____   _____   _____

2. Similarity   _____   _____   _____

3. Contrast   _____   _____   _____

4. Example   _____   _____   _____

5. Emphasis   _____   _____   _____

6. Sequence   _____   _____   _____

7. Generalizing   _____   _____   _____

8. Cause   _____   _____   _____

9. Consequence   _____   _____   _____

10. Exception   _____   _____   _____

11. Summary   _____   _____   _____

ISBN: 978-1-77149-036-8

C. **Improve the coherence of the following paragraph by using transitional words and phrases. Make any necessary changes to the sentences.**

Hannah Taylor was five years old. One day she saw a man eating out of a garbage can. She saw another homeless woman. The woman had everything she owned in a grocery cart. Hannah felt very sad. She thought everyone needed a home. She could not understand why some people were homeless and did not have enough to eat. She talked with her mother many times about homelessness. Her mother told her that if she could do something to change a problem, she would not feel as bad. Hannah founded the Ladybug Foundation in 2004. She wanted to raise the public's awareness of the needs of the homeless. She wanted to raise funds to provide food, shelter, and other necessities for them. Hannah has talked to many people about homelessness. More and more people know about this problem. More and more people want to help. Hannah hopes that everyone can share a little of what he or she has. She hopes that everyone can show his or her care, love, and support for the homeless. She hopes to eradicate homelessness and hunger from Canada.

_____

_____

_____

_____

_____

_____

_____

_____

_____

_____

The Truth about *Water*

Water is essential to all living organisms. From humans to plants and animals to bacteria, everything on Earth needs water to survive. About 71% of the planet's surface area is covered in water, and when seen from space, the Earth looks blue. That is why it is called the "blue planet". Approximately 98% of all water on Earth is salt water, which is found in oceans and seas and is home to hundreds of thousands of marine species. Only about 2% is fresh water – the water we depend on.

We use fresh water for many things. We drink it, we clean with it, and we cook with it. Doing laundry, flushing the toilet, and washing dishes are some of the domestic ways we use water. But we also have industrial and agricultural needs of water. According to statistics by the United Nations, industrial water use takes up about 22% of all water usage. Factories use water during the production process of many things like glass, paper, plastic, and metals. Car washes are another major form of consumption of our freshwater supply. It is in agriculture, however, where most of our water resources are used. Irrigation is responsible for 70% of freshwater use, since farmers need water to keep crops alive and keep livestock healthy.

Freshwater distribution on Earth is imbalanced. Not only is there already a very limited supply of usable water, but most water resources are hard to reach because they are in the form of glaciers and permanent snow in the Arctic and Antarctic regions, or stored underground in groundwater basins or in the atmosphere. The rest can be found in lakes and rivers. Because of this uneven distribution, many places are facing a water crisis and do not have access to safe water. There are people around the world who drink unsafe water, bathe in dirty water, and have no proper facilities for waste disposal. Sub-Saharan Africa, specifically, has the least amount of drinking water in the world. Almost 800 million people on Earth cannot get clean water, with the vast majority of them being from the Third World.

The consequences of a water crisis are great. Only about 10% of waste water gets treated. This leads to widespread water pollution and is the cause of the majority of illnesses. In developing countries with inadequate access to safe water, women

ISBN: 978-1-77149-036-8

and children often bear the responsibility of collecting water for their households. They spend hours finding water sources, often contaminated, and walk miles carrying water back. Lack of sanitation is a very serious and deadly issue as dirty water leads to diseases and infections. Diarrhea, caused by polluted drinking water, bad hygiene, and insufficient sanitation facilities, is one of the leading causes of death around the world. In the children population, it accounts for about 1.5 million deaths each year.

Many of these problems can be prevented. In fact, great progress has been made in globalizing access to safe water. Based on a report by the World Health Organization, within the last two decades, about 1.9 billion people have gained access to improved sanitation facilities, and almost 90% of the world's population can now enjoy improved drinking-water sources. Despite these improvements, 11% of the global population still suffers from inadequate water supply.

A. Answer the following questions.

1. Why is the Earth called the "blue planet"?

_____

_____

2. In what ways is water used for agriculture?

_____

_____

3. How is the distribution of fresh water imbalanced?

_____

_____

4. What role do women and children play in the water crisis?

_____

_____

5. What does "globalizing access to safe water" mean?

_____

_____

Chronological Order

Good and effective writing involves clear and logical organization. One way to achieve this is to arrange events in **chronological order**, that is, in the order in which they occur. Very often, the dates of the events are provided, and transitional words and phrases such as "then", "after that", and "three years later" are used.

B. **Read some facts about other major world events. Compose a brief article about the Earth's history by putting the facts in chronological order. Add appropriate transitional words and phrases wherever necessary.**

The Earth's History

- 4.5 billion years ago, a planet the size of Mars collided with the Earth; some of its debris formed the moon

- dinosaurs became extinct approximately 40 million years before the evolution of great apes

- fish evolved 530 million years ago

- the genus Homo, which includes Homo sapiens, is about 2 million years old

- reptiles evolved 210 million years after fish

- dinosaurs evolved 230 million years ago

- 4.6 billion years ago, the Earth was born

- plants evolved between the evolution of fish and reptiles

- Pangaea, the supercontinent, broke apart 30 million years after dinosaurs first appeared

- the last glacial period, more commonly called the Ice Age, ended 10 000 years ago

- the first sign of life appeared approximately 1 billion years after the Earth's formation

- Snowball Earth, a period when the Earth was covered in ice, occurred 650 million years ago

ISBN: 978-1-77149-036-8

Yoga:

a Most Healthful Form of Exercise

Sports have always been a popular way to stay in shape. In more recent decades, the increased popularity of aerobic exercise routines has resulted in millions of gyms – equipped with devices such as rowing machines, elliptical trainers, stationary bicycles, treadmills, and "StairMasters" – being built all over the world, and even more millions of aerobic workout DVDs being sold to people who believe that, in order to be healthy, they need to move around a lot. This is not an incorrect assumption; physical movement gets the heart pumping, increasing the amount of oxygen in the blood and turning fat into needed energy. But now some people are turning to another form of exercise that seems quite the opposite of the frantic aerobic workout – but which provides just as many, if not more, health benefits: yoga.

Yoga originated in India centuries ago as a spiritual practice, a type of meditation that was meant to provide the practitioner with a deeper understanding or insight into the nature of our existence. The word "yoga" comes from the Sanskrit (a classical language of India) word yuj, meaning "yoke" – and we take this to mean the coming together of the mind, body, and spirit. To be able to achieve this, inner peace must first be realized, which means that the physical body and the spiritual and mental mind must be trained and disciplined. This used to be done through the practice of "asanas" or postures. These days, these postures form the basis of the exercise we know as yoga.

There are actually many different kinds of yoga. Hatha yoga is perhaps the most well-known and widely practised, with postures that cater to all levels of practitioners. Other yoga styles have developed from this one. Ashtanga yoga involves performing postures in a faster-paced, flowing sequence. Viniyoga involves gentler, synchronizing breathing techniques with the postures. The postures of Kundalini yoga are meant to unlock a powerful energy that is supposed to exist at the base of the spine. Ananda yoga involves hatha yoga poses and meditation, and is meant to promote self-awareness. Jivamukti yoga combines intensely physical postures with chanting and meditation. There are many other forms.

Some of these ancient forms have been adapted and marketed in yoga schools and studios, which are becoming as popular as all the fitness centres we now see, or have even become an integral part of them. For example, Bikram yoga, which is an ancient yoga practice in a heated room,

   ISBN: 978-1-77149-036-8

has now been adapted for modern fitness buffs as "hot yoga". "Power yoga" is a step up from the rigorous Ashtanga postures, making sure you build up a sweat. "Forrest yoga" involves yoga sequences along with other core strengtheners based on a different type of workout called "Pilates".

Recently, people in the United States have started signing up for a new kind of yoga class: Happy Face Yoga. This yoga program consists of a series of 30 facial exercises such as sticking out your tongue, raising your eyebrows, pushing your nose up, and pressing your cheeks in, along with the usual deep breaths and relaxing moments in between. Of course, some people think Happy Face Yoga is just as silly as the faces of the people who are doing it, but let's not forget that just as our bodies have muscles, so do our faces – up to one hundred individual muscles in ten muscle groups.

Whether or not you believe in "facial yoga", the benefits of yoga cannot be disputed: it firms and tones muscles, builds self-esteem, and provides an understanding of anatomy as well as an avenue to personal spirituality, self-reflection, creativity, and imagination. Why not give it a try?

A. Complete the following charts on the different types of yoga.

Ancient Forms	
Type	**Feature**
Viniyoga	
Ashtanga yoga	
Kundalini yoga	
Jivamukti yoga	
Modern Forms	
Type	**Feature**
Power yoga	
Forrest yoga	
Happy Face yoga	

Argumentative Writing

In **argumentative writing**, we try to convince others to agree with us and adopt our way of thinking. We start by stating an argumentative proposition, which sets the tone of the argument and enables the reader to know our stand. In addition to explaining and supporting our proposition with details, evidence, and examples, we should also anticipate and overcome objections that the opposition might raise. Drawing up a chart to compare the two sides of the argument helps us consider how to refute the opposition's arguments.

B. Below are some points about the harmful effects of yoga. Decide on an argumentative proposition related to yoga. Then draw up a chart to compare the two sides of the argument with the information from the passage and the points below. Add some points of your own.

Harmful effects of yoga:

*   common side effects include knee pains and backaches
*   can harm muscles if body is not flexible
*   may cause bone fractures or ruptures
*   some experience adverse gastric or sleep problems after practising yoga
*   may cause frustration for those who fail to do some poses
*   has been reported that one may become more irritable and agitated
*   Kundalini yoga poses done incorrectly can have adverse mental effects
*   instructors might not be fully aware of the techniques

Proposition: _____

For

Against

C. **Based on the chart you developed in (B), write your argumentation.**

_____

_____

_____

_____

_____

_____

_____

_____

_____

_____

_____

_____

_____

_____

_____

_____

_____

_____

_____

_____

_____

Tips for Effective Public Speaking

It has been said that most people fear speaking in front of a large audience even more than death! Whether or not this is really the case, there are many things we can do to help make public speaking a less frightening ordeal for ourselves. Of course, not everyone will have a job or career that requires them to speak to large groups of people, but we can all benefit from feeling comfortable and confident when we speak in groups of any size. Let's not forget that students are required to give presentations in class from time to time, and being mindful of just a few tips for effective public speaking will mean that you can focus your attention on the research, without getting overly anxious about the speaking part to follow.

1. Do your research. (   ) Knowing that you have done your best to know your subject matter will give you the confidence that you know what you are talking about and can answer any questions. This confidence will be evident in the way you act.

2. Know how to organize your thoughts. Every good presentation or speech follows a logical sequence. Your presentation will need an introduction, in which you tell your audience your "thesis statement", possibly with an anecdote the audience can relate to. Next, the body of the speech will contain all the information (with each piece of information stated one at a time, without going back-and-forth) that supports your thesis statement. Last is the conclusion, explaining everything you have just said "in a nutshell". (   )

3. Know your audience. The type of audience you speak to will have an impact on what you say and how you say it. For example, you wouldn't want to give a speech about how you hated school to a group of students! (   ) Use humour when you can, but be careful that any jokes you tell are not rude in any way and are appropriate for your audience.

4. Use visual aids. Make use of visual aids such as PowerPoint to highlight crucial ideas or information. You should arrive early at your venue and, if possible, even run through the use of the equipment with the IT (Information Technology) person on hand – if you are lucky enough to have one. (   )

ISBN: 978-1-77149-036-8

5. Throw in an element of drama. Understand that, as a public speaker, presenter, or debater, you are also an actor. You are not having an ordinary conversation. So, speak with conviction, and with a greater sense of yourself – and perhaps even a bit of drama. People want to hear someone who believes in what they are saying. You should speak clearly, with your chin held high, in order to project your voice out into the room. Understand the importance of pausing for effect. Sometimes a long silence gives people a chance to consider what you have just said. You must be mindful of body language. Make eye contact with your audience, all over the room, and maintain it. Learn how to move about, to walk and hold your arms and hands, and to gesticulate to emphasize a point. (   )

6. Know how to avoid "the jitters". Have you ever started speaking to an audience and then, after about a minute or so, your hands started to shake? This is a common reaction to nervousness, caused by adrenaline coursing through your body. That chemical is really a bodily reaction to stress, stemming from our days as cavemen – the "fight or flight" mechanism in action. Of course, you don't want to do either of these things at the lectern, so here is a tip to help reduce that flow of adrenaline: just before you go on stage, jump up and down very quickly, and open and close your hands very quickly many times, for about 30 seconds to a minute, until the muscles start to feel fatigued. (   )

A.   Each of the following statements goes with a tip mentioned in the preceding passage. Decide on the matching statements and tips. Write the letters in the parentheses where the statements should go.

a.   This will help to avoid any buildup of adrenaline as you start to get into your presentation.

b.   And if the education levels of your audience vary, you may want to choose simpler, less nuanced ways of expressing yourself, and avoid idiomatic expressions.

c.   As the old saying goes: "Say what you are going to say, say it in full, and then say it again."

d.   When it comes to using machinery of any kind in your presentation – Be prepared!

e.   There is no substitute for knowing your topic.

f.   To do this well, you must practise in front of a mirror, or ask people to listen and give you some feedback.

27

Speech Writing

Before you start writing a speech, you have to determine the theme or message that you want to convey, and identify the occasion and audience. Stick to that theme throughout the speech and use the language appropriate for the occasion and audience.

A good speech follows a formal structure:

- Introduction - Explain clearly what the theme of your speech is. To get the audience's attention, you can raise a thought-provoking question or recite a relevant quotation.

- Body - Come up with a list of points that explain and support your theme. Group the points according to common topics, and organize them so that each point builds upon the previous one. Illustrate your points with relevant examples and personal stories.

- Closing - Reinforce the theme by summarizing the main points, and make a conclusion to your speech. You can also end it with another thought-provoking question or get your audience to act on your message.

B. **You are asked to deliver a speech at the opening ceremony of your school's "Share with Others Day". Complete the writing plan below in point form.**

Theme: _____

Occasion: _____

Audience: _____

Introduction: _____

_____

Body: _____

_____

_____

_____

Closing: _____

_____

ISBN: 978-1-77149-036-8

C. **Write a speech based on your writing plan in (B).**

_____

_____

_____

_____

_____

_____

_____

_____

_____

_____

_____

_____

_____

_____

_____

_____

_____

_____

_____

_____

_____

A **Volunteer** and a **Tourist**?

What do a volunteer and a tourist have in common? Nothing. But can you be a volunteer and a tourist at the same time? Absolutely.

Voluntourism – a new trend combining volunteering and tourism – is catching on fast, with more and more people looking for opportunities to help others while visiting interesting places. Louis Palmer, a freshman from the University of Toronto, recently returned from a trip to Guizhou, China. It was not the usual sightseeing trip. Rather, Louis went on a one-week cycling trip through Guizhou organized by Protect the Earth, Protect Yourself (PEPY), a volunteer agency there to help improve the lives of rural children. Louis enjoyed the bike tour, but what was more, he had the chance to pitch in by teaching children at a rural elementary school. Louis's family and friends chipped in to sponsor his bike ride, and the funds collected were also used for building schools in rural areas in Guizhou and buying stationery for children.

Like PEPY, many organizations provide voluntouring projects. Earthwatch, for example, is a non-profit organization focusing on bringing science to life for those concerned about the Earth's future. It offers opportunities for people to join their teams of scientists on a diverse range of projects all over the world. It has also set up "teen teams" whereby young people aged 16 to 17 can work with, and learn from, leading scientists.

On the other hand, Habitat for Humanity, a voluntary agency well known for building houses for the poor and homeless, has developed a voluntouring package for participants to help out in their building projects across the world, mainly in developing countries. They provide affordable housing for the deprived. Jimmy Carter, the former president of the U.S.A., is a regular participant in Habitat for Humanity projects. You don't have to possess building skills to be part of its volunteering team; you can pitch in as long as you know how to hold a paintbrush or a hammer.

But just like in any other field, there are always black sheep that exploit the goodwill of voluntourists. They may come up with phoney schemes, like charging a voluntourist a premium just for a chance to hand out school supplies to children at a remote school. Would-be voluntourists should therefore be scrupulous and check out the organizations before taking part in their programs. Daniela Papi, founder of PEPY, advises anyone interested in voluntourism

ISBN: 978-1-77149-036-8

to do their homework beforehand. "Ask for a list of past participants and their contacts. Any reputable operator should be able to provide you with such a list."

It is not difficult, though, to figure out which organizations are genuine and which are phoney. Genuine voluntourism operators have long-term goals and they regularly assess the success of their projects. These are the ones that you can count on if you are thinking of a voluntour for your next vacation.

A. Check the main idea of each paragraph.

<u>Paragraph 2</u>

A. The definition of voluntourism

B. How Louis Palmer experienced voluntourism in Guizhou, China

<u>Paragraph 3</u>

A. The variety of voluntouring projects organized by Earthwatch

B. The mission of Earthwatch, another organization providing voluntouring projects

<u>Paragraph 4</u>

A. The projects developed by Habitat for Humanity for those interested in voluntouring

B. The projects offered by Habitat for Humanity to those who do not have building skills

<u>Paragraph 5</u>

A. Daniela Papi's advice to would-be voluntourists

B. Beware of phoney voluntouring schemes

B. If you had the chance to go voluntouring, which one of the three volunteer organizations – PEPY, Earthwatch, or Habitat for Humanity – would you join? Explain your choice.

_____

_____

_____

28

Editing

Editing is a very important process to ensure that our writing is the best that we can make it. In editing, we focus on the language (spelling, punctuation, subject–verb agreement, tenses, sentence structures, etc.) and organization of writing.

C.   Edit the following sentences for any language problems.

1.   Even breif periods of voluntouring gives everyone involved insight into the lifes of people in others countries.

_____

_____

2.   According to the travel industry association of America over 55 million American has participate in a voluntouring project.

_____

_____

3.   One-quarter of people planing for a vacation is considering a service-orient one.

_____

_____

4.   Some of the work voluntourists do on their trips include; teaching English, planting trees, build bridges, repairing trail.

_____

_____

5.   Jamie found two organizations who provide voluntouring projects on the internet but neither of them was non-profit organization.

_____

_____

D. Edit the following paragraph focusing on its organization.

Make sure you have a topic sentence, supporting details, and a concluding sentence. Check if there are good transitions between sentences, and cut out redundancy.

PEPY organizes different programs in Cambodia to help foster and improve the education of children in the country, especially those living in the rural areas. The average rural Cambodian is estimated to have 2.94 years of education. The Road-to-Literacy program (RTL) is one of the programs organized by PEPY. This program aims to increase literacy for children in rural Chanleas Dai, Siem Reap Province. As Kofi Annan said, "Literacy is, finally, the road to human progress and the means through which every man, woman, and child can realize his or her full potential." Kofi Annan was the seventh Secretary-General of the United Nations. RTL decided to create a school-based library for students of the Poverty Reduction Strategy (PRS) of Cambodia. A group of volunteers cleaned up and renovated a room with books originally donated by Room to Read, a non-governmental organization. This room was previously locked most of the time in fear that the books might get ruined or stolen. The library is now brightened and more donated books have been added. It opens during school hours. Teachers can arrange library classes to incorporate more books into their curriculum. Students are encouraged to read more. Library use has largely increased since the renovation.

_____

_____

_____

_____

_____

_____

_____

ISBN: 978-1-77149-036-8

Creating Canada

In 1867, three colonies in British North America united to form the Dominion of Canada. Confederation, the act of uniting the colonies, was the result of both internal and external factors. Other colonies joined later.

A. **Read about some of the factors that led to the Confederation of Canada. Match the factors with the descriptions. Then identify the internal and external factors and answer the question.**

Political Deadlock American Civil War Fenian* Raids
Repeal of the Corn Laws Transcontinental Railway
Reciprocity Treaty Abrogation Manifest Destiny

* Fenians:

an Irish Republican organization founded in the United States

Factors that Led to the Confederation of Canada:

A

It was a belief held by many in the United States that it was their destiny to expand throughout the continent and assimilate the surrounding colonies.

B

A built-up military presence in the U.S. North, and the fact that Britain had supported the U.S. South in the war, made the colonies fear retaliation.

C

Canada East and Canada West were given equal representation in the elected assembly of the new Province of Canada. They could not make political decisions because each colony would oppose the other.

D

The 1854 free-trade agreement between British North American colonies and the United States ended, triggering economic uncertainty in some colonies.

E

A railway to connect eastern and western colonies would make transporting people and goods easier, but it would not be easy to build without a central government.

F
British North American colonies were targets of small attacks from Irish-Americans wanting to end British rule in Ireland and in British North America.

G
Agricultural trade between Britain and its colonies had once been favourable for the colonies, with non-colonial countries being charged a tariff – but that was gone.

Confederation of Canada

internal factors: ◯ ◯ ◯

external factors: ◯ ◯ ◯ ◯

Do you think the events and policies in the United States played an important role in the formation of the Dominion of Canada? Why?

_____

_____

_____

B. **Fill in the blanks to complete the paragraph about the history of Canada's first provinces.**

	Nova Scotia	Upper	Province	Quebec
Ontario	Lower	colonies	New Brunswick	Dominion

The Confederation of Canada was the union of three British North American 1._____ . Areas across the land were still being developed and established in the early years, and would undergo a few name changes. Canada East and Canada West, formerly known as 2._____ Canada and 3._____ Canada, were known for a few years as the 4._____ of Canada. This colony, along with the colonies 5._____ and 6._____, came together in 1867. With Confederation, Nova Scotia and New Brunswick kept their names as new provinces of Canada. Canada East became the province of 7._____ and Canada West the province of 8._____ . These three colonies became the four provinces that made up the 9._____ of Canada.

Expansion of Canada

1850 – 1890

Canada was already a large country at the time of Confederation. In the years after Confederation, Canada expanded and grew even more, and the map of Canada changed drastically.

A. Fill in the blanks to complete the timeline. Use the abbreviations to help write the provinces and territories. Then write the year that each map represents.

Red River   Britain   Confederation   Rupert's Land   Dominion

1867

_____ (ON), _____ (QC), _____ (NS), and _____ (NB)

- Four provinces united to form the Dominion of Canada, an event called _____ .

1869

An organized group of Métis, concerned about their land rights and way of life, formed the _____ Resistance. Their resistance delayed Canada from taking control of Rupert's Land until 1870.

1870

_____ (NT)

- Canada bought _____ from the Hudson's Bay Company and renamed it.

_____ (MB)

- This province was established as a small square around the Red River.

1871

_____ (BC)

- Canada promised a rail link across the _____, convincing the people of this colony to become a part of Canada.

1873

_____ (PEI)

- As part of the deal that brought this colony into the union, Canada bought the land back from landowners in _____ so the residents could now own the land.

ISBN: 978-1-77149-036-8

1.

Canada in _____

2.

Canada in _____

B.   Fill in the blanks to learn more about the events in Canada after Confederation.

Canadian Pacific
Supreme Court   Indian Act

In 1875, Canada established its own _____ . Prior to this, Canadians had to travel to London, England for a high court decision. The formation of the court allowed room for the important function of interpreting division of powers between the federal and provincial governments in Canada.

The _____ of 1876 helped curtail resistance to settlers by the original habitants. This Act limited First Nations peoples to small parcels of land and denied them important aspects of their cultural heritage.

In 1881, the _____ Railway was formed. It was the promised connection of British Columbia, and all the former colonies, to the rest of Canada. The rail line was completed in 1885, successfully making Canada accessible across the country, from "sea to sea".

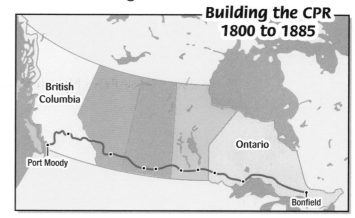

Building the CPR
1800 to 1885

Events and Development of Early Canada

1850 – 1890

Canada's creation and expansion involved many events and developments that impacted communities and groups. Each development had complications as the groups did not always agree.

A. **Identify which communities or groups these developments would have involved. Write the letters.**

A politicians   **B** First Nations   **C** settlers

D Chinese labourers   **E** Métis   **F** business people

Building the Canadian Pacific Railway

Communities/Groups Involved
☐ ☐ ☐ ☐

The CPR was promised by the federal government to bring colonies into Canada and unify the nation. It would provide quick, safe, long-distance travel. The competition to secure the contract to build the railway was fierce. The construction was difficult and expensive, and required thousands of labourers to accomplish the task.

Settlement of the Northwest

Communities/Groups Involved
☐ ☐ ☐ ☐

Canada had planned to take over this enormous area since Confederation. Many people wanted to push settlement west after Confederation and put pressure on their leaders to make it happen. Control of this area was necessary as it would allow passage to the other side of the country, keeping it out of the hands of the Americans. The government had to negotiate with the people who resided in these lands.

Creation of the North West Mounted Police

Communities/Groups Involved
☐ ☐ ☐

They patrolled Manitoba and the region that would become Alberta and Saskatchewan. They were few but effective. Their duties included aiding settlers, helping First Nations peoples transition to reserves, resolving small disputes, and fighting in small wars. The government could not have controlled such a vast space without them.

ISBN: 978-1-77149-036-8

B. **Read the points of view of each side of the Red River Resistance. Write the letters on the side that they belong. Then answer the question.**

Red River Resistance – Points of View

The Red River Resistance was the first crisis that the Canadian government had to deal with after Confederation. With the purchase of Rupert's Land from the Hudson's Bay Company in 1869, the Canadian government faced a lot of resistance from the organized Métis, under the leadership of Louis Riel, living in the area. The result of the conflict was the formation of the province of Manitoba. Although at the time it was only a small-sized settlement around the Red River, it was politically equal to Ontario and Quebec.

A There is plenty of room for more settlers.

B Our unique culture, a mix of Cree and French-Canadian ancestry, will disappear if it is not protected.

C We have rights and we want to keep them!

D The Red River settlement is a part of Rupert's Land that was purchased by the Canadian government.

E The land around the Red River is perfect for farming; it will be beneficial for many!

F The United States will take over this land if we don't start surveying now.

G The Canadian government didn't consult us as to what will happen to this land.

H We've been on this land for generations!

Métis

Government/ Settlers

Why do you think it was important for Manitoba to be politically equal to Ontario and Quebec although it was only a fraction of their size?

_____

_____

Distinguished Canadians

1850 – 1890

Many individuals and groups have helped shape Canada into what it is today. Many have fought for the abolition of slavery, improving work conditions for labourers, and for their peoples' rights.

A.   Fill in the blanks and identify the individuals who helped shape Canada.

resistance   prime minister
anti-slavery   Nova Scotia   medical

**Louis Riel   John A. Macdonald
Emily Stowe**

1. He was a politician who argued for the unification of the colonies. He became Canada's first _____ . He played a pivotal role in Canada's formation and early expansion.

2. He was a Maritime politician who tried to keep _____ from Confederation. As the owner of a major newspaper, his influence was wide. He eventually joined Canada's federal cabinet.

    Joseph Howe

3. She was the first female doctor to practise in Canada, despite being denied access to _____ school for being a woman. She was a life-long advocate of women's rights.

4. He was a leader of the Métis of the Red River. He led his people through _____ and rebellion, fighting to preserve their rights and heritage. He was also a founder of Manitoba.

5. She was an educator, newspaper editor, and lawyer, as well as a widowed mother. She was black, and dedicated her work and life to _____ and women's rights.

    Mary Ann Shadd

ISBN: 978-1-77149-036-8

B. **Match the groups that played a part in Canada's development with the descriptions. Then circle the correct words and answer the question.**

Chinese railway workers   Métis nation   Knights of Labor
Underground Railroad   Women's Christian Temperance Union

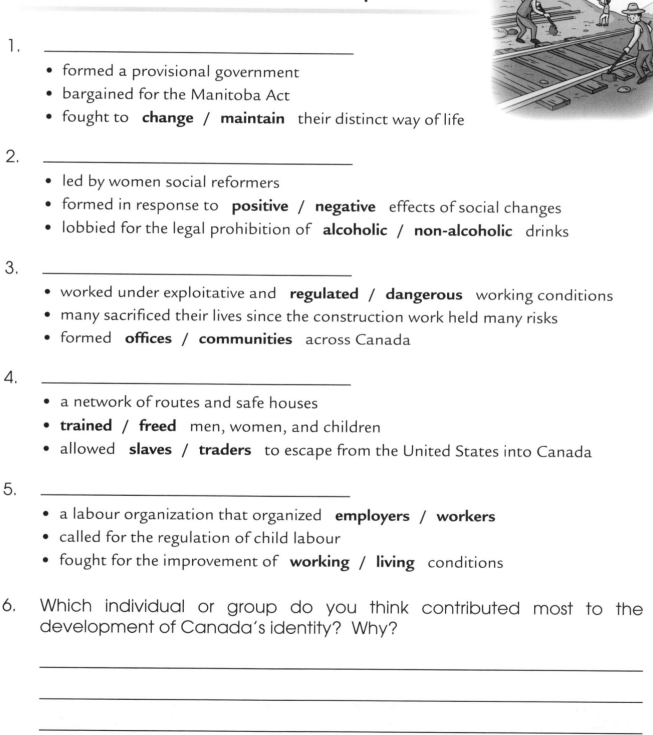

1. _____

   • formed a provisional government
   • bargained for the Manitoba Act
   • fought to **change / maintain** their distinct way of life

2. _____

   • led by women social reformers
   • formed in response to **positive / negative** effects of social changes
   • lobbied for the legal prohibition of **alcoholic / non-alcoholic** drinks

3. _____

   • worked under exploitative and **regulated / dangerous** working conditions
   • many sacrificed their lives since the construction work held many risks
   • formed **offices / communities** across Canada

4. _____

   • a network of routes and safe houses
   • **trained / freed** men, women, and children
   • allowed **slaves / traders** to escape from the United States into Canada

5. _____

   • a labour organization that organized **employers / workers**
   • called for the regulation of child labour
   • fought for the improvement of **working / living** conditions

6. Which individual or group do you think contributed most to the development of Canada's identity? Why?

   _____

   _____

   _____

ISBN: 978-1-77149-036-8

Social, Economic, and Political Changes

1850 – 1890

The late 1800s saw many changes in Canada. The technological advancements from the Industrial Revolution affected almost every aspect of daily life. Social and economic changes from events and developments like Confederation shaped this young country and led to political and legal actions that further impacted Canada.

A. **Fill in the blanks to learn how the Industrial Revolution affected the development of Canada.**

First Nations   transportation
wheat   changed   railway
jobless   Industrial   immigration

The latter half of the 1800s was a period of profound change in Canada, due in many ways to the 1._____ Revolution. In Europe, the Revolution created efficient factory production which left many people 2._____ . In search of better opportunities, people moved to Canada. The invention of the steam engine made 3._____ faster and easier both on land and on sea, increasing 4._____ to Canada. As the immigration rate grew, more people moved west, which increased the need for a 5._____ . The railway moved settlers across the country and made living in the west more attractive and practical. The railway also made it easier to transport goods such as 6._____ and timber.

However, the Industrial Revolution negatively affected the 7._____ peoples and the Métis. More people in the west meant fewer buffalo for the First Nations peoples and the Métis. The increase in population depleted the First Nations peoples' and the Métis' main food sources and also changed their environment. This significantly 8._____ their way of life.

ISBN: 978-1-77149-036-8

B. **Identify the policy and acts. Then write the letters to show the causation for each chain of events.**

Political and legal actions happen due to needs or wants of the public, and these actions have impact.

Policy or Act

National Policy   **British North America Act**
Indian Act   **Chinese Immigration Act**

1.

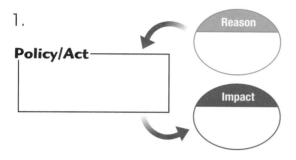

Policy/Act

Reason

Impact

A For the British North American colonies to unite under one constitution, they needed a set of rules for the new dominion that they could all agree on.

B The new Canadian federal government and the provinces distributed power and responsibilities.

2.

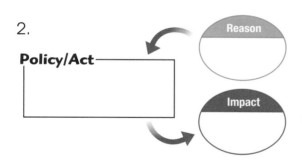

Policy/Act

Reason

Impact

A The government gained control over many aspects of First Nations life, from government to education, and even the practice of cultural traditions.

B The Canadian government thought First Nations peoples should give up their culture and assimilate into the rest of society.

3.

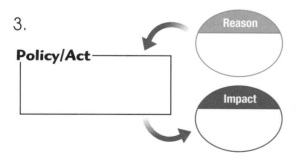

Policy/Act

Reason

Impact

A Protective taxes on imported products were introduced, immigration rates rose, and the Canadian Pacific Railway was built.

B John A. Macdonald's political party needed a plan that would develop and expand the Canadian economy, and help them win the 1878 election.

4.

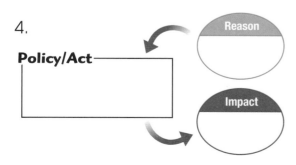

Policy/Act

Reason

Impact

A This Act imposed unaffordable entry tax. Immigration was severely limited, and those already in Canada were unable to bring family members over.

B Once the railway was completed, the Canadian government wanted to restrict Chinese immigration.

Conflict and Cooperation (1)

Conflict between groups is a normal aspect of development. Looking at significant conflicts between 1850 and 1890, we can often see how and why Canada is what it is today. However, there are also examples of different groups coming together to achieve a common goal.

A. **Read about the conflicts. Put the parties concerned on the appropriate sides.**

Equal Representation Representation by Population	Métis Canadian Government	Confederationists Anti-Confederationists

1. Conflict Over Settling Land in North Western Canada

_____

- wanted to keep their unique culture and way of life
- concerned about the decline of buffalo – a staple food in their diet

VS.

_____

- had to send in settlers quickly before the United States claimed the land
- knew buffalo and farmland could not co-exist

2. Conflict Over Confederation

_____

- a central, federal government would be destructive to the power of individual colonies
- some colonies identified better as part of the United States or Britain than as a province of Canada

VS.

_____

- a national railway would be built
- it would be easier to trade between colonies

3. The Debate Over Division of Power in the Government

Supporters of _____

Each side would have representatives based on their numbers. The side with a larger population would have more representatives, and more power. Without this method, there is no room for a majority or decisions to be made, which may lead to a political deadlock.

VS.

Supporters of _____

Equal representation has been in place since Canada East and West united. It would mean that there is an equal number of representatives for each side. Without it, some sides would not have enough representation to have a say.

ISBN: 978-1-77149-036-8

B. Fill in the blanks to learn about an important example of cooperation in Canada's history. Then answer the question.

The Great Coalition

Conferences	George Brown	political
Confederation	cooperation	unification
	social Maritime	

There were many conflicts in Canada's early history, but there were also instances of 1._____ .

One of the most significant alliances in Canada's formation is what is known as the Great Coalition. Three 2._____ parties, each with a different view on many political and 3._____ issues, came together because they agreed strongly on one objective: Confederation. John A. Macdonald of the Liberal Conservatives, 4._____ of the Clear Grits, and George-Étienne Cartier of Parti Bleu led the conferences that convinced two 5._____ provinces, New Brunswick and Nova Scotia, to eventually join them.

In the end, it took three politicians who saw the importance of cooperation to start a conversation on the 6._____ of Canada. The Charlottetown, Quebec, and London 7._____ were held to conduct speeches and debates regarding this issue. This coalition eventually led to Canada's 8._____ .

Province House, Prince Edward Island
Location of 1864 Charlottetown Conference –
the "Birthplace of Canada"

9. Although all three leaders had the same objective, why do you think it took three conferences before the alliance known as the Great Coalition was formed?

_____

_____

_____

1890 – 1914

The Underprivileged in Canada

Industrialization affected different groups in Canada. Poor community members of urban cities such as the unemployed and the elderly were particularly vulnerable to the negative consequences of urban growth.

A. Fill in the blanks. Then answer the questions.

Toronto's Urban Poor in the Late 1800s

> **poor overcrowded poverty industrialization agricultural higher accommodations sanitation**

1._____ in urban areas in Canada emerged rapidly as urban cities grew in the late 1800s. 2._____ , the sharp increase in population, and lack of jobs in the rural 3._____ sector had negative effects on many urban dwellers.

Toronto's 4._____ and unemployed population, for example, often had to huddle in small, one-room, low-rent 5._____ in increasingly poor neighbourhoods. Lack of proper 6._____ , morality, and space led to the prevalence of diseases and alcoholism, and a 7._____ crime rate. There was also a correlation between 8._____ dwellings and mental illness among the urban poor.

9. Why do you think the population increased in big cities like Toronto in the late 1800s?

_____

_____

10. Compare the urban dwellers in Toronto in the 1800s to today's. Write one similarity and one difference between them.

Similarity: _____

Difference: _____

B.   Read the passage. Then answer the questions.

Help for the Elderly

In Canada, the elderly poor became an issue in the late 19th and early 20th century. As industrialization swept across the country, more and more people moved into cities to work in warehouses and factories. This meant the loss of the rural agricultural life and it greatly affected the elderly. People who lived on farms worked there until they were old. Then the farm and the work were passed down to the next generation, with the elderly being taken care of by their families. The farm was also a self-sustaining source of income. Thus, the elderly had income and family support.

In the cities, however, wages were low and the family unit collapsed. The elderly who could not work had neither money nor family to continually support them. More and more seniors ended up in poorhouses or begging for charity.

The government believed that supporting the elderly was a family responsibility. However, as the elderly were recognized as a distinct group, people became more aware of their plight. In 1908, the Government Annuities Act was introduced. It was not successful though, as people had to purchase these government annuities and most elderly could not afford them. This period was particularly difficult for them. It was not until 1926 that the first old age pension was enacted.

1.   How did industrialization affect the elderly?

_____

_____

2.   What role did the government play in the plight of the elderly?

_____

_____

_____

3.   In what way are the elderly treated better today than those in the early 20th century?

_____

_____

_____

1890 – 1914

Changes in Canada

From 1890 to 1914, Canada grew in size and population. With this growth came political and legal changes, as well as social and economic changes. These changes affected everyone in society; even children were affected when developments concerning them were specifically put in place.

A.   Fill in the blanks.   Then match the changes with their effects.   Write the letters.

Political and Legal   Social and Economic

Effects

1.   Changes: _____

- Klondike Gold Rush → **Effect**

- reciprocity → **Effect**

2.   Changes: _____

- increase in Chinese head tax → **Effect**

- creation of Alberta and Saskatchewan as provinces → **Effect**

- federal Department of Labour → **Effect**

- Alaska boundary dispute resolution → **Effect**

A This change caused a steep decline in Chinese immigration due to prohibitive costs, causing separation of families.

B It caused mass immigration, mainly from the United States, to the Yukon, and led to the formation of the Yukon Territory in 1898.

C Britain voted in favour of the United States instead of Canada, causing Canada to become angry toward Britain and consider self-governance.

D It was created in response to the formation of labour unions. It helped resolve disputes between unions and employers.

E The government collected taxes from the growing population of these provinces and provided services in return.

F Prime Minister Wilfrid Laurier negotiated lower tariffs on American goods, which many Canadians were opposed to. This eventually contributed to his election loss in 1911.

ISBN: 978-1-77149-036-8

B. Fill in the blanks to learn about the changes that specifically affected children in Canada. Then identify each sentence as "Cause", "Development", or "Result".

1. **inequality orphans ill-treatment**

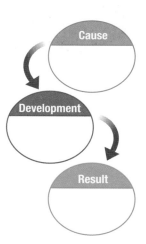

(A) Britain created the Home Children program which sent _____ or children from poor families to British colonies.

(B) A combination of pollution, poverty, and social _____ created dreadful circumstances in Britain, particularly for children.

(C) From 1869 to the early 1940s, approximately 118 000 Home Children came to Canada, and were offered as indentured workers. It was later revealed that many suffered from _____ .

2. **labour foster protection**

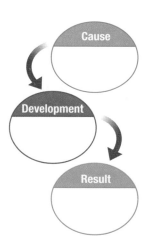

(A) Exploitation of children for their _____ , the increase in children without families, and the growing number of children living on the streets led to the call for children's _____ .

(B) Children were protected under new laws and found placement in _____ homes when necessary.

(C) Children's Aid Societies were founded across Canada.

3. **residential culture identity**

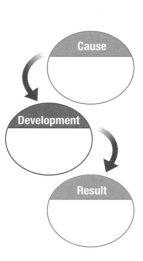

(A) New generations of First Nations peoples and Métis were separated from the older generations, resulting in the loss of their language and cultural _____ .

(B) The number of _____ schools for First Nations and Métis children increased to assimilate the children into the now European-dominant Canadian society.

(C) A massive influx of immigrants spread across western Canada, encroaching on the _____ of the First Nations.

1890 – 1914

Diverse Faces of Canada

There were many reasons why people wanted to leave their home countries for Canada. The diverse cultures and faces that made up Canada was the result of people from all over the world coming to Canada.

A. **Draw lines to match the groups with their common reasons for leaving their home countries.**

Americans •

Europeans
Asians •

Mormons
Jews
Doukhobors •

• populations in older countries were growing, leading to poverty and overcrowding

• possible persecution based on religion or beliefs

• best homestead lands in newer countries were already claimed

B. **Fill in the blanks to complete the paragraph. Then label the map and answer the questions.**

encouraged   settle   ethnic   immigration   Britain

Canada's _____ policy was exceptionally open when Clifford Sifton was Laurier's Minister of Interior. He _____ immigrants to come to Canada. He wanted people to come from parts of the world besides _____ because he believed they were the type of people that could _____ the land. As a result, a large number of immigrants of various _____ backgrounds came and settled in Canada during this period.

Ethnic Backgrounds of Canadians in 1911	
Asian	1%
British	55%
First Nations	2%
French	28%
German	6%
Russian	1%
Other European	6%
Other	1%

ISBN: 978-1-77149-036-8

Origins of Canada's Immigrants in 1911

China   Finland   Germany   Britain
Hungary   Italy   Japan   Poland   Russia
Sweden   Ukraine   United States

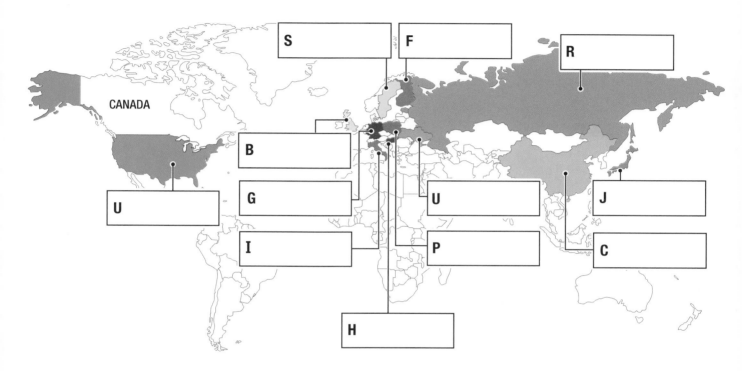

1. Which two ethnic backgrounds made up the highest percentage of the Canadian population in 1911? Why?

    _____

    _____

2. What countries could the "other European" population originate from?

    _____

    _____

3. How did the influx of immigrants affect the First Nations population?

    _____

    _____

1890 – 1914

Groups in Action

Between 1890 and 1914, many changes happened in Canada. This period saw high population growth and growing industrialization, which changed the way people worked. The women's suffrage movement was active during these years because women's right to vote was a big issue at the time.

A.   Fill in the blanks.   Then write a sentence to describe each term.

> government   unions   unify   workers   cheap   industrialization

In the 19th century, workers were underpaid, overworked, and overlooked. They formed labour 1._____ to strengthen their unity against their employers.   Labour unions represented and furthered the interest of the workers. For many, improved working conditions could save lives. The central labour organization was the Trades and Labour Congress of Canada, which aimed to 2._____ unionists across the country.

Labour unions fought an uphill battle because industry owners had both the legal system and the 3._____ on their side.   Their efforts were also set back by employers who found a source of 4._____ and willing labour in new immigrants to Canada.

In 1889, the federal government established the Royal Commission on the Relations of Labour and Capital.   It looked into the working conditions in Canada and made recommendations for improvement.   It recorded the impact of 5._____ , and recognized unions as a proper form of organization for workers.   However, the government was reluctant to act on these recommendations.   More recognition for the labour issue came in 1894, on the first Monday of September, when Canada celebrated its first Labour Day, the national holiday recognizing 6._____ .

7. labour unions _____

Trades and Labour
Congress of Canada _____

B. **Read the passage. Then answer the questions.**

"*Suffrage*" *means the right to vote in an election.*

The Women's Suffrage Movement

There were many organizations that fought for change. Besides labour unions, which fought for the rights of workers, the women's suffrage movement fought a long and hard battle for women's rights in Canada. Women did not have the right to vote in Canada and many suffragist groups were formed to fight for this right. The suffrage movement gained valuable support from the National Council of Women of Canada (NCWC) – a respected and influential advocacy group for women and children which was founded in 1893 and is still active today – when it spoke out for suffrage. In Manitoba, one suffragist group gained national attention by selling tickets to a mock legislative debate called "The Women's Parliament" to raise funds for their cause. The debate portrayed a make-believe country where men want the right to vote, and all of the political positions were occupied by women.

Women did not gain the right to vote in federal elections in Canada until 1918. The voting right, however, was not extended to all women; even for men, the privilege to vote depended on a person's ethnic background. At the provincial level, women's suffrage succeeded first in Manitoba in 1916. Women in Quebec were the worst off, being denied the right to vote by male legislators and leaders of the Catholic Church until 1940. Despite being extended the right to vote, however, women were not welcomed right away into positions in parliament.

1. Summarize the women's suffrage movement.

    _____

    _____

    _____

2. How did the women and their movements from this period contribute to women's rights then and now?

    Then: _____

    _____

    Now: _____

    _____

Individuals Making a Difference

Many individuals impacted and shaped Canada during 1890 – 1914. They came from many disciplines, and left their marks in various ways.

A. Match the information with the correct persons.

A was an Onondaga from the Six Nations of the Grand River First Nation Indian reserve

B died while still in office as the Leader of the Opposition

C wrote 20 novels, most of which were set in her home province of PEI

D had a political career and was a member of the Alberta Legislature for five years

E invented the gramophone, telephone, and the metal detector

Five Important Persons Who Shaped Canada during 1890 – 1914:

L. M. Montgomery

* _____
* helped her husband with his ministerial duties and ran the family home while maintaining her writing career
* lived in Ontario from 1911 until her death in 1942

Nellie McClung

* a suffragist, feminist, and social activist
* the author of 16 books on different topics, ranging from gambling to women's suffrage
* _____

Tom Longboat

* _____
* forced to attend residential school at age 12
* the 1907 Boston Marathon winner, setting a record time that was faster than any of the previous winners of the event

Wilfrid Laurier

* elected as the seventh prime minister and the first French-Canadian prime minister
* an astonishing and powerful speaker
* _____

Alexander Graham Bell

* an American citizen born in Scotland and resided in Canada
* _____
* a founding member of the National Geographic Society

   ISBN: 978-1-77149-036-8

B. **Read about two Canadian poets. Write three similarities and three differences between them. Then answer the question.**

Pauline Johnson

Emily Pauline Johnson was born in 1861 to an English mother and a Mohawk chief father. Known as Pauline, she started writing poetry in her teens. It was unusual for a woman to have such a career. She toured throughout Canada, the United States, and England. Pauline's poems reflected both her Mohawk and English heritage, but they were also patriotic to Canada. She was well-known for her performances, and she was able to support herself with her career until her death in 1913.

Émile Nelligan

Émile Nelligan was born in 1879 to a French-Canadian mother and an Irish-immigrant father. Against his parents' wishes, Émile was only interested in writing poetry. His poems were romantic and full of symbolism. They were published to high acclaim, and Émile earned an income publishing poems. Unfortunately, Émile's career was very short. After writing 170 poems between the ages of 16 and 19, Émile was admitted to an asylum for the mentally ill. He lived there without writing any more poetry and died in 1941.

Similarities

- _____
- _____
- _____

Differences

- _____
- _____
- _____

In what way did Pauline Johnson contribute to Canadian heritage and identity?

_____
_____

1890 – 1914

Conflict and Cooperation (2)

The growth and change that occurred in Canada from 1890 to 1914 was not without conflict. Tension between French and British interests grew while pre-existing conflicts, like those between workers and employers, intensified. However, there were displays of cooperation as well. New immigrants to the Canadian Prairies, for example, relied on one another for successful settlements.

A. Identify the group on each side of the conflict.

A French   C miners
B British   D mine owners

1. **Manitoba Schools Question**

We were here before Manitoba was a province and our language is supposed to be protected!

A single school system would suit us better, and we are in the majority.

2. **Naval Service Act**

It is our duty to provide what we can for the British Royal Navy. The threat from Germany is real! They may take over the seas!

If we use our resources to support Britain's navy, what will we do when we receive threats of our own? We need our own navy!

3. **Vancouver Island Coal Mine Strike**

You won't work? We will replace you with cheaper labour. Demonstrations won't help!

Long hours, low pay, and hundreds of miners killed in accidents! This is not a fair or safe working environment. We're going on strike!

4. **Boer War**

We must show loyalty to Great Britain. It is also a chance to show the world what Canada can do!

We should not be Britain's puppet! The war is too far – South Africa! And it isn't even our war!

ISBN: 978-1-77149-036-8

B.   Read the paragraphs. Then answer the questions.

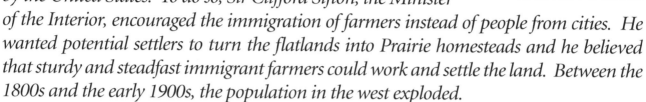

Settling the Canadian Prairies

Settling the West was important to keep it from being claimed by the United States. To do so, Sir Clifford Sifton, the Minister of the Interior, encouraged the immigration of farmers instead of people from cities. He wanted potential settlers to turn the flatlands into Prairie homesteads and he believed that sturdy and steadfast immigrant farmers could work and settle the land. Between the 1800s and the early 1900s, the population in the west exploded.

Immigrants came from all over Europe: Britain, Ukraine, Germany, Hungary, and Scandinavia. They had a lot of work to do and survival could not have been possible without cooperation among them. The settlers were all farmers so they shared agricultural and labour skills and lived similar rural lifestyles. If a family was in trouble, neighbours would step in and lend a hand. Many of the immigrants came from areas close to one another so they also shared a language. For example, immigrants from Belgium settled in French communities since they spoke the same language. There were also public places in which settlers could come together and socialize.

Many of these cultures formed block settlements which were areas where groups of a particular ethnic background had gathered together. Incoming immigrants knew where they could settle and this made it easier for them to adapt and adjust to life in their new homeland.

1.   Why did Sir Clifford Sifton prefer immigrant farmers to city dwellers?

   _____

   _____

2.   What did the new immigrants have in common?

   _____

   _____

3.   In what ways did the immigrants help one another in settling the Prairies?

   _____

   _____

ISBN: 978-1-77149-036-8

GEOGRAPHY

Physical Environment and Human Settlements

Various factors of the physical environment affect people's decision of settling in a place. Many of these factors also shape human settlements and form patterns. There are three main types of settlement patterns: linear, scattered, and clustered.

A. Circle the correct words to show how physical environments affect human settlements.

Landforms

- People tend to settle in low-lying areas with flat land that is ideal for agricultural purposes.
- Rugged mountains are **favourable** / **not favourable** for human settlements.

Soil Types

- Different types of soil are suitable for growing different crops, which is a crucial factor that **miners** / **farmers** have to consider.

Close Proximity to Waterways

- Settlements close to oceans have access to fish as a **power** / **food** source.
- Being near bodies of water also favours the transportation of people and goods.
- Settlements are built near **freshwater** / **saltwater** sources such as rivers and lakes for easy access to water for daily use and irrigation.

Availability of Natural Resources

- **Wood** / **Oil** can be used to build houses.
- Coal and **metal** / **oil** can be the power sources for homes, farms, and factories.
- Other natural resources provide job opportunities in **tourism** / **mining**.

Climate

- Most people prefer a **cold** / **mild** climate to an extreme one.
- This is a particularly important factor for those who rely on **farming** / **manufacturing** to make a living.

Vegetation

- An area with lots of hardwood trees provides **leaves** / **wood** for building houses.
- An area covered by large areas of **grassland** / **shrubs** is ideal for raising farm animals.

ISBN: 978-1-77149-036-8

B. **Identify and write the type of settlement pattern each map shows and match the patterns with the descriptions. Then answer the question.**

Types of Settlement Patterns

linear   clustered   scattered

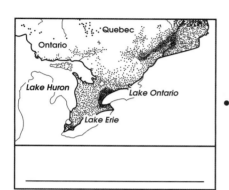

_____

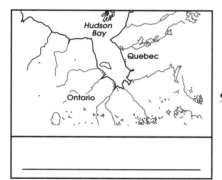

_____

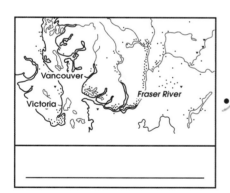

_____

clustered

scattered

linear

• This pattern has individual buildings spread out, and is usually found in rural areas, where resources are limited and can only support a small number of people.

• This pattern has buildings that follow a natural or human-made line, such as a river, a railway, or a shoreline.

• This pattern occurs when a lot of people gather in a place that is rich in resources. This is a high density area, usually with high-rise and multi-family buildings.

Do some research. Give one example of a city or town in Canada for each type of settlement pattern.

Examples of the Three Types of Settlement Patterns:

linear: _____Victoria a ah..._____

clustered: _____Toronto_____

scattered: _____Ottawa   Ontario Essex_____

Global Human Settlement Patterns

The world's population is unevenly distributed. There are places that are densely populated and others that are sparsely populated. Some places are uninhabitable because of hostile physical environments.

A. Match the terms with their definitions. Then answer the question.

population density •

population distribution •

• how people are spread out within an area or across the world

• the number of people living per unit area, such as per square kilometre, of a given place

Which one above assumes that the population is evenly distributed within an area?

_____

B. Find the population density of the two countries. Then describe them.

	Canada	Singapore
Population (Feb 2015)	35 622 082	5 448 991
Area (km²)	9 984 670	718
Population Density (no. of people/km²)		

Population Density

$$= \frac{\text{no. of people in an area}}{\text{area in km}^2}$$

high:
greater than 150 people/km²

moderate:
between 50 and 150 people/km²

low:
fewer than 50 people/km²

Canada : _____ population density

Singapore: _____ population density

ISBN: 978-1-77149-036-8

C. **Read the descriptions and label the choropleth map*. Then circle the correct answers and answer the questions.**

* A choropleth map is usually used to show population density. The darker the colour is, the higher the population density.

Population Density
Bangladesh: 1257 people/km²   Spain: 94 people/km²
Greenland: 0 people/km²   Brazil: 23 people/km²

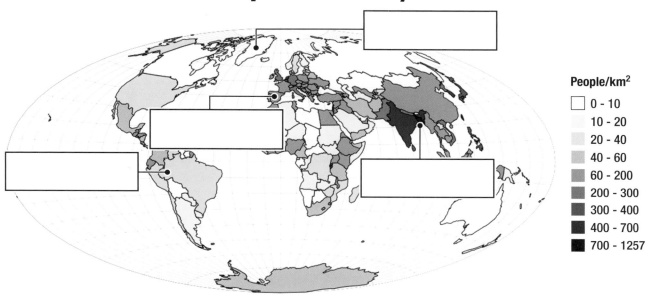

World Population Density 2013

People/km²
☐ 0 - 10
10 - 20
20 - 40
40 - 60
60 - 200
200 - 300
300 - 400
400 - 700
700 - 1257

1. a. densely populated region: **North America / North Asia / South Asia**

    b. sparsely populated region: **Australia / Central America / Southeast Asia**

2. What physical factors do you think account for the low population density of Greenland?

_____

_____

3. Why do you think places with population density much higher than that of Bangladesh, like Singapore, are not shown on the map above?

_____

_____

Global Settlement Trends

Urbanization has been a global settlement trend for decades. Canada, with its immigration policy and the resulting fast-growing population, is one of the most urbanized countries in the world.

A. Fill in the blanks to learn about urbanization. Then answer the questions.

> urbanization decline growing
> cities unplanned rural sustainable
> outward degradation inequality

Urbanization

People are in constant motion. One of the most common and significant moves globally is the migration from 1._____ to urban centres. This often takes place within a country, or even within a small region. More and more people leave villages and farms to live in 2._____ . The result is a global trend toward increased 3._____ , very often with rural land being converted to urban areas, and existing urban spaces expanding 4._____ .

According to the United Nations, less than 30% of the world's population lived in urban settlements in 1950, but in 2014, the urban population increased to 54%, and this percentage is 5._____ . Asia and Africa together have almost 90% of the world's rural population, but with increased urbanization in these regions, the rural population is expected to 6._____ . Rapid and 7._____ urban expansion poses great challenges to the 8._____ development of cities. There are different forms of pollution and environmental 9._____ , and many poor urban dwellers face 10._____ and live in sub-standard conditions.

ISBN: 978-1-77149-036-8

11. What do you think the global trend of human settlements will be in ten years? Why?

_____

_____

_____

12. Why do you think many urban dwellers live in sub-standard conditions?

_____

_____

_____

B. Read the graph. Then answer the question.

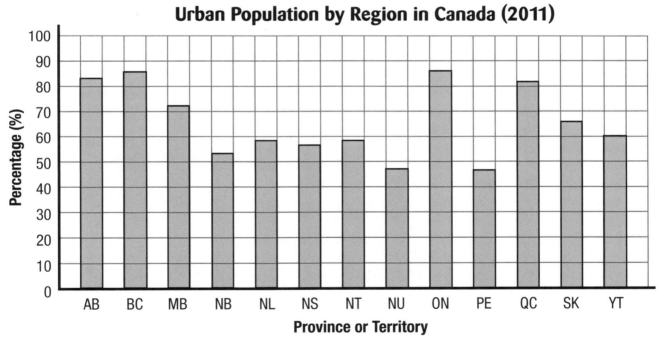

Urban Population by Region in Canada (2011)

Y-axis: Percentage (%)
X-axis: Province or Territory (AB, BC, MB, NB, NL, NS, NT, NU, ON, PE, QC, SK, YT)

From the graph above, what can you tell about urbanization in Canada?

_____

_____

ISBN: 978-1-77149-036-8

Impact of Human Settlements

Human settlements, wherever they are, involve the conversion of land use. They, together with the results of human activities and the generation of waste and garbage, have great impact on the environment.

A. **Complete the flow chart to learn about some ways in which human settlements affect the environment.**

Pesticides
Deforestation
Wildlife Habitat Loss
Water Pollution
Desertification

Human Settlements

1. _____
To meet the needs of the population, land is cleared by removing trees in forests.

2. _____
With the forests gone, animals are often forced to move elsewhere. Some species have even become extinct.

Agricultural Land Use
Some land is converted to farms to provide food for people.

3. _____
These are used to ensure a high yield.

Soil Contamination
Chemicals from pesticides enter the soil and contaminate it.

4. _____
Rainwater and water used for irrigation is drained into nearby bodies of water after coming into contact with contaminated soil.

Unsustainable Farming Practices
An example of this is intensive farming, in which farmers use any method and as many inputs as they can to increase the yields of crops.

5. _____
Unsustainable farming practices rob the soil of its nutrients. Wind and water cause further damage by carrying away the top layer of soil, leaving behind an infertile mixture of sand and dust.

ISBN: 978-1-77149-036-8

B. Fill in the blanks to learn more about the impact of human settlements. Then answer the question.

Impact of Human Settlements

radioactive   pollutants
aquatic   garbage   roads
smog   contaminate
industrial   vehicle

Human settlements often result in large scale
1._____ development, particularly
in the manufacturing and construction sectors.   Harmful industrial emissions
are a major contributor of atmospheric 2._____ which can bring
about serious environmental issues such as 3._____ and acid rain.
Besides, industrial by-products, such as chemical solvents, paints, and even
4._____ materials, are discharged from factories.   These harmful
substances not only 5._____ the soil but also inevitably lead to water
pollution, threatening freshwater supply and 6._____ animals' lives.

With human settlements come the development of transportation systems.
More forests are cleared for the construction of 7._____ and railway,
resulting in wildlife habitat loss. 8._____
emissions also aggravate air pollution.

Another inevitable issue brought about by human
settlements is the production of large amounts of
human waste and 9._____ , which also
cause soil contamination and water pollution.

10. Light pollution from large cities is also a serious consequence of human
settlements.   How do you think artificial lights negatively affect the
environment?

_____

_____

_____

Sustainable Human Settlements

With many environmental issues arising from human settlements, it is increasingly important to take steps toward building sustainable communities, like the city of Växjö. There are many practices that communities can adopt to achieve this, but there are also challenges that hinder the successful development of these projects.

A. **Put the descriptions in the correct boxes to show some possible features of a sustainable community.**

Features of a Sustainable Community

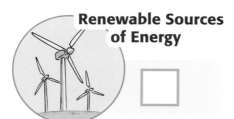

Renewable Sources of Energy

☐

Energy-efficient Buildings

☐ ☐ ☐

Comprehensive Public Transportation Systems

☐ ☐

Waste and Water Recycling

☐ ☐

Ⓐ making use of the sun's lighting and heating capabilities

Ⓑ promoting the use of sustainable energy including renewable sources such as hydroelectricity, solar energy, and wind energy

Ⓒ developing programs of recycling and composting waste, turning it into fertilizers for plants, and increasing soil productivity

Ⓓ developing a community-wide transportation system to encourage people to take public transit instead of driving their own cars

Ⓔ implementing programs of recycling grey water, that is, domestic waste water from sinks, bathtubs, showers, and washing machines, by filtering, treating, and then reusing it to help conserve water supply

Ⓕ constructing buildings using recycled and environmentally friendly materials, especially those from local sources to reduce the environmental costs of transporting them

Ⓖ installing energy-efficient appliances

Ⓗ driving less to use less gas and reduce emissions that pollute the air

ISBN: 978-1-77149-036-8

B. Read the passage. Then answer the questions.

Växjö, the Greenest City in Europe

Lake Trummen in Växjö, Sweden was once heavily polluted by the area's sewage and waste water from factories. Efforts made in the 1960s and 1970s successfully restored it through ambitious environmental projects. The restoration of the lake triggered the city's interest in environmental sustainability.

In 1991, Växjö introduced the world's first carbon tax, and in 1996, it was committed to becoming fossil fuel free by 2030. Some other city-wide efforts include the use of biofuels for public transit, energy-efficient street lighting, use of solar panels for alternative energy production in buildings, expansion and improvement of walking and cycling paths, and the recycling and management of industrial waste.

However, the sustainable development of the city was not without challenges. For example, the lack of financial resources for building environmentally friendly infrastructure at the start of the project, and later, its population growth posed problems for Växjö to become the greenest city in Europe.

1. Give two ways in which the government promoted environmental sustainability in Växjö.

   _____

   _____

2. What challenges were there in developing sustainable communities in Växjö?

   _____

   _____

   _____

3. Write two things you can do to help in the sustainable development of your community.

   _____

   _____

Land-use Issues

Competition for land is an inevitable consequence of human settlement. There are various categories of land use. Different people have different views and concerns about how land should be used, and this can often lead to land-use conflicts.

A. **Read what each speaker says and identify the category of land use each is concerned with. Then determine whether each speaker is for or against the building of a new mall and condominiums in the rural community.**

environmental   transportation   public
commercial   residential   agricultural

Category of Land Use

for / against ✔ / ✗

1. Mr. Smith, a farmer, says, "This land is perfect for farming, so losing this land would greatly impact the rural community".

   _____ ◯

2. Mrs. Nathwani says, "As a business owner, I believe the mall would be perfect for me to open a second store!"

   _____ ◯

3. Miss Jones, a bus driver, says, "With this development, we could add bus routes and buses to our community."

   _____ ◯

4. Mr. Singh, a bird watcher, says, "The forest on this land is a breeding ground for a rare bird species."

   _____ ◯

5. Mrs. Preston, a mother of three, says, "My family wants to live in affordable housing in a growing community."

   _____ ◯

6. Mr. Chen, the community's mayor, says, "This development would help our community thrive, and attract funding for building a hospital."

   _____ ◯

ISBN: 978-1-77149-036-8

B. **Read about the land-use conflict in Georgina, Ontario. Then answer the questions.**

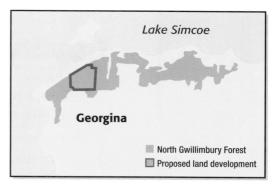

Lake Simcoe

Georgina

■ North Gwillimbury Forest
□ Proposed land development

Land-use Conflict – Georgina

Just an hour's drive north of Toronto, Ontario, you can find the small town of Georgina. Almost 30 years ago, a land development company won a hard-fought battle to build an enormous retirement village in part of the North Gwillimbury Forest. Running along the southern shores of Lake Simcoe, the North Gwillimbury Forest is a wetland that stretches around 15 kilometres, making it one of the ten largest forest areas in the Lake Simcoe Watershed. However, the company went bankrupt before any building or development could begin. In the mid-2000s, most of the property was designated a provincially significant wetland to protect the area from development and to protect the lake's wildlife and water quality. Today, the current property owner, a large development company, is looking to build a subdivision on this land, which has sparked a big fight with the small town of Georgina. As the policies about development are reviewed, debated, and remade, the developer is squaring off against the citizens and organizations like the North Gwillimbury Forest Alliance.

1. What are the different categories of land use that are factors in this case?

    _____

2. When there is competition for land, what are some things stakeholders can do to have their voices heard?

    _____

    _____

3.

    Housing development is a solution to increasing housing demand with the rise in population, but this cannot be achieved without causing various environmental impacts. If you lived in Georgina, would you want this land to be developed or preserved? Why?

    _____

    _____

    _____

Quality of Life

In different regions of the world, and even in different regions within a country, the quality of life varies. There are different things that indicate quality of life. These indicators can be used to measure and compare the quality of life of different places.

A.   Match the quality of life indicators with their descriptions. Write the letters.

Quality of Life Indicators

- **birth rate:**   number of people born, usually expressed as "per 1000 people per year"
- **death rate:**   number of deaths, usually expressed as "per 1000 people per year"
- **fertility rate:**   prediction of the average number of children born to a woman in her lifetime
- **crime rate:**   number of victims of crime per 1000 people
- **national debt:** amount owed by a country's government
- **literacy rate:**   the calculation of the number of people able to read and write divided by the total population and multiplied by 100
- _____ : rate of people within an area at or below a level of income called the poverty line
- _____ : market value of goods made in a country divided by its population
- _____ : remaining number of years people at a certain age can expect to live
- _____ : number of people who do not have work and are actively looking for work
- _____ : market value of goods made in a country
- _____ : number of deaths of children under one year old, per 1000 people in a given year
- _____ : appropriate, timely medical care without discrimination
- _____ : the time it takes for a population to double
- _____ : proportion of people within a reasonable distance to the supply of water of a certain standard of quality
- _____ : education to a certain level without discrimination, which may mean regardless of gender, race, or income, or with support for disabilities
- _____ : measure of the wealth of people of a place, calculated by dividing income by the number of people in that place

A.   per capita income
B.   poverty rate
C.   gross domestic product (GDP)
D.   unemployment rate
E.   life expectancy
F.   infant mortality rate
G.   doubling time
H.   access to education
I.   access to clean water
J.   gross domestic product per capita
K.   access to medical care

B. **Graph the data from the highest unemployment rate to the lowest. Then answer the questions.**

Canada: 7%   Pakistan: 6%   Portugal: 13%   Spain: 24%   South Africa: 25%
France: 10%   Greece: 26%   Iraq: 11%   China: 4%   United States: 6%

Unemployment Rate in Ten Countries (2014)

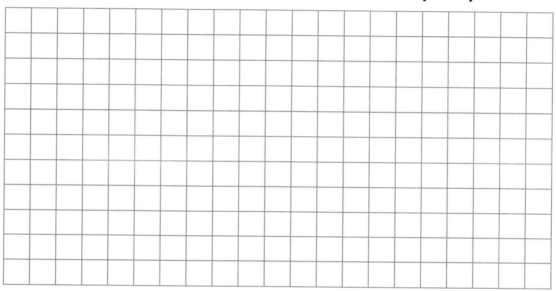

1. a. What is the highest unemployment rate? _____

    b. Which country has the highest unemployment rate? _____

    c. What does the unemployment rate say about the quality of life in this country?

    _____

2. a. What is the lowest unemployment rate? _____

    b. Which country has the lowest unemployment rate? _____

    c. What does the unemployment rate say about the quality of life in this country?

    _____

Quality of Life – Interrelationships among Factors

The various factors that contribute to quality of life do not exist in isolation. They are very often related to one another. Problems in one area may lead to other problems, but improving one area can also positively affect other areas.

A. Read to find out how access to clean water affects other factors that contribute to quality of life. Write the numbers in the circles. Then answer the question.

Access to clean water is vital in every human settlement. It is a natural resource that humans rely on for survival – for drinking, cooking, and washing. Agriculture, including crop growing and livestock rearing, also needs easy access to a consistent supply of clean water. If the water source is far away from a settlement, people must spend hours every day transporting water. This takes farmers' time away from tending to their livestock and crops, to the point that it may not be possible for them to grow or provide enough food for their families or the trade market①. It also takes families' time away from caring for their children and the ill. It prevents children from attending or getting to school②, and others from learning a trade or maintaining a job③. Moreover, unclean water can lead to water-borne diseases, strain the health system④, and even cause death⑤.

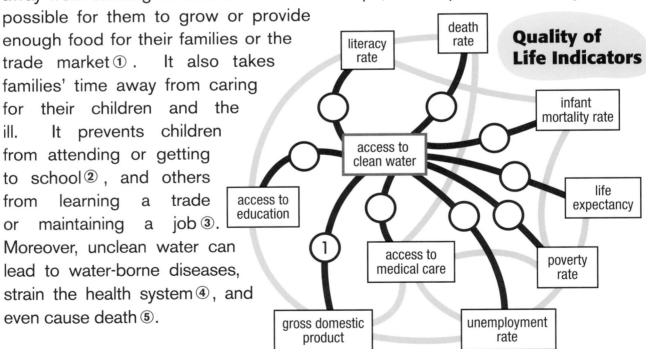

How does access to natural resources affect quality of life?

_____

_____

ISBN: 978-1-77149-036-8

B. **For each group, write the quality of life indicators in the correct boxes to show which one may affect the other two. Then answer the question.**

Group A
access to education
literacy rate
per capita income

Group B
infant mortality rate
access to education
poverty rate

Group C
fertility rate
doubling time
birth rate

Group D
crime rate
unemployment rate
poverty rate

Group A

Group B

Group C

Group D

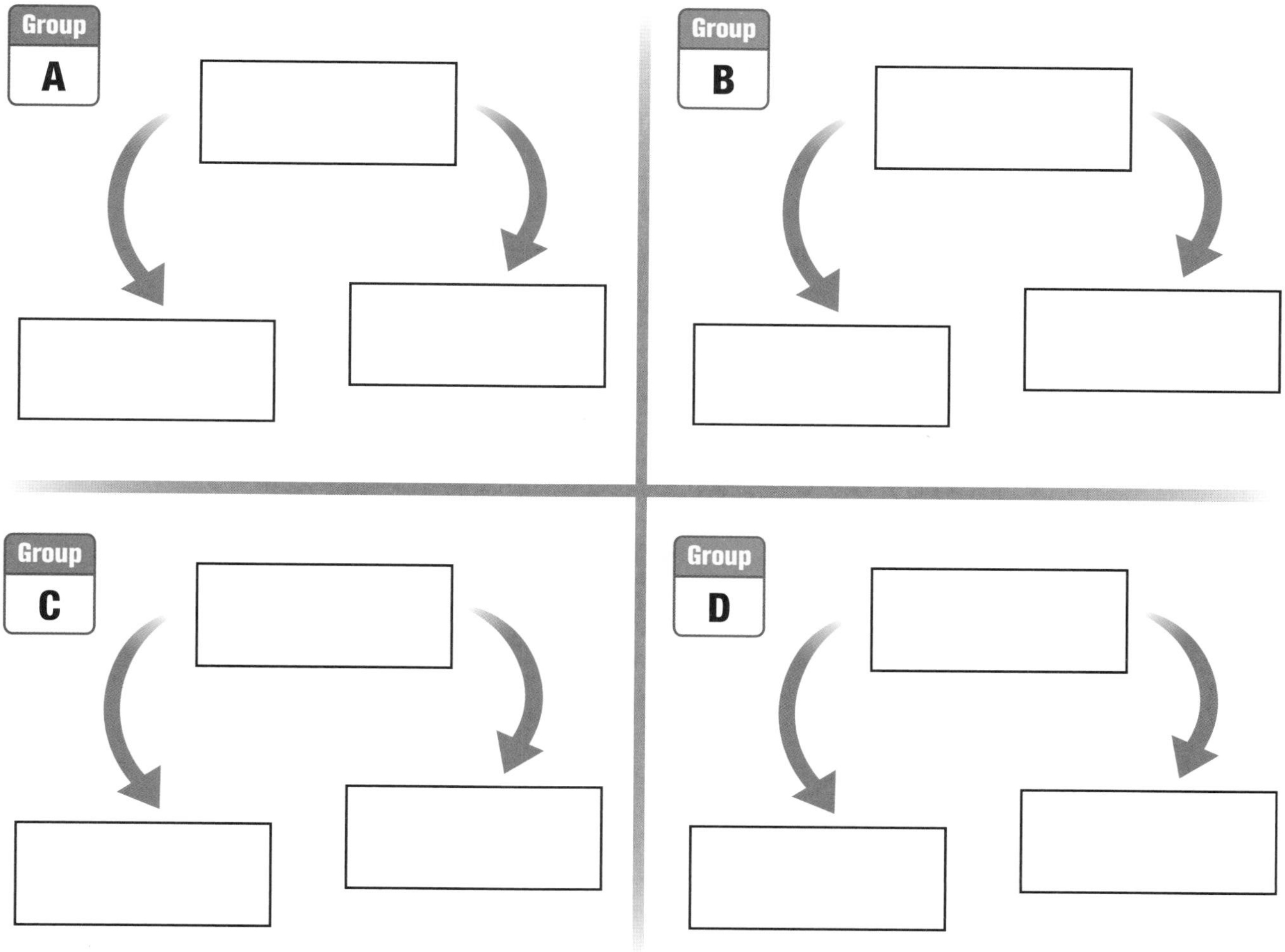

Look at Group D again. Describe briefly how these factors are interrelated.

_____

_____

Quality of Life – Correlations between Indicators

Just as factors that contribute to the quality of life are interrelated, there are also correlations between the quality of life indicators. When two indicators are correlated, both indicators experience changes simultaneously.

A. **Colour the legend and the demographic map to show the data. Then answer the questions.**

Percentage of Population below the Poverty Line in South American Countries (2012)

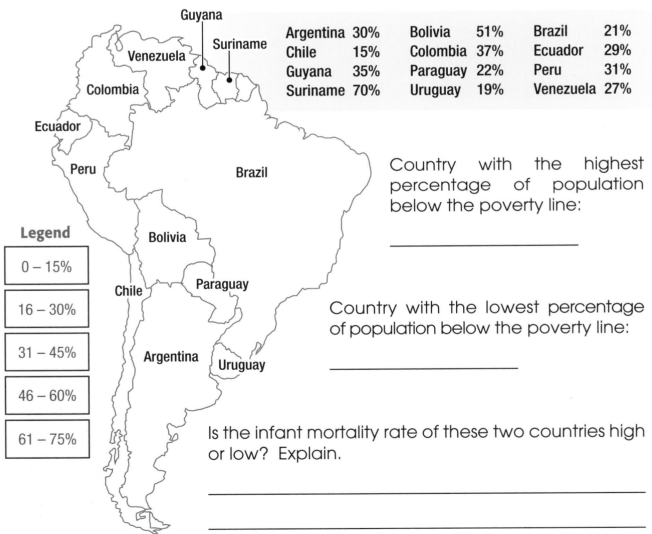

Argentina	30%	Bolivia	51%	Brazil	21%
Chile	15%	Colombia	37%	Ecuador	29%
Guyana	35%	Paraguay	22%	Peru	31%
Suriname	70%	Uruguay	19%	Venezuela	27%

Legend

| 0 – 15% |
| 16 – 30% |
| 31 – 45% |
| 46 – 60% |
| 61 – 75% |

Country with the highest percentage of population below the poverty line:

_____

Country with the lowest percentage of population below the poverty line:

_____

Is the infant mortality rate of these two countries high or low? Explain.

_____

_____

      ISBN: 978-1-77149-036-8

B. **Construct a bar graph to show the infant mortality rate. Then answer the questions with the help of the data in (A) and the graph below.**

Infant Mortality Rate in South American Countries (2012)

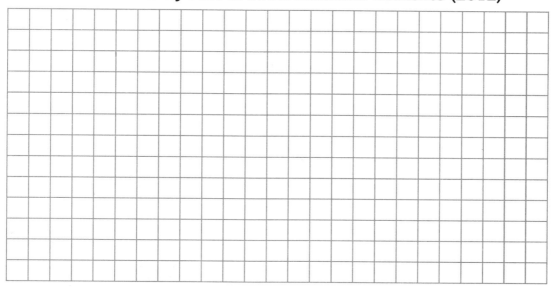

Deaths per
1000 live births

Argentina – 11
Bolivia – 41
Brazil – 21
Chile – 7
Colombia – 16
Ecuador – 19
Guyana – 36
Paraguay – 22
Peru – 22
Suriname – 29
Uruguay – 9
Venezuela – 20

1. Check if there is a positive correlation between the percentage of population below the poverty line and the infant mortality rate in the given country; otherwise, put a cross.

   Bolivia _____

   Chile _____

   Colombia _____

   Uruguay _____

   A positive correlation means that if the percentage of population below the poverty line is high, the infant mortality rate is also high, and vice versa.

2. Why do you think one of the countries in question 1 does not show a positive correlation between the two indicators of quality of life?

   _____

   _____

3. Write about the quality of life in countries with a low percentage of population below the poverty line and a low infant mortality rate.

   _____

   _____

10

Fair Trade and Quality of Life

As people are more conscious about Fairtrade certified products, they become more concerned about fair trade's impact on producers and consumers. Fair trade impacts society at the social, economic, and environmental levels, thereby affecting people's quality of life.

Fill in the blanks to learn about fair trade and its impact. Then answer the question.

Fair Trade   sustainable social producers

Fair trade is a _____ movement that aims to support and help _____ in developing countries achieve better trading conditions and therefore improve their quality of life while promoting _____ development.

Impact of Fair Trade

1.   **Economic Impact**   farmers stable consumer equipment

Loans and other forms of financial assistance are provided for producers, smallholder _____ and artisans in particular, to help them get the necessary _____ and materials and employ local workers to start their businesses. Fairtrade certified producer organizations have better access to larger _____ markets. Sales can increase up to 15% after certification so the producers would make greater profits. Also, these producers are ensured _____ market prices so that they can have secure profits and save money.

     ISBN: 978-1-77149-036-8

2. **Social Impact**   ethical   community   housing   businesses

Fair trade provides producers with opportunities for education and training in basic skills needed for running small _____ , as well as math and language skills.   The producers can then pass on this knowledge to their children and workers, thereby allowing for the sustainable development of their _____ . In addition, profits from fair trade are invested in building local public schools, health and medical clinics, safe low-income _____ , food banks, and facilities that provide clean water and sanitation. Fair trade also works to promote _____ treatment of workers by monitoring employers to ensure that they do not exploit their workers.

3. **Environmental Impact**   organic   productivity   natural   composting

Environmental care and protection is an important pillar of fair trade standards because a healthy environment is a prerequisite for high _____ from farmlands.   Fair trade helps protect the environment through emphasizing subsistence farming, supporting _____ production, and encouraging the production of environmentally friendly items.   It has also brought environmental innovations like _____ into farming communities, thereby achieving the sustainable management of _____ resources.

4.

> *Write three ways in which fair trade helps improve quality of life.*

_____

_____

_____

_____

_____

11

Organizations for Improving Quality of Life

Many non-governmental organizations (NGOs) around the world are working to improve quality of life. Some of them focus on children's rights, while others put their efforts into resolving environmental issues.

A. **Unscramble the words to complete the names of the organizations. Then fill in the blanks to complete the descriptions.**

Organizations for Improving Quality of Life

> human slavery family
> sports medical access

1. **Right to ＿＿＿＿＿＿ (ylPa)**

   Games and ＿＿＿＿＿＿ are the tools this organization uses to improve the lives of disadvantaged children around the world.

2. **International Planned ＿＿＿＿＿＿ (Pahoodrent) Federation**

   This group advocates for women's reproductive health and provides ＿＿＿＿＿＿ planning services.

3. **＿＿＿＿＿＿ (reFe) The Children**

   Started by a child who was inspired by the plight of child slaves in developing countries, this organization's goal is to eliminate the ＿＿＿＿＿＿ and exploitation of children.

4. **＿＿＿＿＿＿ (teraW) For People**

   Believing that access to water is a basic human right, this group works to improve quality of life by trying to secure ＿＿＿＿＿＿ to this basic human need.

5. **＿＿＿＿＿＿ (reenGpaece)**

   This environmental group works to protect the Earth's diverse life, as well as its ability to continue to nurture life, including ＿＿＿＿＿＿ life.

6. **Doctors Without ＿＿＿＿＿＿ (Broedrs)**

   We aim to provide ＿＿＿＿＿＿ assistance for the sick and injured in disasters and wars, wherever it is needed, without political, religious, or economic prejudice.

B. Write which group from (A) can help in each scenario below. Then answer the question.

1

A boy is injured, caught between two factions in his country's civil war. Unfortunately, the dispute has disabled the medical system that used to be in place.

Who can help?

_____

2

A village affected by drought does not have the equipment necessary to build the infrastructure they now need.

Who can help?

_____

3

A ship has hit rocks and there is a growing potential for oil to spill extensively. This poses a great threat to the ecosystem, which provides resources for the booming economy of nearby communities.

Who can help?

_____

4

The growing demand for chocolate around the world has the potential to increase the demand for child labour in regions where the cacao bean is grown.

Who can help?

_____

Select one NGO and describe briefly how it helps improve quality of life.

_____

_____

_____

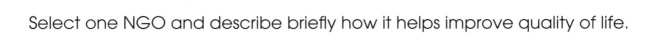

12

Economic Systems and Sectors

Goods and services are produced and distributed to people through what is known as an economic system. Countries around the world operate under different types of economic systems, and the economic activities of a country can be categorized into four basic sectors.

A.   Read the paragraph. Then answer the questions with the words in bold.

Four Economic Systems

*The command economy and the market economy are two starkly contrasting economic systems. The **command** economy is centralized, where the government controls what is produced and what is distributed to whom. The **market** economy is the opposite. It allows for individual ownership of business or industry, and everything is produced and traded according to what and how much people want. In the developed world, most countries have economies that are a mix of the two – aptly called a **mixed** economy. A fourth economic system, the **traditional** economy, is rarer in today's world. Economic decisions are based on how things have always been done – custom and tradition. In this system, there is not a lot of room for change, but there are also no ups and downs like those found in mixed or market economies.*

Which economic system...

a.   is most likely to see mass production of unnecessary, frivolous goods?   _____

b.   is most heavily controlled by the government?   _____

c.   has product advertising as a common feature?   _____

d.   is the most decentralized, without the involvement of the government in any market processes?   _____

e.   benefits from two contrasting systems?   _____

f.   is likely to have the greatest gap between the rich and the poor?   _____

g.   has people likely to know what to expect, generation after generation?   _____

ISBN: 978-1-77149-036-8

B. Identify the four economic sectors. Match the occupations with the sectors and give one more example for each. Then answer the questions.

Secondary   Tertiary   Quaternary   Primary

1. **Four Economic Sectors:**

   - _____ **Sector**
     concerned with extracting or producing raw materials

     e.g. _____ ; _____

   - _____ **Sector**
     concerned with turning raw materials into goods

     e.g. _____ ; _____

   - _____ **Sector**
     concerned with providing services

     e.g. _____ ; _____

   - _____ **Sector**
     concerned with information generating or sharing

     e.g. _____ ; _____

A doctor

B lumberjack

C carpenter

D computer programmer

2. Would there be any problems if a country's economy is highly dependent on the primary sector? Why?

   _____

   _____

3. Why does a country with a high employment rate in the primary sector tend to rank lower on the HDI* than those countries with most people working in the tertiary and quaternary sectors?

   *Human Development Index (HDI) is a summary measure of a country's average achievement in its people's health, education, and standard of living.

   _____

   _____

ISBN: 978-1-77149-036-8

SCIENCE

ISBN: 978-1-77149-036-8

1

Cell Theory

Teddy, did you know that all cells come from pre-existing cells?

- The cell theory is one of the major foundations of biology, and is comprised of three main postulates and two exceptions.

- Without technology and dedicated individuals, the formulation of this theory would not have been possible.

A. **Fill in the blanks to complete the postulates of the cell theory and its exceptions. Then give each picture a caption with the postulate or the exception that it illustrates.**

Postulates of Cell Theory

1. All living things are made up of _____ .

2. All cells are a _____ to carry out functions to sustain life. _____ flow occurs within cells.

3. All cells come from _____ cells.

first
pre-existing
viruses
structure
energy
cells

Exceptions

1. The _____ cell did not come from an already existing cell.

2. _____ do not contain a cell structure, so they are not living.

Picture 1
Animals:

Plants:

Picture 2

Yeah, I understand that, but where did the first cell come from?

ISBN: 978-1-77149-036-8

B. To complete the timeline, fill in the blanks with the names of people and events that led to the Cell Theory.

Thedor	Robert	Anton	Zacharias		cell	microscope	membrane
Rudolph	Charles-Francois	Matthias			arise	products	live

Events that Led to the Cell Theory:

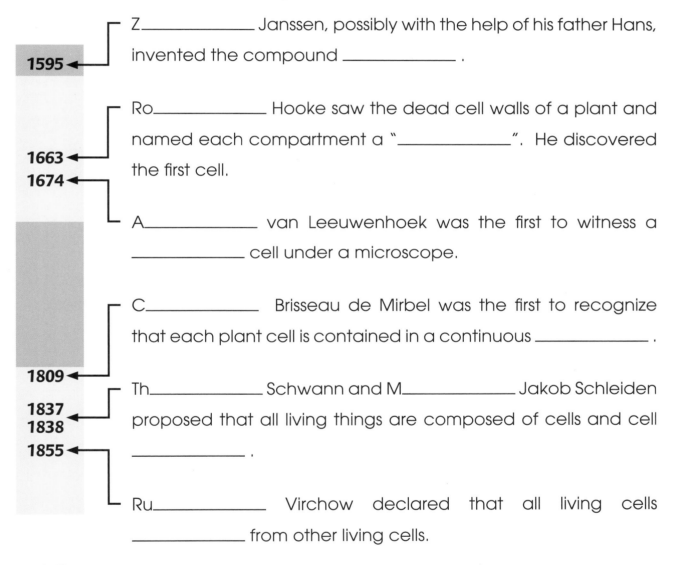

1595 ← Z_____ Janssen, possibly with the help of his father Hans, invented the compound _____ .

1663 ← Ro_____ Hooke saw the dead cell walls of a plant and named each compartment a "_____". He discovered the first cell.

1674 ← A_____ van Leeuwenhoek was the first to witness a _____ cell under a microscope.

C_____ Brisseau de Mirbel was the first to recognize that each plant cell is contained in a continuous _____ .

1809 ←

1837 ← Th_____ Schwann and M_____ Jakob Schleiden proposed that all living things are composed of cells and cell

1838 ← _____ .

1855 ← Ru_____ Virchow declared that all living cells _____ from other living cells.

Science Fact

Long ago, it was believed that life could arise out of non-life. Spontaneous generation, as it was known, was a way for people to explain how maggots could appear on rotting meat, or how frogs could rise up from the muddy banks of the Nile River.

2

Animal and Plant Cells

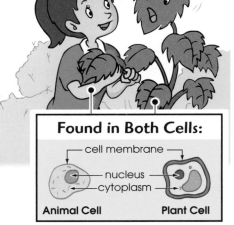

Don't you know that we have some structures in common?

Found in Both Cells:

cell membrane
nucleus
cytoplasm

Animal Cell   Plant Cell

- Both animal and plant cells contain some of the same types of structures, but not all.
- Photosynthesis and respiration are important functions of plant and animal cells, respectively.

A. **Unscramble the words to label the diagram of a typical animal cell. Then use the same words to complete the passage. Words can be used more than once.**

1. **A Typical Animal Cell**

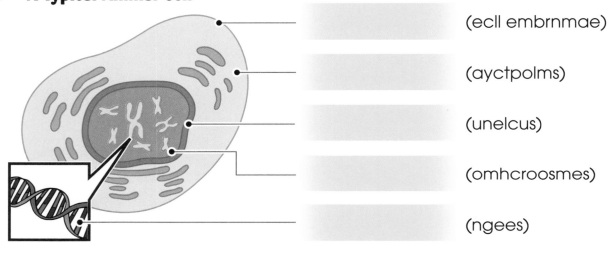

(ecll embrnmae)

(ayctpolms)

(unelcus)

(omhcroosmes)

(ngees)

2. The a._____ is the control centre of the cell. It contains

the b._____ , which are thread-like structures that contain

genetic information. This information, stored in c._____ , is

the information needed to define the characteristics of the individual.

The material that suspends the d._____ and other structures in

the cell is called the e._____ . The whole cell is enclosed in a

f._____ , which is not a complete barrier, but rather one that

allows some materials to pass in and out of the cell.

B. **Fill in the blanks with the words in the diagram.**

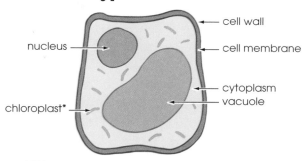

A Typical Plant Cell

cell wall

nucleus

cell membrane

cytoplasm
vacuole

chloroplast*

*Chloroplasts are members of a class of organelles known as plastids.

1. A _____ is a protective and supportive structure external to the cell membrane that is found in plants, fungi, bacteria, and algae.

2. A _____ contains chlorophyll, which is a green pigment used in photosynthesis.

3. A large part of the cytoplasm is occupied by a _____, which is a fluid-filled cavity that may contain water, minerals, sugars, and proteins.

4. A _____ is an organelle found in both plants and algae. It is involved in food production and storage.

C. **Read what Amy says. Complete the flow diagrams with the words in bold.**

*Green plant cells perform a chemical reaction called photosynthesis, where they use the **energy** from the sun to change **carbon dioxide** and water into food and **oxygen**.*

*Animal cells undergo respiration, where they change sugar (food) and **oxygen** into **carbon dioxide**, **water**, and energy.*

Photosynthesis

_____ + water + _____ ⟶ sugar + _____

Respiration

sugar + _____ ⟶ _____ + _____ + energy

One of the main functions of the plant cell wall is to prevent the cell from bursting when it absorbs water.

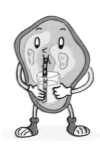

3

Structures and Organelles in Cells

I can see it clearly under an electron microscope.

- Advances in microscope technology have made it possible to identify the various structures and organelles inside cells.

- These organelles have particular jobs to do inside the cell.

A. **Read what Simon says. Identify whether the microscope is a "light" or "electron" microscope. Then sort the structures into the correct groups.**

Using a light microscope, we can observe many different structures inside a cell. These include the nucleus, cell membrane, and the cell wall (in plant cells only). Other specialized structures in the cytoplasm, known as organelles, can only be seen under an electron microscope.

_____ microscope

- _____

- _____

- _____

- _____

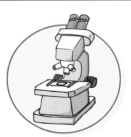

_____ microscope

- _____

- _____

- _____

- _____

- _____

endoplasmic reticulum

cytoplasm

cell membrane

Golgi apparatus

lysosomes

cell wall

mitochondria

nucleus

ribosomes

ISBN: 978-1-77149-036-8

B. **The organelles of the cell have specific forms and functions. Use the diagram and the given words to complete the information chart.**

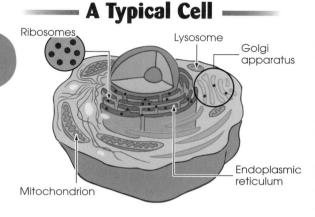

A Typical Cell

canals	cellular respiration	recycle	toxic
proteins	oval-shaped	cytoplasm	sac-like

The Organelles of the Cell

1. R_____ (Form: free or attached)

   Function: assemble _____

2. M_____ (Form: _____)

   Function: make energy through photosynthesis or _____

3. Endoplasmic reticulum (Form: _____)

   Function: carry materials through the _____

4. G_____ a_____ (Form: stacked like pancakes)

   Function: packages proteins and _____ materials

5. Lysosome (Form: _____)

   Function: contain proteins that break down and _____ larger molecules

Science Fact

The number of mitochondria a cell contains seems to be related to the type of cell in which they are found. Cells that need a lot of energy to perform their job typically have a high number of mitochondria.

Diffusion and Osmosis

- Diffusion is the movement of molecules from an area of high concentration to an area of low concentration.

- Osmosis is the movement of water molecules from an area of high concentration to an area of low concentration.

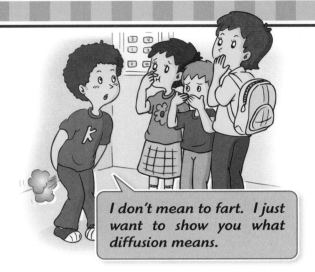

I don't mean to fart. I just want to show you what diffusion means.

A. Fill in the blanks by unscrambling the letters to complete what Sally says. Then write 1 to 5 to number the sentences that describe the movement of molecules during diffusion.

1.

> *Diffusion occurs on a molecular level when molecules move from an area of _____ (ihgh) concentration to an area of _____ (wlo) concentration.*

food colouring (solute)

water (solvent)

Liquid food colouring comes in concentrated form, and when a drop is put into a glass of water, it diffuses.

2. **Movement of Molecules During Diffusion:**
   (Add a drop of food colouring into a glass of water.)

( ) The molecules of the food colouring "glob" collide with other molecules that they are close to, and are sent off in all directions, only to collide with more.

( ) There is no longer a "glob", as the food colouring molecules have spread themselves out evenly throughout the water.

( ) Before meeting with water, the highly concentrated food colouring molecules are close together, forming a "glob" as it begins to fall through the water.

( ) Due to the randomness of the collisions, the food colouring molecules spread out and "intermingle" with the water molecules.

(1) According to the Kinetic Theory of Matter, the molecules in both the concentrated food colouring and water are in constant motion.

ISBN: 978-1-77149-036-8

B.   Fill in the blanks with the given words. Then put ">", "<", or "=" in the circles.

Osmosis

equal   membrane   osmosis   water   out

When salt is used on roadways to combat icy conditions, roadside plants can be destroyed. This happens as a result of 1._____ . Under normal conditions, the concentration of water inside the cells of the plant is 2._____ to the concentration of water outside. Water flows equally in and out of the cells through a selectively permeable 3._____*. When salt is added to roads, it forms a salt solution with the melting ice. The concentration of water inside the plant cells is no longer equal to the concentration outside. More water flows 4._____ of the cells than into the cells through the cell membrane, damaging the cell, and leaving it without the 5._____ it needs to make food.

* a membrane that only allows some materials to pass through it

Plant Cell when Exposed to Salt Water

cell wall   selectively permeable cell membrane

← water molecule

← salt molecule

concentration of water
inside the cell ◯ outside the cell

Plant Cell with Continued Exposure to Salt Water

concentration of water
inside the cell ◯ outside the cell

The size of the arrows indicates the amount of water moving from one place to another.

Science Fact

Turgor pressure is the pressure of the cell's contents against the cell wall. This pressure is a direct result of osmosis and it gives the plant rigidity and strength.

ISBN: 978-1-77149-036-8   Complete Canadian Curriculum • Grade 8   **293**

5

The Organization of Cells

Some life forms on Earth are single-celled; some are multi-celled. Sea sponges are animals that display the move from being single-celled to multi-celled.

- Cellular differentiation is displayed in multi-cellular organisms.
- Cells in multi-cellular organisms are specialized and organized into three levels: tissues, organs, and systems.

A. **Complete the passage about the five differentiated types of cells in a sponge with the help of the diagram. Then fill in the missing information.**

The body of a sponge is made up of different types of cells in a jelly-like mass substance called a mesoglea. 1.C_____ are "colour cells" that function as the sponge's digestive system in that they have flagellum to beat and create the sponge's water current. They also filter the water to trap and engulf food. 2.P_____ are

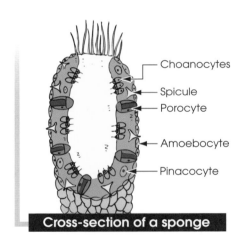

Cross-section of a sponge

cells that make up the pores in the body, making openings that allow water to flow through the body. 3.A_____ move around in the sponge's body, storing and carrying food to other cells that they get from choanocytes. 4.S_____ are made from calcium carbonate. They provide protection and structure. 5.P_____ form the outer covering of the sponge.

6.

Cell and Its Function

- _____ : Make up the pores in the body.
- Choanocytes : _____
- Amoebocytes : _____
- Pinacocytes : _____
- _____ : Protect and support the body.

ISBN: 978-1-77149-036-8

B. **Read what Simon says. Then fill in the blanks.**

> *Organisms on Earth come in many different forms, but all of them are composed of cells. The organization of different types of cells is highly complex. The cells must work together.*

organs
cells
tissues

1. Groups of _____ that specialize in performing the same function are called tissues.

2. Organs are groups of _____ working together.

3. Several _____ that work together to perform a function are called an organ system.

C. **Answer the children's questions.**

1. *Which organ system does the kidney belong to?*

   _____

   digestive system
   excretory system
   respiratory system
   circulatory system
   nervous system

2. Amy asks, "Which system is responsible for the ingestion and breakdown of food into tiny pieces so that it can pass into cells?"

   _____

3. Kevin asks, "Which system is comprised of these organs: heart, arteries, veins, and capillaries?"

   _____

White blood cells have a lifespan of about two days, while red blood cells can live for four months.

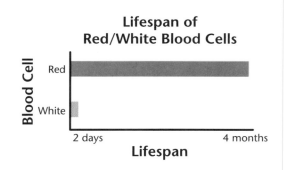

Lifespan of Red/White Blood Cells

Blood Cell

Red

White

2 days   4 months

Lifespan

About Systems

- Systems are groups of parts that work together to do something. They can be found in nature or constructed by humans.

- Systems can be made up of smaller systems, or subsystems, that work together to make up the whole.

This is my audio system.

A. **Circle the letter for the correct ending to each sentence that describes systems.**

1. Systems are designed to

    A. get things done.

    B. run without stopping.

    C. break down eventually.

There are many ways to describe systems.

2. Systems can

    A. be human-made only.

    B. be human-made, or occur in nature.

    C. only occur in nature.

3. Systems are characterized by

    A. parts that work together to accomplish a task.

    B. mechanical parts.

    C. electrical parts.

4. The goal of a system is to

    A. produce resources.

    B. retain as many resources as possible.

    C. use resources more efficiently.

ISBN: 978-1-77149-036-8

B. Look at the pictures. Identify the various types of systems.

mechanical system   body system   optical system
electrical system   hydroelectric power system

1. _____

2. _____

5. _____

3. _____

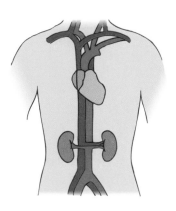

4. _____

C. Identify three different subsystems that work inside the larger system of a bicycle.

_____

_____

_____

_____

_____

_____

Many systems contain smaller systems, or subsystems, working together to make the larger system work.

Science Fact

Some systems are very old. The cuneiform writing system of the Sumerians, for example, was invented about 5000 years ago. This Sumerian system was one of the first writing systems in the world.

Cuneiform Writing

Examples:

bird   water

7

Systems: Input and Output

- All systems have a purpose – something they are meant to create.
- Systems include an input and an output.

> Look at my vaned lighting system at home. The purpose of this system is to give me light. This system allows me to work at night.

A. Identify the purpose, input, and output of the different systems. Fill in the missing information.

1. **System: home heating**

   Purpose: heat home

   ↘ Input: fuel

   ↗ Output: _____

2. **System: bicycle**

   Purpose: move from one place to another

   ↘ Input: _____

   ↗ Output: _____

3. **System: digestive system**

   Purpose: digest food

   ↘ Input: _____

   ↗ Output: _____

4. **System: farm**

   Purpose: _____

   ↘ Input: _____

   ↗ Output: _____

5. **System: grandfather clock**

   Purpose: _____

   ↘ Input: _____

   ↗ Output: _____

ISBN: 978-1-77149-036-8

B. Identify the input and output of each system. Write "input" or "output" in the boxes.

1.

2.

3.

4.

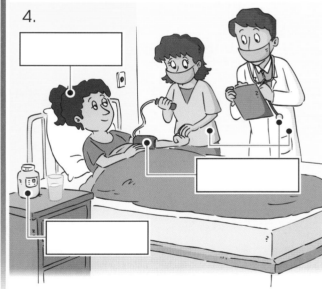

Science Fact

Sometimes the output of one system can be the input of another. For example, the output of the logging industry's timber could be the input for a home heating system as logs for a fireplace.

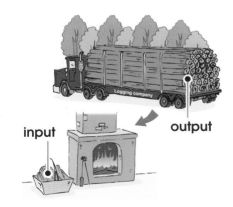

input   output

The Work Systems Do

- The terms energy, force, work, and efficiency have scientific meanings that differ from their meanings in our everyday use of the words.

- Work, in the scientific sense of the word, is only being done if the force is causing movement of an object in the same direction as the force being applied.

Dad, look at the windmill. Is work being done?

Yes. The wind is doing the work.

A. **For each picture, write the term that is being used. Then write whether it is an everyday use or a scientific use of the term.**

Term: energy force work efficiency

1.

You must have hit the ground with tremendous force to cause this much damage.

_____ ; _____ use

2.

They have lots of energy.

_____ ; _____ use

3.

Our new machine works with a higher efficiency than the old one. We get a lot more output for the same amount of input.

_____ ; _____ use

4.

I'm going to be late for work.

_____ ; _____ use

ISBN: 978-1-77149-036-8

B. **Fill in the blanks with the given words to define the scientific meanings of the terms.**

useful   work   pull   effort

scientific meanings

Energy: the capacity to do 1._____

Force: a push, 2._____ , or other factor that makes an object change speed, shape, or direction

Work: the amount of 3._____ expended in moving an object

Efficiency: how much of the energy used is 4._____

C. **Read each situation. Decide whether or not work is being done. If so, explain how it is being done; otherwise, suggest ways to make work happen.**

1. A conveyor belt is moving heavy auto parts through a factory.

   Is work being done? _____

   Explain: _____

2. The circulatory system moves oxygen to cells throughout the body.

   Is work being done? _____

   Explain: _____

3. A man pushes a piano, but no matter how hard he pushes, it does not move.

   Is work being done? _____

   Explain: _____

Science Fact

The Industrial Revolution certainly made work easier and more efficient for humans, but it also brought about major changes to society, including pollution and job displacement.

Work, Mechanical Advantage, and Efficiency

- Work, mechanical advantage, and efficiency are all elements of simple machines, complex machines, and mechanical systems.

> Jason, do you know that the output force increases if we use a longer screwdriver to open the can? It is because we gain a mechanical advantage from it.

A. Fill in the blanks to complete the paragraph. Then use the formula to calculate the amount of work being done in each situation.

Force is a push or pull that is exerted on an object. It is measured in 1._____ (N). 2._____ is done when a continuous force is applied to an object and the object moves a certain distance in 3._____ (m) in the direction of the force. It is measured in 4._____ (J) and can be calculated using the formula:

work	joules
metres	Newtons

See how much work I have done!

distance travelled

Work = Force x Distance

5. A car was pushed across a parking lot. Two students applied a force of 800 N for a distance of 40 m. How much work was done?

6. 4 kJ of work was done when a box was pushed along the floor for 10 m. What amount of force was applied? 1 kJ = 1000 J

ISBN: 978-1-77149-036-8

B. Use the formula to determine the mechanical advantage (MA) of each simple machine. Then answer the question.

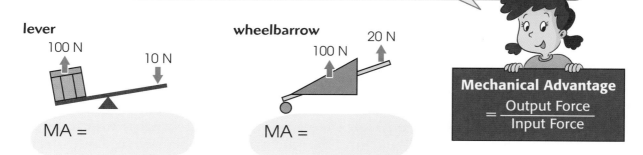

Many machines and mechanical systems are designed to multiply an input force. This multiplied force makes work easier for us. To calculate the mechanical advantage of a machine, simply divide the output force by the input force.

lever

100 N   10 N

MA =

wheelbarrow

100 N   20 N

MA =

Mechanical Advantage
$$= \frac{\text{Output Force}}{\text{Input Force}}$$

Which has greater mechanical advantage? _____

C. Use the formula to determine the efficiency of each simple machine. Then fill in the blank.

We know how efficient a machine is by comparing its output work to its input work. To calculate efficiency, simply divide the output work (W_{out}) by the input work (W_{in}) and then multiply by 100%. The higher the percent, the higher the efficiency.

Machine A

Work Input: 35 000 kJ

Work Output: 30 000 kJ

Efficiency =

Machine B

Work Input: 100 000 kJ

Work Output: 75 000 kJ

Efficiency =

Efficiency of a Machine
$$= \frac{W_{out}}{W_{in}} \times 100\%$$

Machine _____ is more efficient.

In 1763, James Watt had an idea for improving the incredibly inefficient steam engine of the time. His design made the new steam engine four times as powerful, making it much more efficient.

10

Evolving Systems

an automated system

- Automated systems work with little or no human direction.

- Automation can have social, economic, and environmental impacts.

Please take a look at our business hours. If we are closed, you may use the automated teller machine to access your account.

A. **Two different tasks are given for each area of work or production. Decide whether or not each situation is an automated task. Write "automated" or "not automated" on the line.**

1. a. mail delivery   _____

    b. mail sorting   _____

2. a. long-distance phone calls   _____

    b. operator-assisted phone calls   _____

3. a. garden hose and spray nozzle   _____

    b. automatic sprinklers   _____

4. a. automatic weaving machine   _____

    b. knitting needles   _____

5. a.    b.

    _____   _____

B. Complete the sentences to find out some of the positive and negative impacts of automation on society.

environment   economic   social

1. One of the _____ impacts of automation is the deterioration of workmanship in goods that are now mass-produced.

2. Positive _____ impacts of automation are increased productivity and reduced costs.

3. A negative _____ and _____ impact of automation is job losses.

4. Automated devices can be sophisticated and powerful, but in industries such as shipping and nuclear power, errors may have a catastrophic impact on the _____ .

C. Think about an automated system that you use. Write a paragraph to describe the social, economic, or environmental impact it has had since its automation.

_____

_____

_____

_____

_____

Here are some suggestions.

Movie theatre ticket-booth
Home heating/air conditioning
Automatic ice-maker

Science Fact

Not long ago, the job of a pinsetter was to set up bowling pins that had been knocked down and to roll the balls back to the bowler. This gruelling job became obsolete with the introduction of the automatic pinsetter in 1946.

11

Where on Earth Is Water?

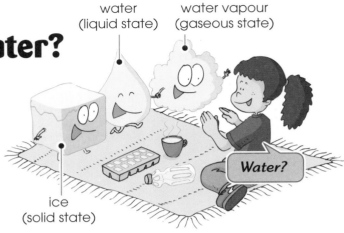

water
(liquid state)

water vapour
(gaseous state)

Water?

ice
(solid state)

- The water cycle ensures that water is constantly recycled around the Earth.
- Water is present in different states all over the Earth.
- All living things need water, and very little is available to humans.

A. Complete and label the diagram with the help of the passage and the given words. Use arrows to show the directions of the movement of water. Then answer the questions.

Fuelled by the sun, water from oceans, lakes, puddles, and even dewdrops on leaves enter the atmosphere through evaporation. There, water exists as a gas. It may condense again on the outside of a cold glass, or around dust particles in the air, forming clouds. From clouds, water may precipitate in the form of snow, hail, or rain, saturating a field and flowing to wherever gravity takes it. No new water is ever formed. All the water that ever was is the same water that exists now, and it is all that we will ever have. This is the water cycle.

1. **Water Cycle**

precipitation   condensation
evaporation   groundwater
runoff   transpiration

2. Which three processes describe how the atmosphere transports water from one place to another?

_____

3. How do plants release evaporated water into the atmosphere?

_____

B. Circle the ten hidden words that show where water is distributed on Earth. Label the circle graph with the help from the information points. Then answer the question.

1.

a	n	p	o	n	d	s		y	w
g	l	o	m	e	c	k	p	g	a
r	c	l	o	u	d	s	T	l	t
o	n	a	c	s	n	t	j	a	e
u	e	r	i	v	e	r	s	c	r
n	a		i	n	t	e	t	i	
d	b	i	x	i	v	w	r	e	v
w	r	c	j	s	o	c	e	r	a
a	c	e	n	t	e	r	a	s	p
t	i		r	h	u		m	a	o
e	o	c	e	a	n	s	s	e	u
r	k	a	b	e	s	i	p	u	r
m	n	p	i	c	w	d	e	w	w
o	c	s		m	h	o	l	e	t

- more than 97% of the water on Earth is salt water
- almost 3% is fresh water (with more than 2% in the polar ice caps or glaciers)

Distribution of Water on Earth

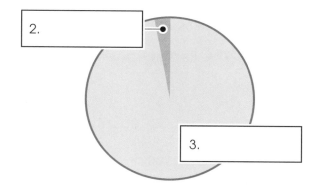

2. _____

3. _____

4.

Humans can only use unfrozen, fresh water for drinking. Approximately what percentage of all the water on Earth is available for human use?

_____

C. Write an example of water on Earth given in part B for each state of matter.

Solid _____ **Liquid** _____ **Gas** _____

_____ _____ _____

🧪 **Science Fact**

Some facts about the distribution of the world's fresh water can be surprising! For instance, there is more water in the atmosphere – in the air – than there is in all of Earth's rivers.

12

What Is a Watershed?

- A watershed is an area of land in which all the water drains into the same body of water.

- Water in a watershed is replenished through precipitation or melted ice from higher ground.

Look at our watershed model. Don't you think it's great?

A.   Check the correct answers.

1.   A watershed is

   Ⓐ   a safe place to store water.

   Ⓑ   a geographical area where all the water runs to the same place.

2.   New water in a watershed comes from

   Ⓐ   precipitation or ice/snowmelt.

   Ⓑ   the mountains.

3.   Water in a watershed travels

   Ⓐ   from low land to high land.   Ⓑ   from high land to low land.

4.   The downward travel of water in a watershed is caused by

   Ⓐ   gravity.   Ⓑ   heat.   Ⓒ   water pressure.

5.   Watersheds are separated by

   Ⓐ   areas of lower elevation.

   Ⓑ   areas of higher elevation.

   Ⓒ   bodies of water.

ISBN: 978-1-77149-036-8

B. **Match each physical component of a watershed with its description.**

river   lake   glacier   wetland   precipitation   groundwater aquifer

1. _____

   a large mass of ice formed by the compaction and recrystallization of snow under freezing conditions; it moves slowly down slopes or moves outward due to its own weight

2. _____

   solid or liquid water that falls from clouds to the ground

3. _____

   an underground layer of water-bearing permeable rock; groundwater can usually be extracted using a well

4. _____

   any inland body of standing water, usually fresh water, larger than a pool or a pond

5. _____

   an extensive network across land; a natural drainage channel for surface water

6. _____

   an area with soft and wet land intermingled with surface water; a marsh

   (valuable because it provides a habitat for many plants and animals and for its ability to clean polluted water)

C. **Colour the map to show the major watersheds in Canada that drain into the oceans below.**

- **Green:** Pacific Ocean
- **Blue:** Atlantic Ocean
- **Yellow:** Arctic Ocean
- **Red:** Gulf of Mexico
- **Brown:** Hudson Bay

 Science Fact

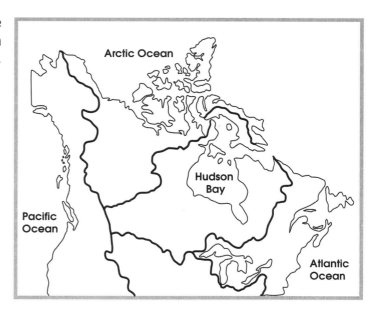

Topography (physical features), soil type, and land use are some of the factors that determine how quickly water reaches its final drainage point – and whether an area is prone to flooding.

13

The Water Table

- Underground water is below the water table when all the spaces among particles of soil and rock are filled with water – in other words, where the earth is saturated.

- The level of the water table increases and decreases due to natural and human-caused events.

Jason, let me show you what "water table" means.

No, it doesn't mean a table with water. A water table is the upper surface of groundwater that is available under the soil.

A. Complete the diagram with the given words. Then follow Wayne's direction.

ground level	water table	saturated zone
bedrock	surface water	unsaturated zone

1.

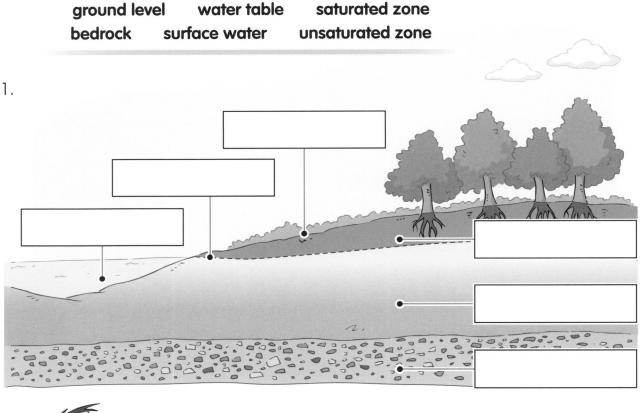

2.

A successful well taps into the groundwater below the water table. Draw a well in the diagram.

ISBN: 978-1-77149-036-8

B. **Write "true" or "false" for each sentence.**

1. Heavy rainfall or water from melted snow and glaciers can cause the water table to rise. _____

2. A water table can change due to natural causes such as drought. _____

3. Groundwater can enter impermeable rock. _____

4. Once lowered, the water table cannot return to its previous level. _____

5. A rising water table will never reach ground level and cause flooding. _____

6. Underground water is replenished by precipitation and water from melted glaciers and snow packs. _____

7. The soil below the water table has air spaces, as it does above the water table. _____

8. Lawn-watering, inefficient showers and toilets, and the bottled water industry are all human causes of lowered water tables. _____

C. **Write the meaning of each word that is related to groundwater.**

1. saturated: _____

2. impermeable: _____

3. groundwater: _____

4. water table: _____

Science Fact

The Russian city of Saint Petersburg is situated on a river delta with a high water table. This makes for shallow wells, but the underground transportation system had to be built extra deep; it is over 100 m below the Earth's surface.

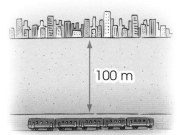
100 m

14

Glaciers and Polar Ice Caps

- Precipitation and temperature affect the size of polar ice caps and glaciers.
- All glaciers and ice caps are dynamic, with patterns of movement.
- Melting ice caps and glaciers affect both local and global water systems.

A. Fill in the blanks with the given words to complete the paragraph.

Glaciers and 1._____ do not stay the same size year after year, or even within a year. These enormous stretches of ice respond to fluctuating 2._____ of the seasons, to 3._____ , and to global 4._____ change. Sometimes, when all factors equal out, they may stay 5._____ for a time. But usually they are dynamic, 6._____ and retreating at distances often only noticeable over years.

ice caps
temperatures
advancing
precipitation
stationary
climate

B. Label the two glaciers below as a valley glacier or a continental glacier.

1.

_____

2.

_____

ISBN: 978-1-77149-036-8

Experiment

Melting glaciers and ice caps affect water systems around the world. Try this experiment to find out how melting ice caps affect sea levels.

Materials:

- a tray of ice cubes
- tape
- two partially filled bowls of water
- a plastic lid small enough to float in bowl

Steps:

1. Put half the ice cubes in the first bowl of water.
2. Put the remaining ice cubes on the plastic "land" that is floating in the second bowl.
3. Mark the top of the water line on each bowl with a piece of tape.
4. Allow the ice cubes to melt.

While you wait, write down what you predict will happen to the water level in each bowl.

Bowl 1 (ice cubes in water): _____

Bowl 2 (ice cubes on "land"): _____

5. Check the water level of each bowl when all ice cubes have completely melted. Write your observation.

Bowl 1 (ice cubes in water): _____

Bowl 2 (ice cubes on "land"): _____

Antarctica is completely covered in an ice sheet that is kilometres thick. The Arctic ice cap, however, is floating on the ocean. Based on your findings in this experiment, which ice cap would have a bigger effect on sea levels when it melts?

_____

Science Fact

Glacier
Antarctic Ice Water

Approximately 75% of the Earth's fresh water is in the form of glaciers, with almost all of that in the Antarctic ice cap.

15

Water Conservation

- Three of the main uses we have for water are domestic, agricultural, and industrial.

- The water we use comes from a watershed and is returned to a watershed.

- Human activity within a watershed affects our water supply.

Domestic Water Use

wash hands

drink

wash dishes

When washing dishes, never let water run while rinsing. Instead, fill one sink with soapy water and the other with rinsing water. It helps to conserve water.

A. Read the descriptions of the different ways we use water. Then answer the questions.

Domestic Water Use

We use water for personal hygiene and cleanliness. We drink and cook with it. Water is flushed down our toilets, pressure-sprayed on our driveways, and used to clean our cars. The water we use is groundwater from a well or lake treated and filtered at a water treatment plant. After we use it, water that disappears into the sewage system is treated, while water that flows into storm drains is not treated, before returning to the water system. Water that soaks into the Earth goes through a natural water filter through soil and rock before reaching the water table.

Agricultural Water Use

The agricultural industry uses the most fresh water because many crops require enormous amounts of water. In dry climates, underground aquifers can be depleted. Conservation efforts are important, and growers are switching to less wasteful irrigation methods. Agriculture can also pollute water systems by leaching pesticides and fertilizers into the water supply.

Industrial Water Use

Industrial demands for fresh water increase with industrialization. Water is used as a solvent, a coolant, and a transport agent. It is also a source of energy in the production of wood and paper products, steel, plastics, and many other items. Toxic waste is an inevitable by-product of industry. It is difficult to filter out because water is a good solvent. In addition, water used to cool industrial machinery is returned to a water body at a higher temperature, causing thermal pollution.

ISBN: 978-1-77149-036-8

1. Name two possible ways that we get our water at home. _____

2. Where does water from a bathtub drain go? _____

3. Where does water sprayed on a paved driveway go? _____

4. Name one agricultural use of water. _____

5. Which agricultural pollutants can leach into the water supply? _____

6. List two ways industry uses water. _____

7. Why would it be better to wash a car on grass than on pavement?

_____

_____

8. What is one way to conserve water in agriculture?

_____

9. What kind of pollution results from the disposal of warm water into a cold water body?

_____

B. **List three different ways you use water in a day. Then describe how you conserve water in at least one of your water uses.**

_____

_____

Science Fact

Desalination, or the removal of salt from salt water to make it fresh water, is one of the ways drier countries deal with water shortages.

16

Fluids and Density

- The particle theory of matter explains how the different states of matter vary in density.

- Liquids and gases are fluids because they flow.

- Mass, volume, and density relate as a property of matter.

Our boxes are the same size, but the cubes in my box are closely packed. The density of my box is higher than that of yours.

A. **Unscramble the letters to fill in the blanks. Then label the diagrams with "solid", "liquid", or "gas".**

Solids have _____ (rmoe) density than liquids, which have more density than _____ (esgas). The particle theory of matter explains this by showing the particles closely packed, as in a solid, or loosely together, as in a gas.

Solid water is one of the few exceptions to this rule; although ice is a solid, it is less dense than liquid water.

General Densities of the Three States of Matter

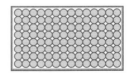   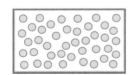   

_____   _____   _____

B. **Circle the fluids in the list of matter.**

We recognize fluids by the fact that they flow under force and take the shape of the container they fill.

orange juice	calculator	chair	honey
helium	shoe	maple syrup	clock
water vapour	oxygen	marble	air

ISBN: 978-1-77149-036-8

C. Fill in the blanks to complete the paragraph about density.

mass   decreases   temperature   volume   density   fluid

Density is the amount of matter in a given 1._____ of fluid. Every fluid has a characteristic density that does not change with a change in 2._____ or a change in volume. Indeed, one litre of milk has the same 3._____ as one tablespoon of milk. However, density can vary with 4._____ . With most fluids, density increases when a fluid's temperature 5._____ . In other words, the colder a 6._____ is, the denser it will be.

D. Use the equation to find the density of water at room temperature.

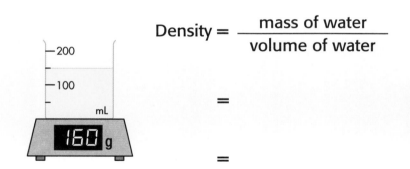

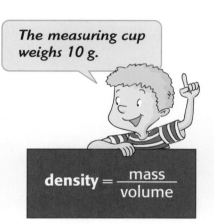

$$\text{Density} = \frac{\text{mass of water}}{\text{volume of water}}$$

$$=$$

$$=$$

$$\text{density} = \frac{\text{mass}}{\text{volume}}$$

The measuring cup weighs 10 g.

The density of water at room temperature is _____ g/mL.

Science Fact

A hydrometer is an instrument that measures the density of liquids. It specifically measures a liquid's density relative to the density of water. These instruments have a wide range of use, from breweries and dairies to the petroleum industry.

hydrometer

17

Viscosity

- Viscosity is not just a measure of the thickness or thinness of a fluid; it measures a fluid's flow, as well as how other substances move through it.

- Generally, heat reduces a fluid's viscosity while cold increases it.

"Oil" reaches the finish line first. So, "ketchup" has a higher viscosity.

A. Fill in the blanks with the given words and circle the correct words to complete the sentences.

> cohesion   adhesion   fluids   viscosity   temperature   viscous

1. _____ are a phase of solids / matter that flow when a force pushes or pulls them.

2. _____ is a measure of a fluid's resistance / reaction to flowing.

3. Generally, the more density / mass a fluid has, the more _____ it is.

4. The viscosity of a fluid usually increases / decreases when its _____ increases.

5. The particles of a fluid have a force of repulsion / attraction called _____ that causes them to move toward each other.

6. _____ is the force between a fluid's particles and the particles of another substance / fluid , such as the fluid's container.

B. Which of the following determine the viscosity of a fluid? Check the correct letters.

Determine the Viscosity of a Fluid

(A) the colour of a fluid

(B) how much space a fluid takes up

(C) the rate of a fluid's flow

(D) the temperature of a fluid

(E) how long it takes for a peanut to sink to the bottom of a fluid

---

Experiment – How the viscosity of a fluid changes with different temperatures

Choose two or more of the following fluids to use in the experiment. You will need two sets of each in small amounts: one to be refrigerated and one to be at room temperature.

Steps:

1. Pour a little more than a teaspoon of liquid into each container. There should be two containers of each liquid.

2. Refrigerate one set of your chosen liquids. Let the other set sit at room temperature.

3. One at a time, pour the room-temperature liquids onto a teaspoon.

4. Record how each liquid flows, numbering them in order of viscosity, from least to greatest.

5. Do the same with the refrigerated liquids.

Materials:

- Fluids: water   maple syrup
  honey   chocolate sauce
  vinegar   ketchup

- small containers, (4 for 2 different liquids, 6 for 3 different liquids)

- teaspoons

Record	
Fluids	Observation
room temp.	
refrigerated	
room temp.	
refrigerated	

How did each room-temperature liquid compare with the same refrigerated liquid? Write down if there was a change and what the change was.

Science Fact

Viscosity is very important in the production of motor oil. Viscosity modifiers are added to oil so it can flow freely through a vehicle's engine in the cold winter and in the hot summer.

Viscosity modifier

Motor oil

18

Buoyancy

I can float because the gas inside me has a lower density than the air.

- Buoyancy is a property of fluids.
- The force of buoyancy exerted on an object depends on a fluid's density.

A. Fill in the blanks with the given words to complete the descriptions.

buoyancy   gravity   densities

Helium balloons, toy sailboats, and cruise liners all float.   Matter floats as a result of another property of fluids: 1._____ .   When the force of 2._____ pushes an object down on a fluid, the fluid pushes back with the force of 3._____ .   If the force of buoyancy is equal to the force of gravity, the object will float. Objects float differently in different types of fluid because of their different 4._____ .   The more density a fluid has, the more buoyancy it can exert on an object.   So, buoyancy is created by the difference in density between the fluid and the object that floats on it.

5.   *Force of* _____ $\textcircled{=}$ *Force of* _____ ➝ **Float**

B. Draw arrows to show the directions of the forces.   Then write what the forces are.

1.

2.

ISBN: 978-1-77149-036-8

C. **Read what Dr. Simmons says. Figure out which glass and pitcher contain "salt water" and "fresh water". Label each container with "salt water" or "fresh water". Then answer the questions.**

An uncooked egg will sink in a glass of fresh water as a result of the low density of the fresh water. If salt is added to fresh water, the result will be different. This is because salt water has a higher density than fresh water. It exerts a stronger force of buoyancy on the egg to keep it afloat.

1.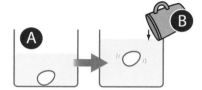

A _____ water

B _____

2.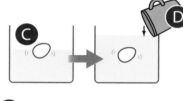

C _____

D _____

3. For question 1, which liquid has a greater density? How do you know?

_____

_____

4. For question 2, which liquid has a greater density? How do you know?

_____

_____

5. Why does matter float differently in different liquids?

_____

6. Is it possible to have buoyancy without gravity?   _____

Any swimmer will notice the difference in buoyancy between a pool of fresh water and an ocean. The Dead Sea has such a high salt concentration and high level of buoyancy force that a swimmer can stop, lay back, and read a book.

19

Compressed Fluids – Hydraulics and Pneumatics

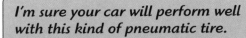

I'm sure your car will perform well with this kind of pneumatic tire.

- Gases and liquids are both fluids, but they are not equally compressible.
- Confined liquids under pressure are the basis of hydraulic systems. Confined air under pressure is the basis of pneumatic systems.

A. **Look at the microscopic view of gas and liquid particles. Draw the particles of gases and liquids when they are confined and put under pressure. Circle the correct words and answer the question.**

1.

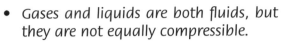

Gas Particles   **Liquid Particles**

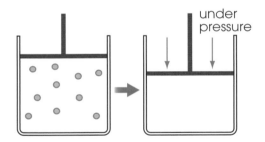

under pressure

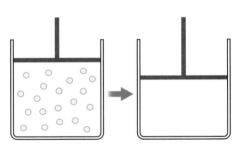

2. Gas particles have   lots of / little   space between them.

3. Liquid particles can move around but have   more / less   space to do so.

4.

How does the particle theory of matter explain why a gas has more compressibility than a liquid?

_____

_____

_____

_____

     ISBN: 978-1-77149-036-8

B. **Fill in the blanks with the given systems.**

hydraulic system   pneumatic system

When force is applied at one point of a _____ , an even stronger force is transmitted at another point further along in the system. Liquids are used as a source of power, and their force can be multiplied many times.

A _____ , usually using air, operates in a similar manner but with different applications. The compressibility of air makes a pneumatic system less suitable for things that require the force a hydraulic system is capable of.

C. **Look at the diagrams of the simple hydraulic systems. Then answer the questions.**

Hydraulic Systems

Which hydraulic system would be good for

a. shooting water a long distance? _____

b. lifting a heavy object? _____

D. **Find an example of one hydraulic system and one pneumatic system in your home, school, or neighbourhood. Describe the work each system does.**

Hydraulic System: _____

_____

Pneumatic System: _____

_____

Science Fact

Hydraulic and pneumatic systems were discovered, but not invented, by humans. The movement of blood through our hearts, arteries, and veins is a hydraulic system. Our respiratory system is a very important pneumatic system.

Hydraulic System
+
Pneumatic System

20

Using Fluids

We make use of one of the properties of fluids – force; it helps us to do work. This jackhammer has a pneumatic system which is powered by compressed air.

Work in Progress

- Properties of fluids affect how they are used.
- Human use of fluid mirrors the way fluid is used in nature.
- Fluid technology has social, economic, and environmental impacts.

A. **Which property of fluid is important to consider when using each of the following? Fill in the blanks using the words in bold.**

1. submarine _____

2. airplane cabin _____

3. streamlined race car

    _____

4. airplane wings in flight

    _____

5. pump for an air mattress

    _____

Properties of Fluids

1. **flow**

2. **pressure**
   - increases with depth
   - is exerted in all directions

3. fluids transmit **force** when confined, causing movement in another part of a system
   - liquids are less compressible than gases, and respond more quickly as a result
   - hydraulic systems use liquids to multiply a force
   - pneumatic systems use gases to multiply a force

B. **Match the human-made uses of fluid with the corresponding natural uses of fluid.**

Ⓐ Fish can inflate and deflate their bladders to give themselves the amount of buoyancy they need at any time.

Ⓑ Valves in our circulatory system direct the movement of fluid, opening for blood flowing in one direction, and closing in response to pressure from reverse flow.

Ⓒ Scuba divers wear a buoyancy compensator vest, which can take in and release gases, to lower themselves and rise to different depths in the water.

Ⓓ Gases produced from the burning of fuel in the internal combustion engine only move in one direction due to valves that prevent two-way movement.

Human-made use
vs
Natural use

◯ and ◯

◯ and ◯

ISBN: 978-1-77149-036-8

C. Read about the impacts of fluid technology on our world. Then answer the questions.

Technology that is based on the properties of fluids impacts our world socially, economically, and environmentally; there are advantages and disadvantages of fluid technology.

Medical hydraulic systems can save many lives, but the costs of tests and treatments mean they are not available to everyone. It is a difficult social dilemma to solve.

Fluid technology is used to make amusement rides run and to allow pilots to train in realistic flight simulators. It increases productivity in backhoes and other heavy machinery. Things are made with less human labour, but this is a disadvantage to the employee who is no longer needed.

Fluid technology has an environmental cost as well. Hydraulic devices can pollute the air. Spills during transport can be harmful to animal and plant habitats as well as our fresh water supply.

While we enjoy the benefits of fluid technology, we must also find better ways to distribute the technology, and use it in a responsible manner.

1. What is one of the social dilemmas regarding fluid technology?

    _____

    _____

2. Give an example of an economic advantage of fluid technology.

    _____

3. Describe how fluid spills harm the environment.

    _____

A Trail of Terra!

The fantastic special effects used in the production of your favourite movies likely owe their success to pneumatic or hydraulic systems.

ISBN: 978-1-77149-036-8

ANSWERS

ISBN: 978-1-77149-036-8

1 Exponents

1. 3 ; 2
2. 4 ; 2
3. $2.5^2 \times 8^2$
4. $1.7^4 \times 5^2$
5. $5^2 \times 9^3$
6. $4.6^2 \times 7^3$
7. $2^2 \times 7.8^4 \times 10^3$
8. $5^3 \times 6.3^3 \times 13 \times 14^2$
9. $3^4 \times 4^5 \times 5.5^2$
10. 27 ; 3 ; 9 ; 3 ; 3 ; 3 ; 3^4
11. 5^3
12. 6^4
13. 3^5
14. 10^4
15. 4^5
16. 2^7
17. 2 ; 16
18. 7 x 7 x 7 ; 343
19. 1.5 x 1.5 x 1.5 ; 3.375
20. $\frac{1}{3} \times \frac{1}{3} \times \frac{1}{3} \times \frac{1}{3}$; $\frac{1}{81}$
21. 8 ; 24
22. 216 ; 9 ; 207
23. 10 + 7.2 = 17.2
24. $3^4 \div 1 + 8 = 89$
25. 3
26. 2
27. 343
28. 76
29. 0
30. 101
31. 11
32. 980
33. 4 ; 64 ; 8 ; 512
34. 91.125 cm³
35. 3375 m³
36. 0.216 m³
37. 1 ; 8 ; 27 ; 64 ; 125 ;
    0.125 ; 1.728 ; 15.625 ; 39.304 ; 74.088
38. 2 ; 2
39. 2.5 ; 2.5
40. 4 ; 4
41. 1.2 ; 1.2
42. base
43. 5^2
44. $2^3 \times 5$
45. 2 x 3 x 7
46. 2×3^2
47. $2^3 \times 3^2$
48. $2^3 \times 7$
49. $2^5 \times 3$
50. $2^2 \times 5^2$
51. $2^2 \times 3 \times 5^2$
52. 3 x 5 ; $3^2 \times 5$; 3, 5, 15
53. $2^3 \times 3 \times 5$; $2^2 \times 3 \times 5 \times 7$; 2, 3, 4, 5, 6, 10, 12, 15, 20, 30, 60

32. $(\sqrt{10})^2, \sqrt{11^2}, 12, \sqrt{169}$
33. 9 cm²
    6 cm x 6 cm = 36 cm²
    3 cm x 9 cm = 27 cm²
    9 cm x 9 cm = 81 cm²
34. 32 cm²
    4 cm x 4 cm ÷ 2 = 8 cm²
    4 cm x 4 cm = 16 cm²
    8 cm x 8 cm = 64 cm²

35.

Square	Side Length	Perimeter
A	4 cm	16 cm
B	8 cm	32 cm
C	16 cm	64 cm

ribbon left: 150 – (16 + 32 + 64) = 38 (cm)
Yes, she will have enough ribbon and 38 cm of ribbon left.

36a.

Field	Side Length	Perimeter
Corn	2.2 km	8.8 km
Carrot	3.2 km	12.8 km

Total fencing: 8.8 + 12.8
= 21.6 (km)
About 21.6 km of fencing is needed.
b. Side length of wheat field: 21.6 ÷ 4 = 5.4 (km)
The side length is 5.4 km.
c. Side length of Tom's Field:
5.4 x 2 = 10.8 (km)
Area of Tom's field:
10.8 x 10.8 = 116.64 (km²)
Area of Jack's field:
5.4 x 5.4 = 29.16 (km²)
No. The area of Tom's field is not two times as that of Jack's.

2 Square Roots

1. 9
2. 11
3. 19
4. 25
5. 30
6. 1.3
7. 0.5
8. 4 ; 16
9. $10^2 = 100$
10. $(1.5)^2 = 2.25$
11. a
12. itself
13. 9 ; 3
14. $\sqrt{121} = 11$
15. $\sqrt{10\,000} = 100$
16. b
17. itself
18. $\sqrt{16}$; $\sqrt{25}$; $\sqrt{36}$; $\sqrt{81}$; $\sqrt{121}$; $\sqrt{144}$
19-22. (Individual guess-and-check)
19. 3 ; 4 ; 3.6
20. $\sqrt{25}$; $\sqrt{36}$; $\sqrt{25} = 5$ and $\sqrt{36} = 6$; $\sqrt{28} \approx 5.3$
21. $\sqrt{144}$; $\sqrt{169}$; $\sqrt{144} = 12$ and $\sqrt{169} = 13$; $\sqrt{150} \approx 12.2$
22. $\sqrt{81}$; $\sqrt{100}$; $\sqrt{81} = 9$ and $\sqrt{100} = 10$; $\sqrt{85} \approx 9.2$
23. <
24. <
25. >
26. <
27. =
28. >
29. $\sqrt{100}, 11, 4^2$
30. $\sqrt{13^2}, 14, \sqrt{255}, 7^2$
31. $5^2, (\sqrt{26})^2, \sqrt{33^2}$

3 Pythagorean Theorem

1. legs ; hypotenuse ; longest
2.

3.  4.

2.8 cm, 5 cm ; 5.7 cm   4.5 cm, 1.6 cm, 4.8 cm
5. B
6. A
7. A
8. 2^2 ; 3^2
9. $h^2 = 4^2 + 5^2$
   $h^2 = 4 + 9$ $h^2 = 16 + 25$
   $h^2 = 13$ $h^2 = 41$
   h = 3.6   h = 6.4
10. $h^2 = 6^2 + 20^2$
    $h^2 = 36 + 400$
    $h^2 = 436$
    h = 20.9
11. $h^2 = 5^2 + 8^2$
    $h^2 = 25 + 64$
    $h^2 = 89$
    h = 9.4

12. $h^2 = 9^2 + 9^2$
    $h^2 = 81 + 81$
    $h^2 = 162$
    $h = 12.7$
13. 8 cm   14. 4.47 cm   15. 4.9 cm
16. 6.63 cm ; 8.31 cm   17. 2.65 cm ; 1.87cm
18. $5^2 + 12^2$ | 13^2 19. $8^2 + 10^2$ | 13^2
        $25 + 144$ | 169 $64 + 100$ | 169
             169 | 169 ✔ 164 | 169 ✘
    It is a right triangle.   It is not a right triangle.
20. $5^2 + 7^2$ | 11^2 21. $6^2 + 8^2$ | 10^2
        $25 + 49$ | 121 $36 + 64$ | 100
             74 | 121 ✘ 100 | 100 ✔
    It is not a right triangle.   It is a right triangle.
22. Side length of square: $\sqrt{8^2 - 5^2} = 6.24$ (m)
    Area of square: $6.24^2 = 39$ (m^2)
23. Length of rectangle: $\sqrt{10^2 - 6^2} = 8$ (m)
    Width of rectangle: $\sqrt{5^2 - 3^2} = 4$ (m)
    Area of rectangle: $8 \times 4 = 32$ (m^2)
24. Base of triangle: $5 + \sqrt{5.8^2 - 5^2} = 7.94$ (m)
    Area of triangle: $7.94 \times 5 \div 2 = 19.85$ (m^2)
25. $\sqrt{2.5^2 + 1.2^2} = 2.77$ (m)
    The length of the ramp is 2.77 m.
26. Walk along the border: $30 + 20 = 50$ (m)
    Walk diagonally: $\sqrt{30^2 + 20^2} = 36.06$ (m)
    Janet will walk less: $50 - 36.06 = 13.94$ (m)
    Janet will walk 13.94 m less.
27.

Length of a: $\sqrt{20^2 + 10^2} = 22.36$ (m)
Length of b: $\sqrt{15^2 + 15^2} = 21.21$ (m)
The second slice of cake is closer.

4   Integers

1. 2
2. 3 ;

3. 6 ;

4. 2 ;

5. 2 ; -2   6. 4 ; -10
7. $21 + 6 - 3$; 24   8. $-9 - 7 + 4$; -12
9. $4 - 15 - 7$; -18   10. $-19 - 7 + 8$; -18
11. positive   12. negative
13. negative   14. positive
15. positive   16. negative
17. -15   18. 56   19. -72
20. -24   21. 45   22. -70

23. 48   24. -64   25. 27
26. -108   27. (-5)   28. (-5)
29. 6   30. (-2)   31. (-4)
32. (-2)
33. positive ; + ; +
    negative ; - ; -
34. -4   35. -5   36. 13
37. -27   38. -14   39. 38
40. 2   41. 5   42. 4
43. -4
44. (-32) ; -44
45. $\boxed{13 \times (-5)}$; $(-65) \div 2$; -32.5
46. $\boxed{(-20) \div (-4)}$; $5 + (-18)$; -13
47. $\boxed{(-4 + 2)}$; $(-11) \times (-2)$; 22
48. $\boxed{(3^2 - 21)}$; $(-12) \div (-2)$; 6
49. $\boxed{(-30) \div 6}$; $(-5) + (-5)$; -10
50. -32 ; 64 ; -128 ; Start with 1. Multiply by -2 each time.
51. -75 ; 149 ; -299 ; Start with 2. Multiply by -2 and subtract 1 each time.
52. -4 ; 2 ; -1 ; Start with 128, divide by -2 each time.
53. -16 ; 5 ; -2 ; Start with -1276. Add 1 and divide by -3 each time.
54. -768, -3072 ; -12 288 ; Start with -3. Multiply by 4 each time.
55a. -42   b. -7
56a. -18°C   b. -18.5°C

5   Order of Operations

1. 8 ; 64 ; 16 ; 64 ; 8 ; 72
2. $5^2 \times 8 - 5^2 = 25 \times 8 - 25 = 175$
3. 52   4. 11   5. 7
6. 0   7. 14   8. 154
9. 9   10. 128
11. $2^2 - 1 = 3$ 12. $22 - 4^2 = 6$
13. $1.8^3 - 0.2 = 5.632$ 14. $1.5^2 \times 10^2 = 225$
15. $1.5^2 \times 2^2 = 9$ 16. $1.331 + 3.3 = 4.631$
17. 202   18. 162
19. 2   20. $(-4)^2 = -4 \times -4 = 16$
                         $-4^2 = -4 \times 4 = -16$
21. $(-2)^3 = -2 \times -2 \times -2 = -8$
    $-2^3 = -2 \times 2 \times 2 = -8$
22. 81 ; -81   23. 25 ; -25
24. -1024 ; -1024
25. +   26. -   27. C
28. A   29. B   30. B
31. $-125 - 49 \times (-216) = -125 + 10 584 = 10 459$
32. $(-11) \times 9 = -99$ 33. $44 \div 4 = 11$
34. $36 \div 9 = 4$ 35. 8
36. 2   37. -215
38. 192   39. A ; 39.06 cm^2
40. C ; 87   41. B ; 227 cm^3

6 Expanded Form and Scientific Notation

1. 20 ; 4 ; 2×10 ; 4×1 ; 2 ; 4
2. $200 + 50 + 3$
   $= 2 \times 100 + 5 \times 10 + 3 \times 1$
   $= 2 \times 10^2 + 5 \times 10^1 + 3 \times 10^0$
3. $800 + 90 + 6$
   $= 8 \times 100 + 9 \times 10 + 6 \times 1$
   $= 8 \times 10^2 + 9 \times 10^1 + 6 \times 10^0$
4. $1000 + 600 + 20 + 5$
   $= 1 \times 1000 + 6 \times 100 + 2 \times 10 + 5 \times 1$
   $= 1 \times 10^3 + 6 \times 10^2 + 2 \times 10^1 + 5 \times 10^0$
5. $40\,000 + 7000$
   $= 4 \times 10\,000 + 7 \times 1000$
   $= 4 \times 10^4 + 7 \times 10^3$
6. 1.75×10^8 7. 1.06×10^5 8. 4×10^4
9. 9.7×10^6 10. 1.52×10^4 11. 7.06×10^4
12. $10\,000$; 4
13. $9.21 \times 1000 = 9.21 \times 10^3$
14. $7.08 \times 10\,000 = 7.08 \times 10^4$
15. $3.145 \times 10\,000 = 3.145 \times 10^4$
16. 2.5 17. $3\,270\,000\,000$
18. 3.145×10^7 19. $1\,008\,000$
20. 8.012×10^6 21. $63\,240\,000$
22. 1.927 23. 10^{13}
24. 10^9 25. 10^7
26. 10 ; 240
27. $5 \times 1000 + 2 \times 100 + 8 \times 10 = 5280$
28. $80\,232$ 29. $302\,021$
30. $212\,070$ 31. 3.7×10^6 ; 3.7×10^4
32. 4.107×10^6
33. 6.54×10^2, 5.46×10^3, 4.56×10^4
34. 1.09×10^7, 9.01×10^7, 1.09×10^8
35. 2.43×10^a, 3.42×10^a, $2.34 \times 10^{a+2}$
36. 4.56×10^b, 4.65×10^b, 6.54×10^b
37. Jupiter, Earth, Venus, Mars, Mercury
38. 5.97×10^{26} kg

7 Ratio and Proportion

1. $\frac{1}{2}$; $2{:}1$; $\frac{2}{1}$; $1{:}5$; $\frac{1}{5}$
2. $1{:}1$; $\frac{1}{1}$; $2{:}3$; $\frac{2}{3}$; $3{:}8$; $\frac{3}{8}$
3. (The pattern will have 4 ▨, 10 ▦, 7 ▧ and 6 ▥.)
4. $\overset{\times 6}{\frac{2}{p}} = \underset{\times 6}{\frac{12}{6}}$
   $p = 1$
5. $\frac{8}{3} \times 9 = \frac{s}{9} \times 9$
   $s = 24$
6. $\frac{3}{7} \times 14 = \frac{q}{14} \times 14$
   $q = 6$
7. $\frac{n}{10} \times 10 = \frac{8}{20} \times 10$
   $n = 4$

8. $\overset{\times 6}{\frac{3}{4}} = \underset{\times 6}{\frac{b}{24}}$
   $b = 18$
9a. $\frac{2}{3} = \frac{10}{n}$ b. $\frac{3}{5} = \frac{15}{m}$
    $n = 15$ $m = 25$
10. $\frac{11}{2} = \frac{p}{10}$; $p = 55$; There are 55 balls in the bag.
11. $\frac{3}{1.5} = \frac{x}{3}$ 12. $\frac{8}{16} = \frac{2}{a}$
    $x = 6$ $a = 4$
13. $\frac{9}{16} = \frac{4.5}{r}$ 14. $\frac{3}{5} = \frac{5}{t}$
    $r = 8$ $t = 8\frac{1}{3}$
15. $100\,000$
16. a. $\frac{1}{100\,000} = \frac{2}{p}$; $p = 200\,000$ (cm) ; 2000 m
    b. $\frac{1}{100\,000} = \frac{6}{q}$; $q = 600\,000$ (cm) ; 6000 m
    c. $\frac{1}{100\,000} = \frac{3.5}{r}$; $r = 350\,000$ (cm) ; 3500 m
17. a. $1{:}2\,400\,000$ b. 108 km ; 84 km
    c.

18. No. of heart stickers: $\frac{4}{5} = \frac{320}{n}$; $n = 400$
    No. of stickers in difference: $400 - 320 = 80$
    There are 80 more heart stickers.
19. No. of heart stickers: $\frac{2}{7} = \frac{n}{14}$; $n = 4$
    No. of star stickers: $\frac{3}{6} = \frac{m}{4}$; $m = 2$
    There are 2 star stickers on the hat.

8 Rate

1. 68   2. 55   3. 17
4. 1.4   5. 2.25   6. 15
7. 1.85 ; 2/L ; 2.10/L ; A
8. 1.60 ; 2.40/kg ; 2/kg ; A
9. $\$1.28 \times 3 = \$3.84$;
   cost of 3 L = $\$1.30 \times 3 = \$3.90$;
   cost of 3 L = $\$1.42 \times 3 = \$4.26$;
   apple
10. cost of 200 g = $\$0.02 \times 200 = \$4$;
    cost of 200 g = $\$0.021 \times 200 = \$4.20$;
    cost of 200 g = $\$0.018 \times 200 = \$3.60$;
    corned beef

ISBN: 978-1-77149-036-8

11.

USD ($)	CAD ($)	HKD ($)
1	1.23	7.75
3	3.69	23.25
5	6.15	38.75
7	8.61	54.25
9	11.07	69.75
10	12.30	77.50
20	24.60	155
30	36.90	232.50

12a. 1.23   b. 6.30   c. 0.13

13. $37.03

14. 180 g ; $\frac{3}{4}$ cup ; $4\frac{1}{2}$ bananas ; $\frac{3}{4}$ teaspoon ; $4\frac{1}{2}$ teaspoons

15. $1.97   16. 1 teaspoon

17. 40 servings

18a. $\frac{3}{2} = \frac{n}{6}$
$n = 9$
9 bananas are needed.

b. $\frac{3}{120} = \frac{n}{240}$
$n = 6$
6 bananas are needed.

19a. 2.22 kg   b. $14.40

20a. $2.88   b. $2.40

21a. Michelle makes: 57 (cookies)
Jane makes: 60 (cookies)
Total no. of cookies made: 117 (cookies)
They made 117 cookies in 1.5 hours.

b. Michelle makes: 114 (cookies)
Jane makes: 120 (cookies)
The ratio is 114:120 or 19:20.

9 Application of Percent

1. 9 ; $\frac{9}{78}$; $\frac{9}{78}$; 11.54% ; 12

2. 5 ; $\frac{5}{51}$; $\frac{5}{51}$ x 100% ; 9.8%

3. 18 ; $\frac{18}{160}$; $\frac{18}{160}$ x 100% ; 11.25%

4. **Way 1:**
Discount: $110.50 x 30% = $33.15
Sale Price: $110.50 – $33.15 = $77.35
Way 2:
Discount in Percent: 1 – 30% = 70%
Sale Price: $110.50 x 70% = $77.35

5. **Way 1:**
Discount: $59.24 x 30% = $17.77
Sale Price: $59.24 – $17.77 = $41.47
Way 2:
Discount in Percent: 1 – 30% = 70%
Sale Price: $59.24 x 70% = $41.47

6. **Way 1:**
Discount: $82.88 x 30% = $24.86
Sale Price: $82.88 – $24.86 = $58.02
Way 2:
Discount in Percent: 1 – 30% = 70%
Sale Price: $82.88 x 70% = $58.02

7. Discount in Percent: 1 – 10% = 90%
Sale Price: ($77.35 + $41.47 + $58.02) x 90% = $159.16 ; $159.16

8. Robot:
PST: $59.50 ; $4.76
GST: $59.50 ; $2.98
Total Cost: $59.50 + $4.76 + $2.98 = $67.24
Remote Car:
PST: $98.70 x 8% = $7.90
GST: $98.70 x 5% = $4.94
Total Cost: $98.70 + $7.90 + $4.94 = $111.54
Riding horse:
PST: $110.54 x 8% = $8.84
GST: $110.54 x 5% = $5.53
Total Cost: $110.54 + $8.84 + $5.53 = $124.91

9. Stove Top: $1139 ; $91.12 ; $56.95 ; $1287.07
Oven: $1513 ; $121.04 ; $75.65 ; $1709.69
Bike: $142.03 ; $11.36 ; $7.10 ; $160.49

10. The total cost of the oven is $1718.73. So, this is not a better buy.

11. $2500 ; 9% ; 5 ; $1125

12. $39 000 x 5% x 3 ; $5850

13. $19.80   14. $7\frac{1}{2}$ 15. 2%

16. $522 = $5800 x r x $2\frac{1}{2}$; $r = 3.6\%$
The interest rate is 3.6%.

17. $19 385 x 5.5% x $\frac{9}{12}$ = $799.63
He will pay back an interest of $799.63 after 9 months.

10 Fractions

1. $\frac{21}{56}$; $\frac{16}{56}$; $\frac{5}{56}$ 2. $\frac{7}{12} + \frac{2}{12}$; $\frac{3}{4}$

3. $2\frac{9}{21} + \frac{16}{21}$; $3\frac{4}{21}$ 4. $1\frac{4}{12} - \frac{1}{12}$; $1\frac{1}{4}$

5. $3\frac{8}{30} + 1\frac{7}{30}$; $4\frac{1}{2}$ 6. $1\frac{3}{4} + 1\frac{2}{4}$; $3\frac{1}{4}$

7. $8\frac{1}{6}$; $3\frac{1}{6}$ 8. $13\frac{7}{9}$; $6\frac{2}{9}$

9. $4\frac{5}{6}$; $2\frac{17}{30}$ 10. $2\frac{5}{8}$; $\frac{1}{8}$

11. $\frac{2}{21}$ 12. $\frac{5}{22}$ x $\frac{11}{4}$ = $\frac{5}{8}$

13. $\frac{19}{12}$ x $\frac{2}{5}$ = $\frac{19}{30}$ 14. $2\frac{1}{2}$

15. $3\frac{3}{16}$ 16. $2\frac{6}{13}$ 17. $17\frac{3}{5}$

18. $1\frac{3}{4} \times \frac{1}{3} = \frac{7}{4} \times \frac{1}{3} = \frac{7}{12}$
He travelled $\frac{7}{12}$ km.

19. $3\frac{3}{4} \times \frac{1}{3} = \frac{15}{4} \times \frac{1}{3} = 1\frac{1}{4}$
$1\frac{1}{4}$ kg of flour was used to make the cake.

20. $\frac{19}{14}$ 21. $\frac{5}{6}$ 22. $\frac{7}{9}$

23. $\frac{11}{50}$ 24. 3   25. $\frac{1}{5}$

26. 16   27. $\frac{8}{13}$ 28. $\frac{1}{33}$

29. 1   30. $5\frac{1}{2}$ 31. $\frac{5}{28}$

32. $8\frac{3}{4} \div 1\frac{1}{4} = \frac{35}{4} \times \frac{4}{5} = 7$
He needs 7 bags.

33. $1\frac{1}{4} \div 5 = \frac{5}{4} \times \frac{1}{5} = \frac{1}{4}$
Each apple weighs $\frac{1}{4}$ kg on average.

34. $(\frac{4}{14} + \frac{5}{14}) \times \frac{8}{15}$
$= \frac{9}{14} \times \frac{8}{15}$
$= \frac{12}{35}$

35. $\frac{10}{3} \times \frac{3}{8} - \frac{6}{7}$
$= \frac{5}{4} - \frac{6}{7}$
$= \frac{11}{28}$

36. $\frac{11}{8} - \frac{2}{5}$
$= \frac{55}{40} - \frac{16}{40}$
$= \frac{39}{40}$

37. $\frac{5}{6}$

38. $1\frac{1}{5}$ 39. $\frac{5}{13}$ 40. $\frac{11}{14}$

41. $(3 - \frac{1}{2}) \div \frac{1}{6} = \frac{5}{2} \times 6 = 15$
There are 15 guests.

42. $3\frac{2}{3} \times 4\frac{1}{2} = \frac{11}{3} \times \frac{9}{2} = 16\frac{1}{2}$
She has $16\frac{1}{2}$ L of juice.

43. $16\frac{1}{2} \div \frac{3}{8} = \frac{33}{2} \times \frac{8}{3} = 44$
The jars can fill 44 cups.

15. $3.\overline{72}$; R   16. $4.8\overline{3}$; R   17. $\frac{1}{6}$; $0.1\overline{6}$
18. $\frac{5}{9}$; 55.56%   19. $0.\overline{6}$; 66.67%
20. $\frac{2}{15}$; $0.1\overline{3}$; 13.33%   21. $\frac{6}{11}$; $0.\overline{54}$; 54.55%
22. $\frac{7}{11}$; $0.\overline{63}$; 63.64%
23. =   24. <   25. <
26. >   27. <   28. >
29. >   30. =   31. <
32. $2.00\overline{6}, 2.00\overline{6}, 206\%, 2.0\overline{6}$
33. $1.0\overline{6}, 1.16, 1\frac{1}{6}, 1\frac{6}{9}$
34. $\frac{33}{90}, 63.3\%, 0.6\overline{3}, \frac{7}{11}$
35. $1.20\overline{7}, 1.\overline{207}, 1.20\overline{7}$
36. 2.81   37. 8070   38. 50.6
39. 1130   40. 140   41. 4
42. 40   43. 4   44. 0.3
45. 90   46. 0.01   47. 2.023
48. 1.08   49. 0.05   50. 0.4
51. 7.2   52. 0.5   53. 0.5
54. 1.2   55. 0.15

56.

0.25	0.025
45	4.5
3.4	0.34

57.

1.4	140
0.279	27.9
0.26	26

58.

0.7	7
1.86	18.6
0.029	0.29

59.

0.18	0.9
0.8	4
1.56	7.8

60.

0.15	3
0.5	10
1.2	24

61.

0.9	300
0.18	60
1.8	600

62. $1.78 \times (1 - 35\%) = 1.78 \times 0.65 = 1.16$
There are 1.16 kg of ground beef.

63a. $0.65 + \frac{7}{12} \times 0.98 = 0.65 + 0.57 = 1.22$
He will get 1.22 L of soup base.
b. $(0.98 - 0.57) \times (1 - 45\%) = 0.41 \times 0.55 = 0.23$
There is now 0.23 L of beef stock.

11 Decimals, Fractions, and Percents

1. $0.\underline{9}9999... = 0.\overline{9}$
2. $1.\underline{13}13131... = 1.\overline{13}$
3. $1.\underline{024}02402... = 1.\overline{024}$
4. $5.0\underline{81}81818... = 5.0\overline{81}$
5. $3.1\underline{234}2342... = 3.1\overline{234}$
6. $2.78\underline{132}1321... = 2.78\overline{132}$
7. $1.17\underline{184}18418... = 1.17\overline{184}$
8. $4.0\underline{53}053053... = 4.0\overline{53}$
9. 0.6 ; T   10. $0.\overline{2}$; R   11. $0.0\overline{675}$; R
12. 2.875 ; T   13. $0.58\overline{3}$; R   14. 1.48 ; T

12 Nets

1. top ; side ; front   2. front ; side ; top
3. side ; top ; front   4. C ; B ; E
5. cross out the front view ;
6. cross out the side view ;
7. cross out the front view ;
8. cross out the top view ;
9.   10.   11.

 ISBN: 978-1-77149-036-8

12.

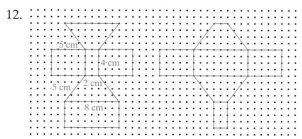

The net is formed by 2 identical trapezoids, 2 identical rectangles, 1 large rectangle, and 1 small rectangle.

13.

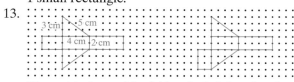

The net is formed by 2 identical right triangles, and 3 rectangles in different sizes.

14. B ;   15. A ;

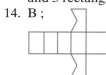

pentagonal prism   rectangular pyramid

16a.

Solid	Rectangular Prism	Triangular Pyramid	Pentagonal Pyramid
No. of Vertices (V)	8	4	6
No. of Faces (F)	6	4	6
No. of Edges (E)	12	6	10
V + F − E	2	2	2

b. 2

17. The solid has 12 edges. It is a hexagonal pyramid.

13 Circumference and Area

1. radius   2. diameter
3. circumference   4. diameter
                     A: 2.7 cm ; 5.4 cm
                     B: 2 cm ; 4 cm
5.

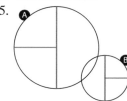

6. The length of diameter is two times the length of radius.
7. π ; 3 ; 9.42 (cm)   8. 2 x π x 10 ; 62.83 (m)
9. 2 x π x 0.5 ; 3.14 (cm)
10. π x 0.68 ; 2.14 (m)
11. π x 7 ; 22 (cm)   12. 2 x π x 1 ; 6.28 (m)
13. 7.32 cm   14. 4 cm

15. 16.13 cm   16. 5 cm
17. π x 1^2 = 3.14 (cm^2)
18. π x 3.9^2 = 47.78 (cm^2)
19. π x 20^2 = 1256.64 (cm^2)
20. A: 153.94 cm^2 ; B: 63.62 cm^2 ; C: 50.27 cm^2
21. area: 153.94 + 63.62 + 50.27 = 267.83 (cm^2)
    radius: $\sqrt{267.82 \div \pi}$ = 9.23 (cm)
    The radius of the big circle is 9.23 cm.
22. $\sqrt{267.83 \div 3 \div \pi}$ = 5.33 (cm)
    The radius of each circle is 5.33 cm.
23.

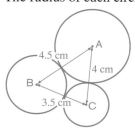

24. The length of $\overline{AB}$ is the sum of the radius of circles A and B, which is 4.5 cm. Use the same way to find the lengths of $\overline{BC}$ and $\overline{AC}$. The lengths of $\overline{BC}$ and $\overline{AC}$ are 3.5 cm and 4 cm respectively.
25. area: π x $(\frac{20}{2})^2$ = 314.16 (cm^2)
    The area of the spinner is 314.16 cm^2.
26. circumference: 20π = 62.83 (cm)
    He will need 62.83 cm of ribbon.

14 Surface Area and Volume

1. πr^2 ; h   2. $\pi 5^2$ x 4 = 314.16
3. $\pi 3.5^2$ x 6 = 230.91   4. $\pi 9.2^2$ x 5.5 = 1462.47
5. A: V = 1017.88 cm^3 B: V = 1628.6 cm^3
   C: V = 603.19 cm^3 D: V = 14.53 cm^3
6. A: 4.02 L   B: 2.62 L   C: 1.36 L
7. 1.85 L   8. 0.68 L   9. 12 cups
10. 8.19 cm   11. 17.41 cm
12.

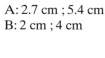

    ; r ; $2\pi r$
13. $2\pi 8^2$ + $2\pi 8$ x 25 = 1658.76 (cm^2)
14. surface area: $2\pi 7^2$ + 14π x 9 = 703.72 (cm^2)
15. surface area: $2\pi 7.5^2$ + 15π x 24 = 1484.4 (cm^2)
16. surface area: $2\pi 4^2$ + 8π x 4.5 = 213.63 (cm^2)
17. h = 9 cm   18. h = 11 cm
19. h = 34.98 cm   20. r = 9 cm ; h = 12.5 cm
21. The volume of the cylinder is 0.24 m^3.
22. The surface area of the cylinder is 2.28 m^2. So, he will need 9 cans of paint.
23. The surface area of each small cylinder will be 1.02 m^2.

15 Volume and Surface Area of Solids (1)

1. volume = 360 cm^3 ; surface area = 336 cm^2
2. volume = 35 cm^3 ; surface area = 76.2 cm^2
3. volume = 156 cm^3 ; surface area = 180.8 cm^2
4. volume = 600 cm^3 ; surface area = 486 cm^2
5. volume = 530 cm^3 ; surface area = 452 cm^2
6. volume = 453 m^3 ; surface area = 436.5 m^2
7. volume = 189 cm^3 ; surface area = 270 cm^2
8.

	A	B	C
V.	176 cm^3	176 cm^3	176 cm^3
S.A.	256 cm^2	240 cm^2	256 cm^2

9. the same
10. different
11. 512 cm^3
12. 152 cm^2
13. 8 blocks
14a. The total surface area to be painted is 2008 cm^2.
  b. The volume will be 5568 cm^3.
15. The total surface area is 250 cm^2.
16a. The volume of each piece of cake is 450 cm^3.
  b. The total surface area of each piece is 447.56 cm^2.
    So, she needs 5 bags of icing.

16 Volume and Surface Area of Solids (2)

1. volume = 1306.9 cm^3 ; surface area = 735.79 cm^2
2. volume = 1428.3 cm^3 ; surface area = 749.9 cm^2
3. volume = 1979.2 cm^3 ; surface area = 1602.2 cm^2
4. volume of cylinder: 785.4 cm^3
   surface area of cylinder: 471.24 cm^2
   volume of cube: 1000 cm^3
   surface area of cube: 600 cm^2
   The cube has a greater volume and surface area.
5. The cylinder of greatest volume is 2199.11 cm^3.
   So, 1720.89 cm^3 of clay is left.
6a. (6 x 6 x π x 20) ÷ (12 x 12) = 15.71
   The height is 15.71 cm.
  b. The total surface area to be painted is 2022.26 cm^2.
7. cylinder A: $\pi(3^2)(5)$ = 141.37 (cm^3)
   cylinder B:

   V = $\pi(6^2)(5)$ = 565.49 (cm^3)
   cylinder C:
   V = $\pi(9^2)(5)$ = 1272.35 (cm^3)
8. 4
9. 9
10. 1800 cm^3 ; 4050 cm^3

11. cylinder P:
   $\pi(5^2)(2)$ = 157.08 (cm^3)
   cylinder Q:
   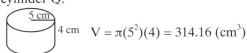
   V = $\pi(5^2)(4)$ = 314.16 (cm^3)
   cylinder R:
   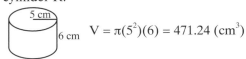
   V = $\pi(5^2)(6)$ = 471.24 (cm^3)
12. 2
13. 3
14. The volume of the container is 2700 cm^3.

17 Angle Properties of Intersecting Lines

1. 180° ; supplementary
2. the same ; opposite
3. 90° ; complementary
4. 180° ; supplementary
5a. complementary   b. supplementary
   c. opposite   d. supplemenary
6a. supplementary   b. complementary
   c. opposite   d. opposite
7. Complementary Angles:
   $\angle b$; $\angle k$; $\angle m$
   Supplementary Angles:
   $\angle d$; $\angle j$; $\angle g$
   Opposite Angles:
   $\angle e$; $\angle l$;
   $\angle i$; $\angle j$
8. complementary ; 90° ; 90° ; 55°
9. opposite ; 62°
10. supplementary ; 180° ; 180° ; 134°
11. $\angle$FOH = $\angle$AOB (opposite angles)
   $\angle$FOH = 35°
12. $\angle$HOI + $\angle$BOI = 180° (supplementary angles)
   $\angle$HOI = 180° – 62° – 35°
   $\angle$HOI = 83°
13. $\angle$DOF = $\angle$AOI (opposite angles)
   $\angle$DOF = 62°
14. $\angle$COD + $\angle$DOF = 90° (complementary angles)
   $\angle$COD = 90° – 62°
   $\angle$COD = 28°
15.
16.
17.
18.

19a. $\angle ABI + \angle DBI = 180°$ (supplementary angles)
     $\angle ABI + (38° + 67°) = 180°$
               $\angle ABI = 75°$
   b. $\angle BCD = \angle ICF$ (opposite angles)
      $\angle BCD = \angle ICF = 39° + 37° = 76°$
   c. $\angle GEF + \angle DEG = 90°$ (complementary angles)
     $\angle GEF + (90° - 38°) = 90°$
             $\angle GEF = 38°$

18. A ; interior
19.

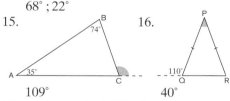

Let x be the measure of the small angle.
$x + x + 10° = 180°$
        $x = 85°$
So, the measure of the angles are 85° and 95° (85° + 10°).

18 Angle Properties in Parallel Lines

1. Corresponding

2. Interior

3. Alternate

4. corresponding ; alternate ; interior
5. corresponding ; alternate ; interior
6. alternate angles: $\angle e$; $\angle h$; $\angle f$ and $\angle g$
    corresponding angles: $\angle c$; $\angle d$; $\angle e$ and $\angle g$
    interior angles: $\angle e$; $\angle c$; $\angle d$ and $\angle h$
7. alternate angles: $\angle s$; $\angle y$; $\angle p$ and $\angle y$
    corresponding angles: $\angle w$; $\angle x$; $\angle s$ and $\angle y$
    interior angles: $\angle r$; $\angle x$; $\angle p$ and $\angle t$
8. $\angle a = 70°$; $\angle b = 110°$; $\angle c = 110°$; $\angle d = 70°$
9. $\angle e = 76°$; $\angle f = 104°$; $\angle g = 104°$; $\angle h = 104°$
10. $\angle i = 100°$; $\angle j = 80°$
11. $\angle m = 130°$; $\angle n = 50°$
12. corresponding ;
    alternate ; $\angle a = 132°$;
    180° ; supplementary ; $\angle c = 48°$;
    alternate ; corresponding ;
    180° ; supplementary ; $\angle f = 40°$
13. $\angle a = 86°$ (corresponding angles)
    $\angle b = 86°$ (alternate angles)
    $\angle e = 180° - 128° = 52°$ (interior angles)
    $\angle f = 128°$ (corresponding angles)
    $\angle d = 180° - 128°$ (supplementary angles)
    $\angle d = 52°$
    $\angle c + \angle b + \angle e = 180°$ (sum of angles in a △)
             $\angle c = 42°$
14. $\angle a + 35° = 90°$ (complementary angles)
         $\angle a = 55°$
    $\angle c = 180° - 55° = 125°$ (interior angles)
    $\angle d = 125°$ (corresponding angles)
    $\angle b = 125°$ (corresponding angles)
    $\angle e = 125°$ (alternate angles)
15. B ; corresponding
16. A ; supplementary
17. B ; interior

19 Angle Properties in a Triangle

1. $\angle a = 48°$; $\angle b = 72°$; $\angle c = 60°$;
    $\angle d = 27°$; $\angle e = 32°$; $\angle f = 42°$
2. A   3. B
4. B   5. A
6. $\angle a + 62° + 45° = 180°$ (sum of angles in a △)
            $\angle a = 73°$
    $\angle b + 45° = 180°$ (supplementary angles)
           $\angle b = 135°$
7. $\angle x + 68° + 68° = 180°$ (sum of angles in a △)
            $\angle x = 44°$
    $\angle y + 44° = 180°$ (supplementary angles)
           $\angle y = 136°$
8. $\angle m + 120° = 180°$ (supplementary angles)
         $\angle m = 60°$
    $\angle n + 60° + 90° = 180°$ (sum of angles in a △)
          $\angle n = 30°$
9. $\angle p = 32°$ 10. $\angle q = 70°$ 11. $\angle r = 69°$
12.   13.

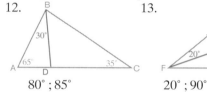

    80° ; 85°   20° ; 90°
14.

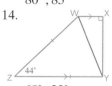

    68° ; 22°
15.   16.

    109°   40°
17. vertex angle: 360° ÷ 5 = 72°
    base angle: (180° − 72°) ÷ 2 = 54°
    The measures of the angles are 72°, 54°, and 54°.
18. $x + 3x + 6x = 180$
           $x = 18$
    Since 1:3:6 = 18:54:108, so the measures of the
    angles are 18°, 54°, 108°.

ISBN: 978-1-77149-036-8

19. $y + 4y + 4y = 180°$
    $y = 20°$
    The measures of the angles are $20°, 80°, 80°$.

20.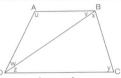
    $\angle u + \angle v + \angle w = 180°$ (sum of angles in a △)
    $\angle x + \angle y + \angle z = 180°$ (sum of angles in a △)
    Therefore, the sum of the angles in the trapezoid is $360°$ $(180° + 180°)$.

20 Constructing Bisectors

1. midpoint ; right

a.   b.

2. vertex ; two

3.

4.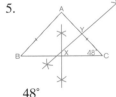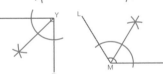

5. 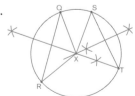   6.

    48°   90°

7.

8a. 2 cm   b. 2 cm
 c. 2 cm   d. 2 cm
9. X is the centre of the circle because the distance between X and any one of the points on the circle is the same.

10a. 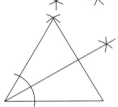   b. perpendicular
                            c. 90°

11. 135° is the sum of 90° and 45°. Bisect a straight line to form two 90° angles. Then bisect one of the 90° angles to form two 45° angles. Connect the 90° angle with the nearest 45° angle to make an angle of 135°.

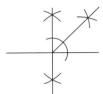

135°

12-13.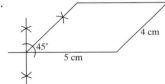

14. equilateral   15. 60°
16. Draw a 90° angle by constructing a perpendicular bisector. Then construct an equilateral triangle on the perpendicular bisector.

150°

17.

45°

5 cm   4 cm

21 Transformations (1)

1. A, E, M ;
   D, F ;
   C, I, J, P ;
   B, G, K, L
2. H, N
3. A and G ; F and J ; D and I ; K and L ; H and P
4. D and M ; B and C ; P and N ; I, J, and L
5. H   6. N   7. E, P
8. A(4,2) ; B(2,-2) ; C(-3,-2) ; D(-5,4) ; E(1,1) ;
   F(-2,3) ; G(4,-5) ; H(-4,0) ; I(-5,-6) ; J(-2,-6) ;
   K(6,-3) ; L(6,-6) ; M(3,4) ; N(0,-4) ; P(-4,-4)

ISBN: 978-1-77149-036-8

9-10.

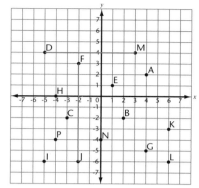

9a. horizontal
 b. (Suggested answers)
    (-5,4), (-4,4), and (-3,4)
 c. They have the same y-coordinates.
10a. vertical
 b. (Suggested answers)
    (-2,3), (-2,2), and (-2,1)
 c. They have the same x-coordinates.
11. a horizontal line
12.

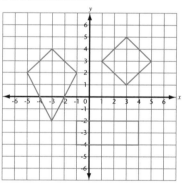

(3,1) ; (-5,2) ; (-1,-4)

13.

	Area (square units)	Perimeter (units)
Square	8	11.31
Kite	12	14.6
Rectangle	10	14

14. triangle: E
    trapezoid: P, T
    L-shape: U, W
15. A   16. B
17. -2,5 ; -2,3 ; -5,3
18. 4,-3 ; 3,-5 ; 2,-3

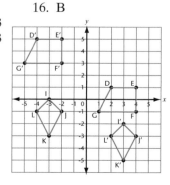

19. Translate 6 units left and 4 units up.
20. Translate 6 units right and 2 units down.

22 Transformations (2)

1.

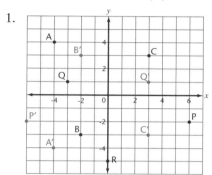

A'(-4,-4) ; B (-2,-3) ; B'(-2,3) ; C(3,3) ; C'(3,-3)
P(6,-2) ; P'(-6,-2) ; Q(-3,1) ; Q'(3,1) ; R(0,-5) ;
R'(0,-5)

2a. stays the same   b. changes in sign
3a. changes in sign   b. stays the same
4-5.

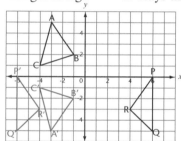

4. A(-3,5), B(-1,2), C(-4,1)
   A'(-3,-5), B'(-1,-2), C'(-4,-1)
5. P(6,0), Q(6,-5), R(4,-3)
   P'(-6,0), Q'(-6,-5), R'(-4,-3)
6. (-15,3), (-18,3), (-18,-1), (-13,-1)
7.

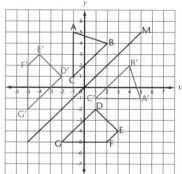

a. A(-1,5) ; A'(5,-1)   B(2,4) ; B'(4,2)
   C(-1,1) ; C'(1,-1)
b. D(1,-2) ; D'(-2,1)   E(3,-4) ; E'(-4,3)
   F(2,-5) ; F'(-5,2)   G(-2,-5) ; G'(-5,-2)
8. The coordinates of each point are interchanged.

ISBN: 978-1-77149-036-8

9a-d.

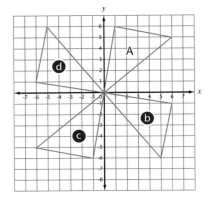

b. (6,-1), (5,-6), (0,0)
c. (-1,-6), (-6,-5), (0,0)
d. (-6,1), (-5,6), (0,0)
10. 90° ; 180° ; 270° clockwise
11a. (2,3), (6,0), (8,7)
b. (-2,-3), (-6,0), (-8,-7)
c. (-3,2), (0,6), (-7,8)
12-14.

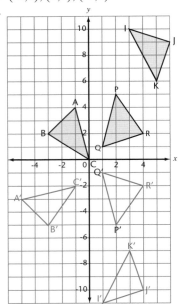

12. I'(1,-11), J'(4,-10), K'(3,-7)
13. P'(2,-5), Q'(1,-1), R'(4,-2)
14. A'(-5,-3), B'(-3,-5), C'(-1,-2)
15a. (-1,4), (2,1), (6,1)
b. (1,4), (-2,1), (-6,1)
16a. (4,-5), (7,-5), (5,0), (2,0)
b. (-5,4), (-5,7), (0,5), (0,2)

23 Number Patterns

1. 3 ; 3
   3 x 3 = 9
   3 x 4 = 12
   3 ; 1
2a. 31   b. 43
 c. 79   d. 106
3a. $4n - 1$ b. 39 ; 63
                            99 ; 119
4a. $3n - 2$ b. 25 ; 49
                            58 ; 97
5a. 4 ; 10 ; 16 ; 22 ; 28
 b. $6n - 2$
 c. 46 ; 88 ; 118
 d. figure 9 ; figure 12 ; figure 18
6a. 3 ; 6 ; 9 ; 12 ; 15 ; $3k$; 90
 b.

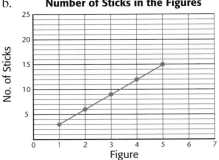

7a.

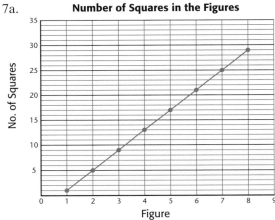

 b. $4n - 3$; 129   c. figure 25
8. 1^2 ; 2^2 ; 3^2 ; 16 (4^2) ; 25 (5^2) ; k^2
9a. 64
 b. 121
 c. 225

ISBN: 978-1-77149-036-8

10a. 20
  b. 16
  c. 19
11a.

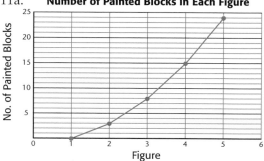

Number of Painted Blocks in Each Figure

  b. $n^2 - 1$ c. 399   d. figure 9

24 Algebraic Expressions

1.

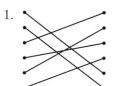

2. $x + y$ 3. xy
4. $4x - y$ 5. $5x + y$
6. $2x + \frac{1}{3}y$
7a. $\$2m$ b. $\$0.25n$
  c. $\$(2i + 5j)$ d. $\$(x + 0.01y)$
8. $(\frac{c}{2} + 4d)$ coins
9a. $\$8m$ b. $\$3p$
  c. $\$(5m + 3n)$ d. $\$(9m + 3k)$
10. $\frac{\$(3m + 3r)}{4}$
11. $(\frac{32}{m} + \frac{d}{3})$ cones and sundaes
12. $\$(9m + 3p + 12)$
13a. 34
  b. 6
14a. 13
  b. 33
15a. 0
  b. 3
16. 94
17. 10
18. 10
19. 38
20. 56
21. -2
22. 3
23. 0

24. 2
25. 11
26. 12
27.

x	y	$2(x + y)$	$2x + y$	$2x + 2y$
-2	0	-4	-4	-4
-1	1	0	-1	0
0	2	4	2	4
1	3	8	5	8
2	4	12	8	12

28. $2(x + y), 2x + 2y$
29. A ; 53   30. A ; 28   31. B ; 8

25 Equations

1. 35 ; 9 ; 70 ; 18 ; 88
2. $= 3 \times 9 + 3 \times 7$ 3. $= 4 \times 20 + 4 \times 6 + 4 \times 5$
   $= 27 + 21$ $= 80 + 24 + 20$
   $= 48$ $= 124$
4. $= 6 \times 5 + 6 \times 5 + 6 \times 5$
   $= 30 + 30 + 30$
   $= 90$
5. $3x$; $2y$; $12x$; $8y$
6. $= 4(5) + 4(4p)$ 7. $= 9(2m) + 9(3n)$
   $= 20 + 16p$ $= 18m + 27n$
8. $6p + 10q$ 9. $10a + 15b$
10. $3b$ 11. 7
12. $4m$ 13. $7p$
14. $2x$; $18z$ 15. $3j$; $2k$; $7i$
16. $3(5 + 7a) = 15 + 21a$
17. $2(4x + y) = 8x + 2y$
18a. $2(3x + 8) = 6x + 16$
  b. $4(p + q) = 4p + 4q$
  c. $5(3 + m) = 15 + 5m$
19a. $6(x + 3y) = 6x + 18y$
  b. $4(m + n) = 4m + 4n$
  c. $9a(b + 15) = 9ab + 135a$
20. $x = 22$
21. $y = 15$
22. $a = 84$
23. 3
24. 6
25. 105
26. 1
27. 32
28. 18
29. x ; x ; 4 ; 4 ; 4
   Left side: $5(4) = 20$
   Right side: $16 + 4 = 20$

30. $2y - 4 - y = y + 8 - y$
     $y - 4 + 4 = 8 + 4$
     $y = 12$
     Left side: $2(12) - 4 = 20$
     Right side: $12 + 8 = 20$

31. $4n - 5 - n = n + 13 - n$
     $3n - 5 + 5 = 13 + 5$
     $\frac{3n}{3} = \frac{18}{3}$
     $n = 6$
     Left side: $4(6) - 5 = 19$
     Right side: $6 + 13 = 19$

32. d ; 74
     $d = 4$
     Left side: $27(4) + 74 = 182$
     Right side: 182
     4

33. Let n be the number of marbles that Annie has.
     $n + 2n = 4n - 8$
     $n = 8$
     Left side: $8 + 2(8) = 24$
     Right side: $4(8) - 8 = 24$
     Annie has 8 marbles.

34. Let r be the growth rate of the plant.
     $21 + 3r = 21 \times 2$
     $r = 7$
     Left side: $21 + 3(7) = 42$
     Right side: $21 \times 2 = 42$
     The growth rate is 7 cm/year.

35. Let m be the number of marbles that Jack has.
     $m + 3m = 2(m + 13)$
     $m = 13$
     Left side: $13 + 3(13) = 52$
     Right side: $2(13 + 13) = 52$
     Jack has 13 marbles.

26 Data Management (1)

1a. sample   b. census   c. sample
    (Check b)
2a. census   b. sample   c. sample
    (Check a)
3a. sample   b. sample   c. census
    (Check b)
4. No. Because there are more people altogether (29) who voted for other types of movies than those who voted for "fantasy" (12).
5. (Individual answer)
6. B and C

7. (Individual answer)
8. The number of male and female teachers in Collingview Public School from 2003 to 2015
9. There will be about 35 teachers in 2018.
10. (Individual answer)
11. **Years of Experience vs Annual Income**

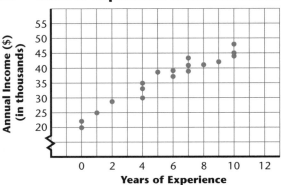

12. The more years of experience, the higher the annual income.
13. It will be about $50k.
14.

Superhero	No. of Children	Sector Angle	Percent
Batman	17	$\frac{17}{65} \times 360° \approx 94°$	$\frac{17}{65} \times 100\% = 26\%$
Spiderman	15	$\frac{15}{65} \times 360° \approx 83°$	$\frac{15}{65} \times 100\% = 23\%$
Superman	13	$\frac{13}{65} \times 360° \approx 72°$	$\frac{13}{65} \times 100\% = 20\%$
X-Men	9	$\frac{9}{65} \times 360° \approx 50°$	$\frac{9}{65} \times 100\% = 14\%$
Ironman	11	$\frac{11}{65} \times 360° \approx 61°$	$\frac{11}{65} \times 100\% = 17\%$
Total	65	360°	100%

15. **Our Favourite Superhero**

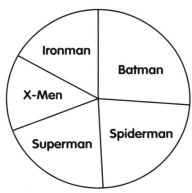

ISBN: 978-1-77149-036-8

16. About 915 children have Batman as their superhero.
17. (Individual answer)

27 Data Management (2)

1.

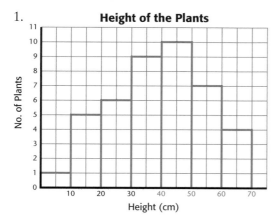

Height of the Plants

2. (Individual answer)
3a. scatter plot
   b. double line graph
   c. circle graph
   d. double bar graph
   e. histogram
   f. scatter plot
4.

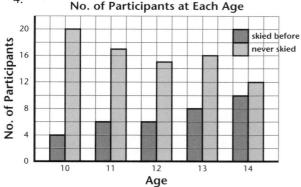

No. of Participants at Each Age

5. A double bar graph is used to represent the data because it can show two sets of discrete data.
6. (Individual answer)
7. She should use a circle graph because it can display a part to whole relationship.
8. 2
9. 5 ; 97
10. 3 ; 7

11. No outliers
12. 5 ; 102 ; 180
13. 6 ; 96 ; 96
14. with the outliers: 47.5 ; 40.5 ; 41
    without the outliers: 39.6 ; 40 ; 41
15a. No. Because the mean is affected by every data point. So, it is not a good idea to use the mean to represent the data if there are some outliers.
   b. Yes. Because every data point is used to calculate the mean. So, the mean is the best average.

28 Probability

1. $\dfrac{\text{favourable}}{\text{possible}} = \dfrac{2}{3}$
2. equal ; 1 ; $\dfrac{5}{5}$; 1
3. numerator ; 0 ; $\dfrac{0}{5}$; 0
4.

Blouse	**Skirt**	**Combination**
plain	black	plain, black
	grey	plain, grey
with ruffles	black	with ruffles, black
	grey	with ruffles, grey
with lace	black	with lace, black
	grey	with lace, grey

5a. $\dfrac{1}{6}$
   b. $\dfrac{1}{3}$
   c. $\dfrac{2}{3}$
   d. $\dfrac{1}{2}$
6. B
7. 31%
8. 0%
9. 69%
10. 81%
11. 100%
12a. $\dfrac{1}{5}$
   b. $\dfrac{2}{5}$
   c. $\dfrac{4}{5}$
   d. $\dfrac{4}{5}$

13a. $\frac{1}{6}$

 b. $\frac{5}{6}$

 c. $\frac{1}{2}$

 d. $\frac{1}{2}$

14. P(not getting a vowel) $= \frac{3}{5}$

 P(not getting a composite number) $= \frac{2}{3}$

 No, the probability of not getting a composite number is higher.

15a. 1 to 14 ; 14 to 1

 b. 6 to 9 ; 9 to 6

 c. 4 to 11 ; 11 to 4

 d. 6 to 9 ; 9 to 6

 e. 9 to 6 ; 6 to 9

16. 45% ; 55% ; 9 to 11

17. 19 to 6

ISBN: 978-1-77149-036-8

1 Polar Bears – Did You Know?

A. 1. C
    2. B
    3. B ; C
    4. A

B. 1. BI
    2. PRP
    3. G
    4. F
    5. TI
    6. PP
    7. BI

C. (Individual writing)

2 Cambodia's Angkor Wat: Endangered by Tourism

A. Paragraph 1: B
    Paragraph 2: D
    Paragraph 3: E
    Paragraph 4: C
    Paragraph 5: A

B. 1. It was built in the early 12th century as a Hindu place of worship, but evolved into a revered Buddhist temple as the religion and inhabitants changed.
    2. For this reason, while other countries in the region, such as Thailand and Malaysia, began to prosper and invite foreign tourists on a large scale, Cambodia, with little infrastructure, was still a place that outsiders knew little about.
    3. A few years ago (2004) over a million foreigners came to Cambodia, and more than half said they had come to visit Angkor Wat.

C. (Individual additional non-progressive verbs)
    Sense: feel ; hear ; see ; taste
    Mental State: believe ; know ; remember ; want
    Emotional State: fear ; hate ; like ; mind
    Existence: appear ; be ; contain ; seem
    Possession: belong ; have ; own ; possess

D. (Individual writing)

3 Canadian Nobel Prize Laureates

A. 1. prestigious
    2. established
    3. bequest
    4. inventor
    5. economics
    6. personal
    7. prestige
    8. attention
    9. impressive
    10. scientists
    11. founded
    12. shared
    13. Peace
    14. efforts

B. 1. came about
    2. broke in
    3. carried on ; took down
    4. died down
    5. get over
    6. has/had gone through
    7. keep to

C. (Individual definitions and sentences)

4 Naming a Public Holiday

A. 1. B
    2. C
    3. B

B. (Individual answer)

C. 1. on
    2. for
    3. from
    4. in
    5. from
    6. in
    7. about
    8. of
    9. to
    10. for
    11. with
    12. for

D. 1. at
   2. of
   3. with
   4. to ; for
   5. with
   6. for
E. 1. for
   2. about
   3. about
   4. about
   5. of
   6. with
   7. of
   8. of
   9. of
   10. in
   11. of
   12. about
F. (Individual writing)

5   The History of Christmas Giving

A. 1. He was actually a man named Nicholas who gave his inherited wealth to the poor and became a monk. He helped the needy and became known as the protector of children and sailors, and was later made a saint.
   2. He gave fruits, nuts, and candies to good children and lumps of coal to naughty ones.
   3. Nicholas tried to help a poor girl who needed a wedding dowry, and he threw a sack of gold coins through her window, which landed in her stocking that had been hanging up to dry.
   4. It attracted shoppers with Christmas-themed window displays and kept its doors open until midnight on Christmas Eve.
   5. (Individual answer)
B. 1. gorgeous, tall, green Christmas
   2. most popular European
   3. precious, heavy gold
   4. special, old German
   5. beautiful, long, silver wire
   6. interesting, miniature, colourful paper
   7. expensive, big, new doll
   8. famous, big, old, American department
C. (Individual writing)

6   The Remarkable Journey of Al Gore

A. 1. Al Gore received about 500 000 more votes than George W. Bush in the 2000 presidential race.
   2. (true)
   3. The documentary *An Inconvenient Truth* was turned into a bestselling book with the same title.
   4. Al Gore shared the 2007 Nobel Peace Prize with the scientists of the Intergovernmental Panel on Climate Change for their efforts in addressing the problem of global warming and climate change.
B. (Individual answer)
C. (Suggested answers)
   1. When did Al Gore run for the presidency against the Republican candidate George W. Bush?
   2. How many more votes did Al Gore receive than George W. Bush?
   3. How did Al Gore present his message about global warming?
   4. Where was the film *An Inconvenient Truth* shown?
   5. Why do many people hope that Al Gore will run for the presidency again?
D. (Suggested answers)
   1. Schools and town halls were the places where Al Gore went to impart his message about global warming. / Al Gore went to schools and town halls where he imparted his message about global warming.
   2. 1965 was the year when Gore enrolled in Harvard University.
   3. The media wanted to know why Gore enlisted in the U.S. military.
   4. There was a time when Gore struggled to make a decision about joining the U.S. military.
   5. This is the cathedral where Gore married Tipper.
   6. Gore gave a speech about why he supported the use of green energy.

7 The Wisdom of a Baseball Player: Yogi Berra's Quotes

A. 1. "Those" refers to stand-up comedians and writers of humour.
   2. He is revered as a humorist because he often came up with quotes containing misused words with comic effects.
   3. It implies "open to all".
   4. (Individual answer)
   5. (Individual answer)

B. 1. Stand-up comedy shows started to be popular long ago.
   2. ✔
   3. I never find it easy to be a person of humour.
   4. It is certainly amusing to read Yogi Berra's one-liners.
   5. Being humorous is completely different from being silly.

C. 1. My brother never finds it hard to make me laugh.
   2. The comedian is so famous that he drew an extremely large audience to his show.
   3. His performance is humorous enough to bring laughter to everyone throughout the two-hour show.
   4. Lester commented quite casually on the controversial issue.
   5. Yogi Berra is widely known for his sense of humour.
   6. His is always quick at coming up with new one-liners.
   7. You can usually discover great philosophy in what he says.

8 Too Much of a Good Thing: the "Law of Unintended Consequences"

A. 1. Purpose: to control the greyback cane beetle that was devastating sugar cane crops
      Consequence: The toad population has now grown to more than 200 million, severely damaging the native Australian ecosystem.
   2. Purpose: to stabilize soil erosion
      Consequence: It grew like a weed, threatened the natural flora, and got in the way of forest rejuvenation.
   3. Purpose: to prevent and reduce forest fires
      Consequence: Old trees that were susceptible to pests and disease were not burned down, allowing accumulated matter on the forest floor to remain, so new seedlings could not sprout and new trees could not grow. Now the forests are seriously threatened by pests such as the pine beetle.
   4. (Individual answer)

B. 1. Surprisingly, the government did not do any research before introducing the species to the country.
   2. Theoretically, the cane toad can control the damage done by greyback cane beetles to the sugar cane.
   3. Ideally, the whole population of cane beetles could be wiped out from Australia.
   4. Honestly/Frankly, I don't think this policy will work without causing other problems.
   5. Clearly/Obviously, the Australian government is facing another serious pest problem – the cane toad.

C. (Individual writing)

ISBN: 978-1-77149-036-8

9 How to Talk Like a Fashion Trendsetter

A. 1. Hipster cool
2. Punk rock
3. Preppy chic
4. Bollywood
5. Goth glam
6. Boho chic
B. (Individual answer)
C. 1. when ; S
2. and ; or ; and ; C
3. whether...or ; CR
4. If ; S
5. and ; C
6. Both...and ; CR
7. or ; C
8. Although ; S
D. (Suggested answers)
1. You can buy either the belt or the necklace.
2. Try both jackets on before you decide which one to buy.
3. My friend, Sean, likes the punk rock style, but I prefer the classic style.
4. Both Sharon and Angela have decided to wear something purple to the prom.
5. Kenneth is saving up his allowance because he wants to buy a pair of leather gloves for his mom's birthday.
6. Jeans are a favourite for many young people and they have been popular since the 1950s.

10 Watch Out for Those Language Bloopers!

A. (Individual answers)
B. 1. We need an energy bill that encourages conservation.
2. Rarely is the question asked: are our children learning?

C. 1. SC
2. A
3. OC
4. SC
5. OP
6. OV
7. S
8. OP
D. (Individual writing)

11 Don't Be a Dope: Drugs in Sports

A. 1. During the two World Wars, soldiers were given cigarettes because cigarettes were considered to be able to provide extra protection against colds and boost concentration.
2. ✔
3. The use of performance-enhancing drugs in competitive sports during the early days was considered acceptable as they helped athletes perform better.
4. Gene doping refers to the activity of altering cells, genes, and other genetic material for the purpose of improving athletic performance.
B. 1. Some new drug-testing policies have been introduced by the World Anti-Doping Agency.
2. The WADA Athlete Guide can be obtained from their website.
3. The hard evidence that some performance-enhancing drugs have resulted in long-term harmful consequences for those who took them cannot be disputed.
4. "Gene doping" is considered to be as sinister as drug doping (by many people).
C. (Suggested answers)
1. The organizing committee had all athletes tested for performance-enhancing drugs before the commencement of the competitions.
2. They want to get the samples examined as soon as possible.
3. Methods of detecting various performance-enhancing drugs need improving.
4. People need educating about the harmful effects of doping.

12 One of the World's Most Published Editorials

A.   (Suggested answers)
1.   They think that if they do not understand certain things, then these things simply do not exist.
2.   Life would lack lustre without childhood dreams and imaginations.
3.   If you have faith, fancy, poetry, love, and romance, you will be able to open yourself up to the beauty and glory of the things you cannot see.

B.   1.   It explained to Virginia that there really is a Santa Claus, just like there is love, generosity, and devotion.
2.   (Individual answer)

C.   1.   IND
2.   SUB
3.   SUB
4.   IMP
5.   IND
6.   IMP
7.   SUB
8.   IND

D.   (Suggested answers)
1.   Cindy wishes she had not asked the silly question.
2.   If I were Keith, I would not have turned down the offer.
3.   If Jan saw fairies, she could take pictures of them.
4.   If Timothy were Molly, he would not have believed in that story.

E.   (Individual writing)

13 Steven Fletcher, an Exceptional Public Servant

A.   1.   A
2.   B
3.   B
4.   C

B.   (Suggested answers)
1.   He was twice elected president of the University of Manitoba Students' Union.
2.   He was recently inducted into the Terry Fox Hall of Fame.
3.   Soon the family moved back to Canada, and Fletcher grew up in Manitoba.
4.   He soon found work in his chosen profession in the environment he loved, and life was good.
5.   A year later, while Fletcher was driving to a job site in northern Manitoba, his vehicle hit a moose.
6.   When his busy schedule allows, he likes visiting the Fort Whyte Centre.
7.   Doctors told him he would be spending the rest of his life in an institution, but Fletcher decided things would be otherwise, and after a long and painful period of rehabilitation, during which time Fletcher regained the ability to speak, he returned to university to obtain a Master of Business Administration Degree.

C.   1.   Fletcher has been inducted into the Terry Fox Hall of Fame and he has received the King Clancy Award.
2.   Fletcher had won the Manitoba kayak competition two times before the accident happened.
3.   If you like the outdoors, you can visit the Fort Whyte Centre and you can hike along the pond and listen to the sounds of water foul there.

D.   (Individual writing)

14 The Seven Sacred Teachings

A.   (Suggested answers)
Wisdom is the ability to think before we act and understand clearly what is good and bad, or right and wrong.
Love means giving kindness without asking for or expecting anything in return.

Respect is the ability to honour others' sincere and healthy beliefs although they may be different from ours.

Courage is being brave enough to stand alone to do what we believe in, and to do things differently because we know the outcome would be better that way.

Honesty means saying, thinking, and doing only the things we really mean.

Humility is the ability to admit that we don't know everything, to admit mistakes, to be successful without being arrogant, to let others take the credit, and to set aside what we want for the needs of others.

Truth is the ability to tell the truth and the desire to be truthful.

B. (Suggested answers)
1. Below is a list of what we consider the "Seven Sacred Teachings".
2. How can we become better people?
3. What a wonderful world it would be if everyone followed the Seven Sacred Teachings!
4. Try to say, think, and do only the things you really mean.

C. (Suggested answers)
1. How can I improve myself?
2. The "Seven Sacred Teachings" include wisdom, love, respect, courage, honesty, humility, and truth.
3. Hand in your project ideas on First Nations culture next Friday.
4. What is the play about, Christine?
5. Come to see my performance, Matthew.
6. Where is the school hall?
7. What a great show!

15 Twenty Thousand "Oskar Schindlers": the Holocaust Rescuers

A. 1. It stands for one who risked one's life to save Jews during Hitler's era of Nazi atrocities in Europe.

2. Most of these diplomats did so secretly, or even against the express orders of their own governments!
3. Although he failed to convince the Canadian government to take in Jewish refugees when he was Canada's top diplomat in France as World War II began, Vanier's continued efforts helped change Canada's immigration policy and enabled more than 186 000 European refugees to settle in Canada between 1947 and 1953.
4. (Suggested answer)
Canada could benefit from accepting Jewish refugees because the capital and expertise they brought to Canada could boost the economy.

B. 1. so that they could travel out of the danger zone ; ADV
2. whom Schindler rescued ; ADJ
3. while he served as the Japanese Consul General in Lithuania ; ADV
4. when he returned to Japan ; ADV
5. which Georges Vanier's son, Jean, founded ; ADJ
6. Exactly how many "Schindlers" there were ; N
7. why someone risked his or her life to save others ; N

C. (Individual writing)

16 An Ancient Story about the Sun and the Moon

A. "The Sun and the Moon" described three physical phenomena. First, it explained how the solar system came about and how it evolved around the sun. It also explained why there are tidal changes in oceans and seas. The eclipse of the moon was accounted for in "The Sun and the Moon" too.

B. (Individual writing)

C. 1. Linda told Julie that the Star and the Crab were children of the Sun and the Moon.
2. Timothy says that there are a lot of similarities among the folktales of different countries around the world.

3. Ginny told Kingsley that her mom had bought her a set of books on Greek mythology.
4. Mom said that she would tell me an interesting folktale before I went to bed.

D. 1. Jerry asked Shirley who had told her that there had been ten suns in the past.
2. The teacher asked the children if/whether they wanted to learn more about their country's legends.
3. Cedric asked where he could find the illustrations of ancient heroes.
4. The librarian reminded us not to write or draw in the books.
5. Mr. Willis told me to create another story about the sun and the moon.

17 Do Aliens Exist?

A. 1. C
2. A
3. C
4. C
B. 1. then
2. that day
3. that night
4. the next day/the following day
5. the year before/the previous year
6. the next Monday/the following Monday
7. eight years before
8. five days from then
9. the next month/the following month
10. three weeks before
11. the weekend before/the previous weekend
12. the next Christmas/the following Christmas
13. that afternoon
C. 1. Jenny said that she had borrowed that book from the library the week before/the previous week.
2. Sandra asked Dave if/whether he believed there really were aliens then.
3. Mr. and Mrs. Hayes said that they had seen a UFO hover over their house six years before.
4. Anna said that they/we could go to the Ontario Science Centre the next weekend/the following weekend.

5. Emily told Sam that a seminar about the existence of life on other planets would be held there the next Friday/the following Friday.

D. (Suggested answers)
1. Nelson asked me, "Will you watch the program about aliens on the Discovery Channel tomorrow?"
2. "Research into the atmospheric conditions of different planetary bodies started some years ago," the astronomer explained to us.
3. "My uncle bought me these cute alien dolls last summer when he came to visit," Tammy said.
4. Ricky's sister told him, "I have to hand in a book report on a science fiction book in two weeks."

18 Saving Lake Winnipeg

A. Paragraph 1: B
Paragraph 2: B
Paragraph 3: B
Paragraph 4: A
Paragraph 5: B
Paragraph 6: A
B. (Individual writing)
C. 1. If I owned a cottage in Manitoba, I would spend every summer there.
2. ✔
3. If Macy had been to Winnipeg before, she would have known more about the city.
4. If the pollution problem of Lake Winnipeg continues, all wildlife will be adversely affected.
5. Lake Winnipeg would recover if everyone started using phosphate-free detergents today.
6. ✔
7. I would teach everyone how to make phosphate-free detergent if I had the formula.
8. If I were a citizen of Manitoba, I would do everything I could to help save Lake Winnipeg.

ISBN: 978-1-77149-036-8

19 Depression in Teenagers: a Very Treatable Condition

A. 1. Depression is a common ailment affecting about one out of every 25 teens each year.
2. ✔
3. Depression can be caused by a chemical imbalance in the brain.
4. Medication is one of the many ways to treat depression.
5. ✔
6. People suffering from depression may have sudden outbursts of anger or tears over relatively small matters.

B. (Individual writing)
C. (Individual writing)

20 The Start of the Sagas

A. 1. Dagur
2. Borr
3. Laxdœla
4. Valkyries
5. Heimskringla
6. Odin
7. Loki
8. Niflheim
9. Bestla
10. Búri
11. Delling
12. Múspell

B. (Individual writing)
C. (Individual writing)

21 Green Iceland: a Letter from Uncle Josh

A. Reykjavik: capital city of Iceland; filled with parks and gardens
The Blue Lagoon: an outdoor geothermal pool with water full of minerals
Gulfoss: a great waterfall in Iceland
Geysir: a place with a lot of colourful bubbling mud pots, steam vents, and a few geysers
Thingvellir National Park: the site of the world's oldest parliament

B. 1. As there are a lot of volcanoes in Iceland, they trap the heat energy and use it to generate electricity and provide hot water.
2. He thinks that Icelanders are trying to live in an environmentally friendly way and they reduce as much as possible the emission of carbon dioxide, which is one of the major causes of global warming.

C. 1. Iceland was ranked as the most developed country in the world in 2007 by the United Nations' Human Development Index.
2. Ocean-fresh seafood is served by many restaurants in Iceland.
3. The ancient language of the Vikings is still spoken by Icelanders.

D. 1. Many Icelanders do believe in the existence of elves.
2. The hotel does provide free shuttle services to many attractions around the city.
3. It's not usual to see polar bears in Iceland but I did see one on my trip there.

E. 1. Never did we expect to see the Northern Lights in Iceland.
2. Little does Keith know about Iceland.
3. Seldom do Icelanders add salt to their food.
4. Hardly had the tourists arrived at the geyser when it erupted.

F. 1. What we all must try is the Icelandic skyr.
2. What some tourists to Iceland want to see are the Northern Lights.
3. What many people do not know is that it is not that cold in Iceland.

22 Magnificent Trees

A.

Name	—	—	General Sherman	The Tule Tree	Pando/ Trembling Giant
Species	Wattieza	Great Basin bristlecone pine	Giant Sequoia	Montezuma cypress tree	quaking aspen
Location	—	White Mountains of California	Sequoia National Park in California	Oaxaca, Mexico	Utah, USA
Age	—	about 5062 years old	about 2100 years old	at least 2000 years old	80 000 years old
Measurement	Height: 8 metres	—	Height: 84 m Base circumference: 31 m	Height: 40 m Base circumference: 50 m	Weight: over 6 000 000 kg
Record	the earliest known tree	the oldest known non-clonal organism still living	the largest non-clonal tree by volume	the stoutest tree	the heaviest living organism

B. (Individual writing)

23 High Flight – a Poem by John Gillespie Magee, Jr.

A. (Suggested answers for 1 – 3)
  1. Noonan has the ability to make references to other great works and reinterpret them to achieve the effect she desires.
  2. It could be interpreted as "broke away from the centre of gravity and soared high into heaven".
  3. Magee expressed in his poem the thrill of being up in the air where few could reach, not even larks or eagles.
  4. B
  5. (Individual answer)
B. (Individual writing)
C. (Individual writing)

24 Hannah Taylor and the Ladybug Foundation

A. 1. It refers to Hannah seeing a man eating out of a garbage can.
  2. It refers to her effort in helping the homeless.
  3. (Suggested answer)
    She wanted to draw more attention to the event.
  4. (Individual answer)
B. (Suggested answers)
  1. too ; also ; furthermore
  2. in the same way ; by the same token ; in like fashion
  3. instead ; nevertheless ; on the other hand
  4. such as ; namely ; to illustrate
  5. indeed ; of course ; above all
  6. then ; later on ; subsequently
  7. usually ; ordinarily ; generally speaking
  8. as ; because ; due to
  9. so ; therefore ; consequently
  10. except ; other than ; exclusive of
  11. in brief ; to sum up ; all in all
C. (Individual writing)

25 The Truth about Water

A. 1. The Earth is called the "blue planet" because about 71% of the planet's surface area is covered in water, and when seen from space, the Earth looks blue.
  2. Water is used by farmers in irrigation to keep crops alive and keep livestock healthy.
  3. Freshwater distribution is unbalanced because most of the Earth's fresh water is in the form of glaciers and permanent snow, in groundwater basins, or in the atmosphere, all of which are hard to reach. The rest can be found in lakes and rivers.
  4. Women and children in developing countries with inadequate access to safe water are often responsible for collecting water for their household.
  5. Globalizing access to safe water means ensuring that more and more people around the world have access to a supply of safe water.
B. (Individual writing)

26 Yoga: a Most Healthful Form of Exercise

A. Viniyoga: synchronizing breathing techniques with postures

Ashtanga yoga: performing postures in a fast-paced, flowing sequence

Kundalini yoga: unlocking a powerful energy that exists at the base of the spine

Jivamukti yoga: intense, physical postures performed with chanting and meditation

Power yoga: more rigorous form of Ashtanga yoga postures to build up a sweat

Forrest yoga: yoga sequences with other core strengtheners

Happy Face yoga: a series of 30 facial exercises, along with deep breathing and relaxation in between

B. (Individual writing)

C. (Individual writing)

27 Tips for Effective Public Speaking

A. 1. e
2. c
3. b
4. d
5. f
6. a

B. (Individual writing)

C. (Individual writing)

28 A Volunteer and a Tourist?

A. Paragraph 2: B
Paragraph 3: A
Paragraph 4: A
Paragraph 5: B

B. (Individual answer)

C. 1. Even brief periods of voluntouring give everyone involved insight into the lives of people in other countries.

2. According to the Travel Industry Association of America, over 55 million Americans have participated in a voluntouring project.

3. One-quarter of people planning for a vacation are considering a service-oriented one.

4. Some of the work voluntourists do on their trips includes: teaching English, planting trees, building bridges, and repairing trails.

5. Jamie found two organizations that provide voluntouring projects on the Internet, but neither of them was a non-profit organization.

D. (Individual writing)

1   Creating Canada

A.   A: Manifest Destiny
      B: American Civil War
      C: Political Deadlock
      D: Reciprocity Treaty Abrogation
      E: Transcontinental Railway
      F: Fenian Raids
      G: Repeal of the Corn Laws
      Internal Factors: C ; E ; G
      External Factors: A ; B ; D ; F
      (Individual answer)
B.   1. colonies
      2. Lower
      3. Upper
      4. Province
      5. Nova Scotia
      6. New Brunswick
      7. Quebec
      8. Ontario
      9. Dominion

2   Expansion of Canada

A.   1867: Ontario ; Quebec ; Nova Scotia ;
            New Brunswick ; Confederation
      1869: Red River
      1870: Northwest Territories ; Rupert's Land ;
            Manitoba
      1871: British Columbia ; Dominion
      1873: Prince Edward Island ; Britain
      1. 1867
      2. 1873
B.   Supreme Court ; Indian Act ; Canadian Pacific

3   Events and Development of Early Canada

A.   A ; C ; D ; F
      A ; B ; C ; E
      A ; B ; C
B.

(Suggested answer)
It was important that they were politically
equal to appease the settlers in Manitoba to
avoid another crisis similar to the Red River
Resistance.

4   Distinguished Canadians

A.   1. prime minister ; John A. Macdonald
      2. Nova Scotia
      3. medical ; Emily Stowe
      4. resistance ; Louis Riel
      5. anti-slavery
B.   1. Métis nation ; maintain
      2. Women's Christian Temperance Union ;
         negative ; alcoholic
      3. Chinese railway workers ; dangerous ;
         communities
      4. Underground Railroad ; freed ; slaves
      5. Knights of Labor ; workers ; working
      6. (Individual answer)

    ISBN: 978-1-77149-036-8

5 Social, Economic, and Political Changes

A. 1. Industrial
    2. jobless
    3. transportation
    4. immigration
    5. railway
    6. wheat
    7. First Nations
    8. changed
B. 1. A ; British North America Act ; B
    2. B ; Indian Act ; A
    3. B ; National Policy ; A
    4. B ; Chinese Immigration Act ; A

6 Conflict and Cooperation (1)

A. 1. Métis ; Canadian Government
    2. Anti-Confederationists ; Confederationists
    3. Representation by Population ; Equal Representation
B. 1. cooperation
    2. political
    3. social
    4. George Brown
    5. Maritime
    6. unification
    7. Conferences
    8. Confederation
    9. (Individual answer)

7 The Underprivileged in Canada

A. 1. Poverty
    2. Industrialization
    3. agricultural
    4. poor
    5. accommodations
    6. sanitation
    7. higher
    8. overcrowded
  9-10. (Individual answers)
B. 1. (Suggested answer)
       People moved to cities where the elderly could not work, and their families could not afford to support them.
    2. (Suggested answer)
       The government initially believed they did not need to provide assistance, holding individual families responsible for the elderly. In 1908, the Government Annuities was introduced, but it was not successful.
    3. (Individual answer)

8 Changes in Canada

A. 1. Social and Economic: B ; F
    2. Political and Legal: A ; E ; D ; C
B. 1. orphans ; inequality ; ill-treatment
       B ; A ; C
    2. labour ; protection ; foster
       A ; C ; B
    3. identity ; residential ; culture
       C ; B ; A

ISBN: 978-1-77149-036-8

9 Diverse Faces of Canada

A.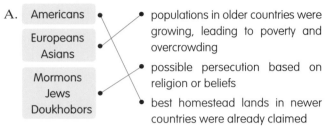

Americans •	• populations in older countries were growing, leading to poverty and overcrowding
Europeans Asians •	
	• possible persecution based on religion or beliefs
Mormons Jews Doukhobors •	• best homestead lands in newer countries were already claimed

B. immigration ; encouraged ; Britain ; settle ; ethnic

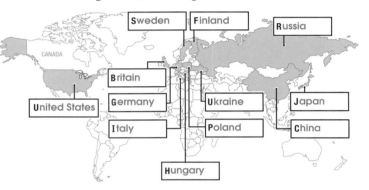

1. They were British and French. They were the first two nations to settle in Canada, which encouraged steady immigration from Britain and France over the years.
2. Finland, Hungary, Italy, Poland, Sweden, and Ukraine
3. (Individual answer)

10 Groups in Action

A. 1. unions
   2. unify
   3. government
   4. cheap
   5. industrialization
   6. workers
   7. (Suggested answer)
      They represent and further the interests of workers.
      It was the central labour organization in Canada and aimed to unify unionists across the country.

B. 1. (Suggested answer)
      Suffragist groups formed in order to fight for women's right to vote in Canada, and gained support from the NCWC. One of the groups in Manitoba gained national attention for this cause. Manitoban women won the right to vote on the provincial level in 1916, and women in Canada won the right to vote in federal elections in 1918. Women in Quebec did not gain the right to vote provincially until 1940.
   2. (Individual answers)

11 Individuals Making a Difference

A. L. M. Montgomery: C
    Nellie McClung: D
    Tom Longboat: A
    Wilfrid Laurier: B
    Alexander Graham Bell: E
B. (Individual answers for similarities and differences)
    (Suggested answer)
    Pauline Johnson wrote poetry that reflected her Mohawk and English background, while remaining patriotic to Canada.

12 Conflict and Cooperation (2)

A. 1. A ; B
   2. B ; A
   3. D ; C
   4. B ; A

B. (Suggested answers)
   1. He believed that these immigrants had the knowledge and skills needed to settle the land.
   2. The immigrants were all farmers with similar skills, lifestyles, and languages.
   3. The immigrants often shared languages and cultures so they could support and socialize with one another.

1 Physical Environment and Human Settlements

A. Landforms: not favourable
Soil Types: farmers
Close Proximity to Waterways: food ; freshwater
Availability of Natural Resources: Wood ; oil ; mining
Climate: mild ; farming
Vegetation: wood ; grassland

B.

This pattern has individual buildings spread out, and is usually found in rural areas, where resources are limited and can only support a small number of people.

This pattern has buildings that follow a natural or human-made line, such as a river, a railway, or a shoreline.

This pattern occurs when a lot of people gather in a place that is rich in resources. This is a high density area, usually with high-rise and multi-family buildings.

(Suggested examples)
linear: Champlain, Quebec
clustered: Toronto, Ontario
scattered: Spirit River in Northern Alberta

2 Global Human Settlement Patterns

A.
population density

population distribution

how people are spread out within an area or across the world

the number of people living per unit area, such as per square kilometre, of a given place

population density

B. 3.57 ; 7589.12
Canada: low
Singapore: high

C.

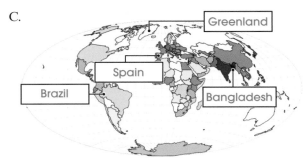

1. a. South Asia
   b. Australia
2. (Individual answer)
3. (Individual answer)

3 Global Settlement Trends

A. 1. rural
   2. cities
   3. urbanization
   4. outward
   5. growing
   6. decline
   7. unplanned
   8. sustainable
   9. degradation
   10. inequality
   11. (Individual answer)
   12. (Individual answer)
B. (Individual answer)

4 Impact of Human Settlements

A. 1. Deforestation
   2. Wildlife Habitat Loss
   3. Pesticides
   4. Water Pollution
   5. Desertification

B. 1. industrial
    2. pollutants
    3. smog
    4. radioactive
    5. contaminate
    6. aquatic
    7. roads
    8. Vehicle
    9. garbage
    10. (Individual answer)

5   Sustainable Human Settlements

A. B
    A ; F ; G
    D ; H
    C ; E
B. 1. (Suggested answer)
       The government promoted environmental sustainability in Växjö by using biofuels for public transit and using solar panels for alternative energy production in buildings.
    2. (Suggested answer)
       The challenges included the lack of financial resources for building environmentally friendly infrastructure and dealing with population growth.
    3. (Individual answer)

6   Land-use Issues

A. 1. agricultural ; ✘
    2. commercial ; ✔
    3. transportation ; ✔
    4. environmental ; ✘
    5. residential ; ✔
    6. public ; ✔

B. 1. They are environmental, transportation, public, and residential.
    2. (Individual answer)
    3. (Individual answer)

7   Quality of Life

A. B ; J ; E ; D ; C ; F ; K ; G ; I ; H ; A
B.
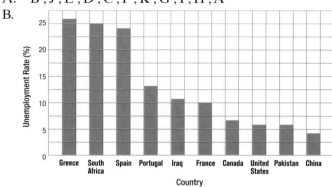
    1. a. 26%
       b. Greece
       c. (Individual answer)
    2. a. 4%
       b. China
       c. (Individual answer)

8 Quality of Life – Interrelationships among Factors

A.

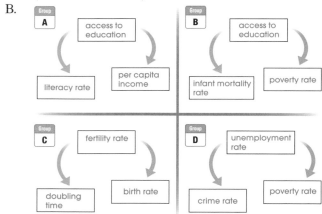

(Individual answer)

B.

Group A
access to education → literacy rate
access to education → per capita income

Group B
access to education → infant mortality rate
access to education → poverty rate

Group C
fertility rate → doubling time
fertility rate → birth rate

Group D
unemployment rate → crime rate
unemployment rate → poverty rate

(Suggested answer)
Unemployment can cause poverty and crime. Some people who are unemployed might commit crime to make money.

9 Quality of Life – Correlations between Indicators

A. (Suggested colours)

Legend
- 0 – 15%
- 16 – 30%
- 31 – 45%
- 46 – 60%
- 61 – 75%

Suriname
Chile
(Individual answer)

B.

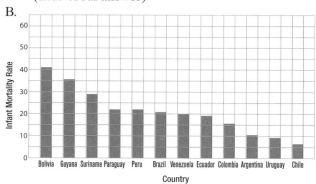

1. Bolivia: ✔
   Chile: ✔
   Colombia: ✘
   Uruguay: ✔
2. (Individual answer)
3. (Individual answer)

ISBN: 978-1-77149-036-8

10 Fair Trade and Quality of Life

social ; producers ; sustainable
1. farmers ; equipment ; consumer ; stable
2. businesses ; community ; housing ; ethical
3. productivity ; organic ; composting ; natural
4. (Individual answer)

11 Organizations for Improving Quality of Life

A. 1. Play ; sports
2. Parenthood ; family
3. Free ; slavery
4. Water ; access
5. Greenpeace ; human
6. Borders ; medical
B. 1. Doctors Without Borders
2. Water For People
3. Greenpeace
4. Free The Children
(Individual answer)

12 Economic Systems and Sectors

A. a. market
b. command
c. market
d. market
e. mixed
f. market
g. traditional
B. 1. Primary ; B ; (Individual example)
Secondary ; C ; (Individual example)
Tertiary ; A ; (Individual example)
Quaternary ; D ; (Individual example)
2. (Suggested answer)
Yes. The primary sector involves the use of natural resources, which are non-renewable. If such a country runs out of natural resources, unemployment would increase and the economy would suffer.
3. (Individual answer)

1   Cell Theory

A. Postulates of Cell Theory:
    1. cells
    2. structure ; Energy
    3. pre-existing
    Exceptions:
    1. first
    2. Viruses
    Picture 1: All living things are made up of cells.
    Picture 2: The first cell did not come from an already existing cell.
B. 1595: Zacharias ; microscope
    1663: Robert ; cell
    1674: Anton ; live
    1809: Charles-Francois ; membrane
    1837-1838: Thedor ; Matthias ; products
    1855: Rudolph ; arise

2   Animal and Plant Cells

A. 1. cell membrane
        cytoplasm
        nucleus
        chromosomes
        genes
    2a. nucleus
    b. chromosomes
    c. genes
    d. nucleus
    e. cytoplasm
    f. cell membrane
B. 1. cell wall
    2. chloroplast
    3. vacuole
    4. plastid
C. Photosynthesis:
    carbon dioxide ; energy ; oxygen
    Respiration:
    oxygen ; carbon dioxide ; water

3   Structures and Organelles in Cells

A. light microscope ;
    • nucleus
    • cytoplasm
    • cell membrane
    • cell wall
    electron microscope ;
    • ribosomes
    • Golgi apparatus
    • endoplasmic reticulum
    • lysosomes
    • mitochondria
B. 1. Ribosomes ; proteins
    2. Mitochondrion ; oval-shaped ; cellular respiration
    3. canals ; cytoplasm
    4. Golgi apparatus ; toxic
    5. sac-like ; recycle

4   Diffusion and Osmosis

A. 1. high ; low
    2. 3 ; 5 ; 2 ; 4
B. 1. osmosis
    2. equal
    3. membrane
    4. out
    5. water
    Plant Cell when Exposed to Salt Water: >
    Plant Cell with Continued Exposure to Salt Water: =

5   The Organization of Cells

A. 1. Choanocytes
    2. Porocytes
    3. Amoebocytes
    4. Spicules
    5. Pinacocytes
    6. Porocytes ;
        Beat and create the sponge's water current. ;
        Store and carry food to other cells. ;
        Form the outer covering of the sponge. ;
        Spicules

ISBN: 978-1-77149-036-8

B. 1. cells
   2. tissues
   3. organs
C. 1. excretory system
   2. digestive system
   3. circulatory system

6   About Systems

A. 1. A
   2. B
   3. A
   4. C
B. 1. optical system
   2. mechanical system
   3. hydroelectric power system
   4. electrical system
   5. body system
C. (Suggested answer)
   3 subsystems are: gears and drivers ; wheels and axles ; frames and materials

7   Systems: Input and Output

A. 1. heat
   2. mechanical energy ; movement
   3. food ; energy
   4. grow food or plants ;
      water, sunshine, and nutrients ;
      food and other plants
   5. tell time ;
      electricity ;
      movements of the clock hands

B.
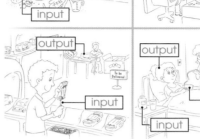

8   The Work Systems Do

A. 1. force ; scientific
   2. energy ; everyday
   3. efficiency ; scientific
   4. work ; everyday
B. 1. work
   2. pull
   3. effort
   4. useful
C. 1. Yes ; The machine is providing the force that moves the objects in the same direction as the force.
   2. Yes ; Red blood cells carry the oxygen molecules from one place to another.
   3. No ; The piano would have to move for work to be done.

9   Work, Mechanical Advantage, and Efficiency

A. 1. Newtons
   2. Work
   3. metres
   4. joules
   5. 800 N x 40 m = 32 000 J ;
      32 000 J of work was done.
   6. 4000 J ÷ 10 m = 400 N ;
      400 N of force was applied.

B. lever: $\frac{100}{10} = 10$

wheelbarrow: $\frac{100}{20} = 5$

lever

C. Machine A: $\frac{30\,000}{35\,000}$ x 100% = 85.7%

Machine B: $\frac{75\,000}{100\,000}$ x 100% = 75%

A

10 Evolving Systems

A. 1a. not automated
   b. automated
   2a. automated
   b. not automated
   3a. not automated
   b. automated
   4a. automated
   b. not automated
   5a. automated
   b. not automated
B. 1. social
   2. economic
   3. economic ; social
   4. environment
C. (Individual answer)

11 Where on Earth Is Water?

A. 1.

   2. evaporation, precipitation, and condensation
   3. Plants release evaporated water into the atmosphere through transpiration.

B. 1.

   2. fresh water
   3. salt water
   4. 1%
C. Solid: glacier
   Liquid: ponds
   Gas: water vapour

12 What Is a Watershed?

A. 1. B
   2. A
   3. B
   4. A
   5. B
B. 1. glacier
   2. precipitation
   3. groundwater aquifer
   4. lake
   5. river
   6. wetland
C.

13 The Water Table

A. 1-2.

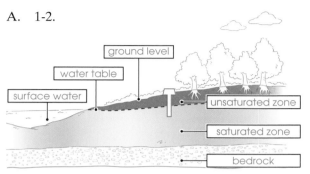

ground level

water table

surface water

unsaturated zone

saturated zone

bedrock

B. 1. true
    2. true
    3. false
    4. false
    5. false
    6. true
    7. false
    8. true
C. 1. where all spaces are filled with water
    2. where water is unable to enter or pass through
    3. water within the soil/rock underground
    4. the top level of the saturated zone underground

14 Glaciers and Polar Ice Caps

A. 1. ice caps
    2. temperatures
    3. precipitation
    4. climate
    5. stationary
    6. advancing
B. 1. valley glacier
    2. continental glacier
    Experiment:
    (Individual record)
    Antarctica would have a bigger effect on sea levels when the ice melts because it is on a land mass and would raise the ocean level if it were to melt.

15 Water Conservation

A. 1. wells, water treatment plants
    2. sewage system
    3. storm drain
    4. irrigation
    5. pesticides ; fertilizers
    6. solvent ; coolant
    7. Soap and dirty water would be filtered through the ground rather than return to a stream or a lake through a storm drain.
    8. Use less wasteful irrigation methods.
    9. thermal pollution
B. (Individual answer)

16 Fluids and Density

A. more ; gases
    solid ; liquid ; gas
B. orange juice
    honey
    helium
    maple syrup
    water vapour
    oxygen
    air
C. 1. volume
    2. mass
    3. density
    4. temperature
    5. decreases
    6. fluid
D. Density $= \dfrac{(160 - 10)}{150}$

    $= \dfrac{150}{150}$

    $= 1 \ (g/mL)$

ISBN: 978-1-77149-036-8

17 Viscosity

A. 1. Fluids ; matter
    2. Viscosity ; resistance
    3. density ; viscous
    4. decreases ; temperature
    5. attraction ; cohesion
    6. Adhesion ; substance
B. C ; D ; E
    (Individual experiment)

18 Buoyancy

A. 1. buoyancy
    2. gravity
    3. buoyancy
    4. densities
    5. Buoyancy ; Gravity
B. 1.

2.

C. 1. A: fresh water
       B: salt water
    2. C: salt water
       D: fresh water
    3. Liquid B has a greater density. After pouring B into A, the solution has a stronger force of buoyancy to exert on the egg to keep it afloat.
    4. Liquid C has a greater density. After pouring D into C, the density of C is reduced, which provides a smaller force of buoyancy to keep the egg afloat.
    5. Different fluids have different densities, and therefore exert different amounts of buoyancy.
    6. No

19 Compressed Fluids – Hydraulics and Pneumatics

A. 1. Gas Particles:

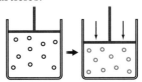

Liquid Particles:

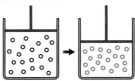

    2. lots of
    3. less
    4. A gas has more compressibility than a liquid because the particles of gas are further apart from one another and there is somewhere for the particles to go. As the particles of liquids are closer to one another, they have less room to compress.
B. hydraulic system ; pneumatic system
C. a. A
    b. B
D. (Individual answers)

20 Using Fluids

A. 1. pressure
    2. pressure
    3. flow
    4. flow
    5. force
B. A and C
    B and D
C. (Suggested answers)
    1. Medical hydraulic systems can save many lives, but the costs of tests and treatment are high, which means they are not available to everyone.

ISBN: 978-1-77149-036-8

2. Increased production
3. They can cause habitat loss and water pollution.

Complete Canadian Curriculum • **Grade 8**

ISBN: 978-1-77149-036-8